America's Best BBQ

REVISED AND UPDATED

100

Recipes from America's Best Smokehouses, Pits, Shacks, Rib Joints, Roadhouses, and Restaurants

ARDIE A. DAVIS, PhB and **CHEF PAUL KIRK, CWC, PhD, BSAS**

REVISED AND UPDATED

AMERICA'S BEST
BBQ

IN SEARCH OF THE BEST BBQ!

SLAB SPECIAL $10.00

BOB'S RIB SHACK AHEAD

PODREBARAC

Andrews McMeel
Publishing

Kansas City · Sydney · London

15 16 17 18 19 TEN 10 9 8 7 6 5 4 3 2 1

ISBN: 978-1-4494-5834-8

Library of Congress Control Number: 2014949621

Cover photo: StockFood America, Inc.
Editor: Jean Z. Lucas
Designer: Diane Marsh
Art director: Tim Lynch
Production editor: Maureen Sullivan
Production manager: Carol Coe
Demand planner: Sue Eikos

ATTENTION: SCHOOLS AND BUSINESSES Andrews McMeel books are available at quantity discounts with bulk purchase for educational, business, or sales promotional use. For information, please write to: Special Sales Department, Andrews McMeel Publishing, LLC, 1130 Walnut Street, Kansas City, Missouri 64106.

For Gretchen.
Ardie

For Jessica.
Paul

Contents

INTRODUCTION

This book honors American barbecue and the people who make it. Here you'll find more than 100 recipes for out-of-this-world appetizers, tender and smoky meats cooked low and slow, sweet and spicy sauces and rubs, homemade sides, and even a few decadent, down-home desserts—if you've saved room. And because food tastes better when you know the people and stories behind the recipes, we'll introduce you to some famous and not-so-famous pitmasters and barbecue personalities, living and dead. Some come from long lines of proud pitmasters, some have been at the craft most of their lives, and others are up-and-coming barbecuers. All view barbecue as an art, craft, and business. It's not a job, it's a profession, and they take great care to ensure that each day's barbecue is even better than the last. We call that a labor of love.

The next best thing to being at one of the best barbecue joints in America is to get it direct—if they will ship it to you. Many of the places in this book sell their sauces, rubs, and other products by phone and online. We list the address, phone number, and Web site when available so that you can buy direct from the source and try it for yourself.

Another great way to enjoy America's best barbecue is to cook it yourself. The usual drill when writers visit a barbecue joint is to take some photos, sample some dishes, and then publish a knockoff recipe from the menu. Most of our recipes and techniques come straight from the source. A frequent reply when we asked for a recipe was "If I tell you, I'll have to shoot you" or "Sorry. Our recipes are trade secrets. We don't give them out." We expected to hear that, but we didn't hear it often. Sometimes, especially when we were strangers to the owner, "No" turned to "OK," or "Sure, I'll give you our recipe," after we got better acquainted. "Yes" was instant from pitmasters who know us. We're honored to know quite a few. Many are friends. Most of the recipes that were given to us haven't been previously published. When original top-secret recipes were denied us, and we thought you would like something similar, we came up with our own

version, thanks to Paul's talents as a championship pitmaster and a certified working chef.

We bring a lot of baggage to this book. We've been involved in the business, sport, and art of barbecue for more than fifty years each. We have many friends in barbecue. Paul also does a lot of consulting and is involved in several restaurants. It's a daunting task to select a hundred places out of more than eight thousand. It's a little subjective, maybe not altogether fair. Occasionally we're influenced by the mystique or personal good memories of a place or both. Our choices reflect our prior knowledge of barbecue joints across the nation and recommendations from trusted friends, family, colleagues, and fans. We also checked books, articles, and online sources for tips. Daniel Vaughn's excellent book, *The Prophets of Smoked Meat*, was invaluable to us in Texas. It was a pleasure to finally meet Daniel in San Marcos.

Barbecue joints are rated various ways in books, articles, and online reviews. Some are rated with numbers; some with stars, rib bones, or other symbols. All ratings are a mix of subjective and objective, including ours. Our best barbecue joints are not ranked from 1, best, and on down. Each joint in this book is, in our view, one of the best in America, with varying qualities. If your favorite barbecue joint isn't in here, maybe we haven't tried it, or maybe we tried it and didn't like it. You will agree with us sometimes; sometimes you won't. We don't always agree with each other about a particular place. We get over it, and so will you!

The menu is similar across America's barbecue joints, with regional variations. The standard meats are pork ribs, beef brisket, pork shoulder, sausage, chicken, and turkey. A few places serve duck, and we wish more would. Some southern joints offer pork only. In parts of Kentucky the featured meat is lamb or mutton. You can get *cabrito* (goat) at many Texas barbecue joints. We've included a good mix of main dishes, and while most of the recipes come from Kansas City and the so-called barbecue belt from North Carolina to Texas, we've loosened the belt a notch or two to include recipes from non-barbecue-belt places. People everywhere love and appreciate good barbecue.

At most barbecue joints, you can expect starters, sandwiches, dinners, sides, and dessert. Some serve traditional breakfasts. Some—very few—serve barbecue for breakfast. Meat is the heart of barbecue, and many joints these days treat starters, sides, and desserts as afterthoughts, serving labor-saving dishes from off-premise suppliers. Real, made-from-scratch American barbecue starters, sides, and desserts

are still out there, and we found them. The ones in this book are the real deal.

More than your standard ribs, beans, and coleslaw (though plenty of those are included), *America's Best BBQ* also includes recipes for burgoo, gumbo, Rocky Mountain oysters, barbecue brisket nachos, smoked catfish, barbecued baloney, bison ribs, barbecue spaghetti, pig salad, fried peach pie, and more recipes that will drive barbecue fans hog wild.

Picking the Best

We're picky about some things and lenient on others. We used two main standards in selecting the best barbecue joints. First, barbecue joints should specialize in barbecue, not just a barbecue item or two as part of a larger menu of nonbarbecue foods. Second, we're OK with gas or electric assist, but the cooking fuel should be enough wood or charcoal to give the meat some smoke flavor. Our only exception is eastern North Carolina whole-hog cooking. Increasing numbers of barbecue joints there have switched from wood to gas. Since little if any smoke penetrates a whole hog during cooking with wood or charcoal, we're OK with that. It's the quality of the hog, the cooking procedure, the sauce, and the presentation that make one hog different from another.

We judge starters on appeal and taste. Many barbecue joints don't offer starters, finding that their customers fill up just fine on meat and sides. Those that do serve starters know that they have to be tempting to make folks risk filling up before they reach the main event. From Brunswick stew to fried cheese grits and more, our starters meet that standard.

We judge main dishes on appearance, tenderness, and taste. Whether served on paper, plastic, Styrofoam, or fine china, the meat has to have eye appeal. Tenderness means that it is easy to chew, not tough or mushy. We love House Park Barbecue's slogan, "Need no teef to eat my beef," and Stevenson's Bar-B-Que proclaims their meat is "Tender as a mother's love." Barbecue should look good, be easy to chew, and be moist and flavorful. Seasonings should complement the meat flavor, not overpower it. The restaurants in this book excel at the meat and bones of barbecue—literally.

We judge sides on appearance and taste. They should look good and complement the meat without overshadowing it. As with starters, a good side makes you want to save a little room. Here you'll find some standout recipes for such classic favorites as beans, slaw, and potato salad, as well as some unique sides we've discovered in our barbecue travels, such as the Vanized Potato, jalapeño hushpuppies, and barbecue corn bread.

We judge desserts on appearance and taste. Things like how decadent and fattening they are never come into play. We don't know the connection between bananas and barbecue, but a good many joints serve banana desserts, and we've included a few here—banana pudding, banana cream pie, bananas Foster. You'll also find the fried pies so ubiquitous in the South, cobbler and crisp, homemade ice cream, and more. A good dessert makes us say, "I shouldn't have eaten that, but I'm sure glad I did," and you won't regret overdoing it with any one of the desserts in this book.

Value is part of the overall equation for any restaurant—good quality, good portions, and a good price. Everything on the menu needn't be great. Some places excel in cooking one meat and fall short on others, but overall, the restaurants in this book are equals. Portions aren't usually a problem at barbecue joints, but the best places make you want to fill up on a little bit of everything—and then go back for more. Price is also a small factor, but since barbecue places usually aren't fancy, you usually get a good deal for your meal. Most places even offer daily specials.

Service is important, too. Contrary to what people who have never waited tables may think, it is not an easy job that anyone could do. We've waited tables, so we know. Building rapport with a wide variety of customers and orchestrating the complete dining experience requires smart work and hard work. A good server can tell you about the pit, the smoke, and the cooking procedures. Tipping isn't necessary at many barbecue joints because they serve on an order/pickup basis, but when you have competent servers, it's nice to reward them with a generous gratuity. They earn it.

Ambience is intangible. It's a feeling that you're welcome when you step inside. It makes you feel glad you're there. As Eldert Walker always says at his restaurant, "Come for the food. Leave with the experience."

Longevity and/or fame is not more important than quality. We avoided places that are past their heyday. Of the few chains that appear here, there is no guarantee that the quality we found at the restaurant listed will be exactly the same at other locations in the chain. What matters most is the quality of the food, the service, and the ambience.

Most of our recipes are scaled down for home-style entertaining; several will serve a crowd. After all, barbecue is best when shared. And when you're putting a lot of time and care into cooking, it should be enjoyed by family, friends, and neighbors.

If you're new to barbecue, our Barbecue Basics at the back of the book will give you the lowdown on barbecue, including what you need to know to select, maintain, and use gas and charcoal grills. We've included some basic meat cooking instructions, plus tips and tricks we've picked up over the years. There's also information on meat cuts and meat doneness to ensure safe and proper cooking.

Remember that barbecue is about making it your own. One cook and another, following the same recipe, will come up with two dishes that don't taste exactly the same. The professionals who contributed our recipes use professional-grade equipment. Their results might not be exactly the same on a home grill, but you'll still end up with some fantastic barbecue, cranked up to new heights of greatness.

We've been fortunate to live lives steeped in barbecue—its history, lore, culture, traditions, and methods. Some of our recipes may trigger good memories of places you've been. Some may introduce you to places you'll want to visit. If you can't get to the places yourself, this can be your armchair tour of the best swine dining establishments in America. We hope you have as much fun reading it as we've had putting it all together. So pull up a chair, grab a Wet-Nap, and dive in.

KEEP CALM AND EAT BARBECUE.

Todd Johns, Plowboys Barbecue, Blue Springs, MO

Starters

Starters should jump-start your appetite. Go easy, lest they fill you up before you get to the main course and dessert. On the other hand, we've been known to fill up on a few remarkable starters that were so good that we passed on the entrée!

The best starters grab your eyes and nose first. They look delicious, smell delicious, and shout out, "You're going to love this!" They should complement your entrée and sides and have come-back appeal that makes you want more.

Some joints will give you smaller portions of certain sides as a starter, such as a cup of gumbo or Brunswick stew.

Stuffed smoked or deep-fried jalapeño peppers, aka Atomic Buffalo Poppers, have populated the menus in many joints over recent years. Likewise, to our delight, we're seeing more fried pickle chips and spears with ranch dressing dip.

Sadly, RMOs (Rocky Mountain Oysters) remain mostly in Rocky Mountain barbecue joints, plus a few joints in Oklahoma and Texas. We hope Steve Holbrook's encore recipe in this volume inspires more pitmasters to add RMOs to the menu. In light of the national obsession with bacon, we expect to see more bacon-wrapped starters and deep-fried bacon in America's best barbecue joints.

RUB (Righteous Urban Barbeque) and Gordon's on the Green are now closed. RUB's Onion Strings and Gordon's Volcanic Goat Cheese are too good to lose, so we moved the recipes to our Legacy Recipes section (page 195).

We have added two new starter recipes that we think will be as big a hit with you as they are with us: BBQ Egg Rolls from Smokey D's in Des Moines, Iowa, and Shrimp and Grits from Lillie's Q in Chicago.

As Woody Guthrie used to say, "Take it easy, but take it!"

Vidalia Onion Dip

Country's Barbecue

3137 Mercury Dr.
Columbus, GA 31906
706-563-7604
http://www.countrysbarbecue.com

Country's Barbecue, which is now a small chain, opened for business in 1975 in an old country store. The food quality and family-friendly ambience quickly caught on. Of the nine Country's today, we like the original on Mercury Drive best. It features a gigantic red wooden rocking chair, very popular with kids of all ages. Of course we can't resist saying that the food at Country's rocks, too!

Chopped pork sandwich, or chopped pork, is what Country's does best—barbecued pork, cooked over hickory and oak, chopped and served with Country's own sauces. Country's does several nontraditional barbecue items such as smoked turkey and homemade corn bread dressing, with a sweet potato soufflé. Its hot roast beef sandwich is topped with Vidalia onions and gravy. It's what we'd expect at a diner instead of a barbecue joint, but it's delicious!

VIDALIA ONION DIP

Makes 5 cups

2 sweet onions, minced

1 cup mayonnaise

1 cup freshly grated Parmesan cheese

1 cup shredded Swiss or
   cheddar cheese

In a large bowl, combine the onions, mayonnaise, and grated cheeses and stir until well blended. Place in a large baking dish or divide among 4-ounce individual ramekins. Cover and refrigerate for 2 hours or overnight. Bake at 325°F for 1 hour, until bubbly and light brown on top. Remove from the oven and let stand for 10 minutes. If there is too much grease, spoon off and discard or absorb the excess in paper towels and discard. Serve with fresh bread or crackers.

One of Country's interesting appetizers is a Vidalia Onion Dip with Frito Scoops. Since the recipe is a trade secret, we will venture this very close adaptation. It's also good as a dip for veggies, potato chips, fries, and onion rings.

2

Onion Rings

Leonard's Pit Barbecue

5465 Fox Plaza Dr.
Memphis, TN 38115
901-360-1963
http://www.leonardsbarbecue.com

eonard's, a Memphis barbecue icon, bears the name of the founder, Leonard Heuberger. He opened the original restaurant in 1922. Leonard's 5-cent barbecue pulled pork sandwiches with vinegar-base sauce and coleslaw became a Memphis classic. Leonard's famous onion rings are a perfect complement to any barbecue item on the menu. As his restaurant grew in popularity, Mr. Heuberger moved to larger quarters. Leonard's became the largest drive-in restaurant anywhere. Now located away from downtown, the décor, murals, and memorabilia pay tribute to Leonard's past and celebrate the present. We've been told that Elvis was a Leonard's fan from his teen years onward, often partying there with friends until daybreak.

Dan Brown and his wife, Janet, own today's Leonard's. Dan has worked there since his teen years, learning the business, recipes, cooking procedures, and traditions directly from Mr. Heuberger. Our recipe for home cooks tastes similar to what you'll get at Leonard's, but don't miss the genuine item on your next trip to Memphis.

ONION RINGS

Serves 6 to 8

1½ cups all-purpose flour

¼ cup cornmeal

¼ cup onion powder

1 teaspoon sugar

2 teaspoons salt

1½ to 1¾ cups milk, or more as needed

1 large egg

½ cup water

Canola oil, for deep-frying

4 large onions, sliced into ½-inch rings

Put the flour, cornmeal, onion powder, sugar, and salt in a large bowl. Add 1½ cups milk, the egg, and the water. Whisk until only slightly lumpy. It should have the consistency of pancake batter. If it's too thick, add ¼ cup milk or more to thin it down.

Put the oil in your deep-fryer and preheat to 365° to 375°F (or in a deep pot and measure the oil temperature with a deep-frying thermometer). Dip the onion rings in the batter. Fry 3 or 4 coated rings at a time, turning the rings when they float to the top. Continue turning the rings until they are golden brown, 3 to 5 minutes. Remove the rings from the grease and drain on paper towels. Serve immediately.

ARDIE'S BARBECUE POSTCARDS

Postcards thrive today, contrary to predictions that e-mail, text messaging, and cell-phone-transmitted photos, videos, and conversations would put the postcard industry out of business. Anywhere you travel you'll find postcards featuring local scenery to send home to friends and relatives. You're home before the card arrives, but the recipients know you thought about them while you were away.

Postcards were in their heyday in the early 1900s. Travel by auto was the norm. Most of the 608 million postcards mailed in 1908 hit the designated mailbox well before the sender returned home. Today there's a huge network of postcard collectors, aka del-tiologists. Some collect, trade, or sell cards on many subjects or locales. Others focus on a few or one category. Ardie collects barbecue postcards. His friend Ken Wilson in Dripping Springs, Texas, got him hooked, bless Ken's soul. Ken has thousands of postcards. He is active in the nationwide network of postcard collectors who meet in person and online to swap or sell cards.

Barbecue postcards are hard to find. Ardie has scanned hundreds of boxes of cards in flea markets and antique stores to no avail. Ken found most of Ardie's cards at post-card collector shows. Some are older, and some are from contemporary barbecue joints. Postcards are an important part of modern barbecue history. They belong in a Barbecue Hall of Fame or Museum, if a real one ever gets legs. All are treasures. Here are a few of Ardie's favorites:

A COMPLETE DINNER OF DELICIOUS BAR-B-QUED SPARE RIBS OR OUR FAMOUS MILK-CORN FED CHICKEN, WITH ALL THE TRIMMINGS, READY TO SERVE.

WE SPECIALIZE IN TAKE-OUT ORDERS. JUST PHONE US

Rudy's Take-Out Carton,
Long Beach, California

Rudy's FOR RIBS

1900 AMERICAN AVE.
Phone 6-1437

WE'RE   EATING

HIGH ON THE HOG

MarTenn COUNTRY HAMS

MarTenn Country Hams, Martin, Tennessee

OKLAHOMA JOE'S   On U. S. 66,   Where Tourists Meet

DIXIE BARBECUE

OKLAHOMA JOE'S   DRIVE IN

BAR-B-QUE PIT PIT

Ladies and Men's Rest Rooms   Albuquerque, N. Mex.

Oklahoma Joe's, Albuquerque, New Mexico

PIT BAR-B-Q

CLEM MIKESKA'S BAR-B-Q
CATERING SERVICE

Clem Mikeska's Bar-B-Q, Temple, Texas

Hog Heaven, San Francisco—"Cornered by a Boar"

The SMOKE HOUSE RESTAURANT

BAR-B-Q

U.S. HIGHWAY 92 . . . 2 Miles West Of . . . LAKELAND, FLORIDA

The Smoke House Restaurant, Lakeland, Florida

Brisket Nachos

Tom's Ribs

North Central San Antonio
121 N. Loop
1604 West at Stone Oak
San Antonio, TX 78232
210-404-RIBS (7427)
http://www.tomsribs.com/home.html

We've found great nachos at barbecue joints across America. Tom's are delicious! Imagine noshing on tostada chips topped with chopped barbecued brisket, warm chile con queso, shredded cheddar and Jack cheeses, and Tom's fresh salsa. Here's our version to make at home. It is a great party platter or plate.

BRISKET NACHOS

Serves 4 to 6

3 ounces tricolored tortilla chips

¼ pound chopped Barbecued Brisket (page 42)

½ cup queso sauce

½ cup cooked or drained canned pinto beans

½ cup shredded cheddar cheese

½ cup shredded Monterey Jack cheese

½ cup homemade salsa or your favorite restaurant or store-bought salsa

Preheat the oven to 400°F. Place the chips on an oven-proof serving plate, then top with half of the brisket, queso sauce, and pinto beans. Repeat with another layer of each, then top with both cheeses and the salsa. Bake for 2 to 3 minutes, until the cheese is melted. Serve warm.

Deviled Eggs

Miss Myra's Pit BBQ

3278 Cahaba Heights Rd.
Cahaba Heights, AL 35243
205-967-6004

Paul loves deviled eggs, and when he heard about Miss Myra's Pit BBQ Deviled Eggs, his mouth watered. While he was initially disappointed to learn that the deviled eggs, like menu items at most restaurants, are named for the restaurant, not the cooking method, he really enjoyed them, finding them a little different from most.

Miss Myra's does serve real pit hickory-smoked barbecue, cooked in a custom-built brick pit at the restaurant, which was opened in 1984 by Myra Grissom and her late husband. Today it is still a family-run operation. Myra's daughter, Rennae Wheat, and husband, Buck Wheat, along with Rennae and Buck's daughter, Myra, and an aunt, Helen Gilbert, keep the busy restaurant going. Myra Grissom still comes to work but has cut back on her work hours.

Although barbecued pork butt is the best seller, the ribs, beef, and chicken with the famous Alabama white sauce (mayo, vinegar, and spices) hold their own with customers. Miss Myra's is a joint where you definitely want to save room for dessert. Try each of the six different pies, plus two pound cakes and banana pudding, at each visit; then pick a regular favorite. Be careful if you start with pound cake, though. It's so good you may never get past it, but we strongly suggest you give the others a chance. Very good eats!

DEVILED EGGS

Makes 1 dozen

6 large eggs

3 tablespoons mayonnaise

1 tablespoon sweet pickle relish

1 teaspoon Worcestershire sauce

1 teaspoon white vinegar

Salt and black pepper

Paprika, for garnish

Pimiento-stuffed green
   olives, for garnish

Put the eggs in a saucepan and cover with cold water. Bring the water to a boil and immediately remove the pan from the heat. Cover and let the eggs stand in hot water for 10 to 12 minutes. Remove from the hot water and run under cold water to cool. Peel the eggs and cut in half lengthwise.

Carefully remove the yolks from the eggs and put them into a medium bowl. Scoop out and discard a little bit of the white to make a more generous cup for filling. Mash the egg yolks, mayonnaise, relish, Worcestershire sauce, and vinegar to make a smooth mixture. Season the mixture with salt and pepper to taste.

Spoon the mixture into the egg whites or pipe with a pastry bag for a more elegant look. Garnish with a sprinkle of paprika and top some of the eggs with a slice of pimiento-stuffed green olive. Chill and serve.

Brunswick Stew

Johnny Harris Restaurant & Barbecue Sauce Company

1651 E. Victory Dr.
Savannah, GA 31404
912-354-7810
http://www.johnnyharris.com

Named after founder John Newman Harris, the restaurant has been a Savannah landmark since the 1920s. Today's roadhouse, with the original ballroom dining area, replaced Harris's former barbecue shack in 1936.

The Donaldson family has sustained the Johnny Harris legacy of great food, great sauce, and southern hospitality from the late Kermit "Red" Donaldson to his son, Phil, and his family. Phil's daughter, Julie Donaldson Lowenthal, has even shared the Johnny Harris story and many treasured recipes in the *Johnny Harris Restaurant Cookbook*.

We are longtime fans of Johnny Harris Original sauce. Simmered until it has about one-third less volume than it started with, the sauce is a rich, hearty complement to barbecue and other foods. A small portion is all you need.

We love the Johnny Harris barbecue and sides, but we have a special liking for the Brunswick stew. Johnny Harris sauce imparts the signature flavor. It's "the main ingredient," Phil told us, so don't try substitutes. Buy some in Savannah or online. Hats off and many thanks to Phil Donaldson for sharing this recipe!

BRUNSWICK STEW

Serves 10 to 12

1 pound smoked pork, cooked and diced

1 pound smoked chicken, diced

½ teaspoon black pepper

½ teaspoon crushed red pepper

1 teaspoon hot sauce, or to taste

2 tablespoons minced onion

1½ cups ketchup

3 cups diced peeled cooked potatoes

3 (15- to 16-ounce) cans niblet corn

½ cup prepared yellow mustard

2 tablespoons salt

½ cup white vinegar

Johnny Harris Original barbecue sauce, to taste

Put all the ingredients in a slow cooker set to medium-low or in a Dutch oven over medium-low heat. Cover and simmer until hot and bubbly, about 2 hours. Taste and add more salt and/or hot sauce as desired.

Burgoo

Moonlite Bar-B-Q Inn

2840 W. Parrish Ave.
Owensboro, KY 42301
800-322-8989 or 270-684-8143
http://www.moonlite.com

In the seventeenth century burgoo was a mush served to sailors during ocean voyages. You wouldn't want to eat it unless you were starving. Today's burgoo is not mush. It tastes so good you can never get enough. Some of the best burgoo in the world is served every day in Owensboro, Kentucky. This recipe makes 3 gallons, which Paul says is "just enough for a big lunch. But I have been told that I am a big eater." It also freezes well. Although Moonlite's recipe has been widely circulated, a book about America's best barbecue wouldn't be complete without this burgoo. Hats off to the Bosley family for keeping this icon of American barbecue going strong!

BURGOO

Makes 3 gallons

4 pounds mutton

1 (3-pound) chicken

¾ pound green cabbage, minced

¾ pound onion, minced

5 pounds potatoes, peeled and diced

2 (17-ounce) cans niblet corn or
   2 cups fresh corn kernels

¾ cup ketchup

3 (10¾-ounce) cans tomato puree

Juice of 1 lemon

¾ cup white vinegar

½ cup Worcestershire sauce

2½ tablespoons salt, or to taste

2 tablespoons black pepper

1 teaspoon cayenne, or more to taste

Put the mutton in a large pot with enough water to cover and bring to a boil over medium-high heat. Reduce the heat to low and simmer for 2 to 3 hours, stirring occasionally. Discard the broth and the bones and finely chop the meat. Set aside.

Boil the chicken in 2 gallons of water in a large kettle over medium heat until tender. Remove the chicken and set aside to cool. Add the cabbage, onion, potatoes, corn, ketchup, and 1 gallon of water to the chicken broth. Bring to a boil.

Meanwhile, chop the chicken meat. Discard the bones and skin. When the potatoes are tender, after 20 or 30 minutes, add the chopped chicken, mutton, tomato puree, lemon juice, vinegar, Worcestershire sauce, salt, black pepper, and cayenne. Simmer over low heat for 2 hours or longer, stirring occasionally as it thickens. Serve with saltine crackers or corn bread if desired.

WHAT TO DRINK WITH BARBECUE

Beverages are essential to the barbecue experience. When the barbecue is world class, just about any beverage will do. Matching the right beverage with the right barbecue can, however—to borrow an expression from Mark Twain—make the difference between a lightning bug and a bolt of lightning.

In the majority of barbecue joints your beverage options are water, iced tea, soda, and beer. Many these days also offer wine. Iced tea has been called "the house wine of the South." Expect iced tea in southern barbecue joints—sometimes sweet, sometimes not, and sometimes you get a choice. The rule is, drink what doesn't distract from the barbecue. If it enhances the barbecue, so much the better!

Sweet Pickles

City Market

633 E. Davis St.
Luling, TX 78648
830-875-9019

City Market's sauce is worth the trip to Luling. Sprinkle some on a post-oak-smoked brisket sandwich for a superb barbecue experience. This mustard-base sauce is almost addictive! We also love the pickles. When you're too far away to enjoy City Market's sweet pickles on-site, try making our version at home. They dance well with raw onions, saltines, and barbecue and are great in tuna salad, deviled eggs, or anywhere else you would use chopped pickles.

TEXAS SWEET PICKLES

Makes 1 gallon

1 gallon dill pickles, drained

5 cloves garlic, minced

1 tablespoon mixed pickling spices

2 cups white vinegar, or as needed

5 pounds sugar

Cut the pickles into chunks and pack into sterilized jars (or back in the drained jar they came in) along with the garlic and pickling spices.

Combine the vinegar and sugar in a 2-quart saucepan and bring to a boil. Simmer for 3 to 5 minutes. Pour over the pickles. Wipe clean the top rim and seal the jar. Leave on the counter at room temperature for about 1 week. Store in the refrigerator and consume within 1 month or can in sterile jars, in which they'll keep at room temperature for up to 1 year.

Note: If you want a sweet-hot pickle, add a 5-ounce bottle of Tabasco sauce to the jar.

Buffalo-Style Chicken Wings

Brooks' House of Bar-B-Q

5560 Hwy. 7
Oneonta, NY 13820
800-498-2445 or 607-432-1782
http://www.brooksbbq.com

When it comes to barbecued chicken in upstate New York, the Brooks family rules the roost. They've been in the poultry business since 1941 and the barbecue business since the mid-1950s. Their barbecue catering business gave rise to a small concession stand, followed by an 80-seat restaurant. In 1965 Brooks' established a permanent home in today's 300-seat restaurant. Brooks' 38-foot-long pit, the "largest indoor charcoal pit in the East," turns out grilled chicken and pork spareribs seven days a week. They also serve oven-roasted turkey and beef with their famous barbecue sauce. Their upstate New York spiedies—marinated grilled boneless skinless chunks of chicken in a roll—are second to none.

Brooks' has come a long way since family patriarch Griffin Brooks and his wife and food management expert, Frances, started their poultry farm in 1941. The Brooks' ownership passed on to son John and daughter-in-law Joan in 1975, and since 2005 John and Joan's son Ryan and daughter-in-law Beth have carried the torch into the third generation. After you try Ryan's recipe for chicken wings, you may switch your preference from Buffalo-Style Chicken Wings to Oneonta Chicken Wings!

BUFFALO-STYLE CHICKEN WINGS

Serves 4

Brooks' Grillin' Rub

2 pounds chicken wings, wings and drums separated and tips removed

1 cup Brooks' Mild, Medium, or Hot Chicken Wing Sauce

Blue cheese dip or dressing, for serving

Celery and carrot sticks, for serving

Preheat a grill to high and then turn down to medium when ready to start grilling.

Shake Brooks' Grillin' Rub on the chicken wings. Place the wings on the grill and turn frequently until done, 25 to 30 minutes. Remove from the grill and let rest for 5 minutes. Place the cooked wings in a bowl, cover with the wing sauce, and shake to coat the wings. Serve with blue cheese dip or dressing and celery and carrot sticks.

Gumbo

BB's Lawnside Bar-B-Q

1205 E. 85th St.
Kansas City, MO 64131
816-8BB-RIBS (822-7427)
http://www.bbslawnsidebbq.com

indsay Shannon, proprietor, with his wife, Jo, calls BB's a "roadhouse juke joint." True to Lindsay's description, the building looks like a roadhouse. From streetside there is a large parking lot, no lawn. Inside there's a full-service bar on one end and dining tables with blues band space on the other. The walls and ceilings sport blues, barbecue, and swine signs, posters, pictures, and other memorabilia. There is living history here as well, with live blues and great barbecue. Blues entertainers such as Shine Top Jr. Boogie Piano, Lee McBee & the Confessors, and the Scotty Boy Daniels Band appear often, as does a roadhouse full of other blues talent.

Lindsay, a blues and barbecue expert, pegs the 1930s as the start of the barbecue and blues tradition in Kansas City. Thanks to BB's and several other Kansas City venues, the tradition thrives today. Lindsay even takes time off from the restaurant every Sunday night to host a blues show on a local radio station.

BB's head pitmaster, Mike Nickel, knows his way around the barbecue pit as well as Lindsay knows "where bar-b-q meets the blues." Barbecue is in Mike's blood. When he isn't cooking at BB's, he's competing in barbecue cooking contests. At BB's, Mike has the honor of cooking with one

of the most unusual and historic barbecue pits in the nation. In fact, the pit may be unique; we know of no other custom-built pit made from granite stones salvaged from the old Kansas City crosswalks, when the streets were paved with gravel. It's no stretch of the imagination to say that Big Joe Turner, Charlie Parker, Count Basie, Ma Rainey, and other blues greats walked on those very stones! The thick granite stones hold heat well, enhancing BB's slow and low barbecue method of cooking. The pit still works well after more than fifty years of smoking.

There is something magical about picking up a hickory-smoked rib cooked in a historic pit and savoring each bite as you listen to the blues. Here's how Lindsay puts it: "When the blues music floats off the bandstand, it wafts across your plate of barbecue, imparting a flavor you can only get in Kansas City at BB's."

BB's also makes great gumbo. Try a cup as a starter or get a bowl and make it your main course. Here's the recipe, straight out of BB's recipe and operations manual—the "Bible."

GUMBO

Makes 8 to 10 quarts

1 pound (4 sticks) butter

½ cup water

4 large onions

4 large green bell peppers

1 celery stalk, any leaves removed

Salt and black pepper

Garlic powder

5 store-bought smoked sausages
   (1½ pounds), thinly sliced

2 smoked ham ends or about
   1 pound sliced smoked ham

2 smoked turkey ends or about
   1 pound sliced smoked turkey

3¾ (28-ounce) cans Hunt's
   crushed tomatoes

2 (49-ounce) cans Swanson's
   chicken broth

2 (3½- to 4½-pound) whole
   chickens, cooked

1 (16-ounce) package frozen okra

1 teaspoon crushed red
   pepper, or to taste

1 (6-ounce) bottle Louisiana hot sauce

Put the butter in a large skillet or stockpot with the water and heat over medium-high heat. Chop the onions, green peppers, and celery and add them to the pot. Sauté the vegetables until they soften, 7 to 8 minutes; then sprinkle lightly with salt, pepper, and garlic powder and stir. Transfer to a 10-quart pot.

Cut up the sausages, ham, and turkey and add to the vegetables. Then add the crushed tomatoes and chicken broth, stirring to mix well. Bring to a boil over high heat for about 15 minutes. Once the crushed tomatoes and broth mix throughout the veggies and meats, reduce the heat to low and simmer for about 15 minutes.

Meanwhile, remove the skins from the cooked chickens, pull the chicken meat off the bones in small to medium chunks, and add them to the pot. Then add the okra, red pepper, and hot sauce. Simmer for 15 minutes more. Do not let it boil. Serve.

Shrimp and Grits

Lillie's Q

1856 W. North Ave.
Chicago, IL
773-772-5500
http://www.lilliesq.com

Chef Charlie McKenna's grandmother Lillie would be proud that his South-in-your-mouth barbecue joint bears her name. Likewise, his dad, Quito, the Q in the name. Grandmother Lillie taught young Charlie the basics of the art of southern cooking. Quito, a championship barbecue pitmaster, taught him how to barbecue. With training like that, who needs the CIA (Culinary Institute of America)? Although most pitmasters don't have CIA credentials, Charlie has put his combination of learning from Lillie, Quito, and the CIA to good use. His persistence at getting it right, his attention to details, and his years of experience at barbecue pits and in upscale restaurants make him one of the most creative, talented pitmasters in America. We have met few who compare.

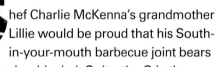

YOU WANT TO KNOW HOW GOOD MY RIBS ARE?

SO GOOD THAT GOD WOULD CALL *ME*, NOT ADAM, TO MAKE ANOTHER EVE!

Quito McKenna, Chef Charlie McKenna's dad,
Lillie's Q, Chicago, IL

Charlie McKenna's gift to Chicago and America is upscale barbecue, creative sides, and non-Q that resonate splendidly on the palates of young, upwardly mobile professionals as well as bubbas like us. Charlie's southern roots reverberate throughout the menu. Before we met him, we wondered how compatibly a CIA-trained chef with a high-end restaurant pedigree could function in a fire-and-smoke barbecue environment. No cause for concern here. In fact it's reason to celebrate!

We loved the entire menu of culinary gems at Lillie's Q. We could make a meal on the award-winning Brunswick Stew alone, savoring each spoonful between bites of pork rinds sprinkled with powdered pimiento cheese. Oysters, fried pickles, boiled peanuts, Kool-Aid pickles, hushpuppies, chicken wings, pulled pork, pulled chicken, tri-tip, hot links, baby back ribs with house-enhanced traditional southern sides, plus smoked fried chicken, crawfish rolls, and the CLT—chicken bacon, lettuce, tomato, and mayo on white bread—will bring you back to Lillie's Q on a regular basis. Sample the excellent variety of house-made sauces to see what you like best with each menu item. If you like the Q on North Avenue, there's also a French Market Store at 131 N. Clinton St. that sells half of the Bucktown menu.

We liked Charlie's "non-Q" shrimp and grits in a small cast-iron skillet so much that we had to have the recipe to share with you. Where else can you get non-Q this good in a barbecue joint?

SHRIMP AND GRITS LILLIE'S Q

Serves 2 to 4

SHRIMP

½ pound (2 sticks) butter

2 tablespoons olive oil

¾ cup chili sauce

2 tablespoons Worcestershire sauce

2 tablespoons fresh lemon juice

2 large cloves garlic, minced

2 teaspoons minced parsley

1 teaspoon cayenne

1 teaspoon paprika

1 teaspoon dried oregano

1 teaspoon Lillie's Q Hot Sauce
   or Louisiana hot sauce

1 pound shrimp, peeled and deveined

GRITS

2 cups heavy cream

2 cups water, or more as needed

1 pound (4 sticks) butter

1 cup stone-ground grits

Cayenne

Salt

Combine all the shrimp ingredients except the shrimp in a medium saucepan and bring to a simmer for 10 minutes. Allow to cool to room temperature. Place the shrimp in a baking pan, cover with the sauce, and marinate for 4 hours.

Preheat the oven to 350°F. To make the grits, bring the cream, 2 cups water, and butter to a simmer in a medium saucepan. Slowly whisk in the grits in a steady stream. Cook, stirring, for 45 minutes or until the grits are soft. Season with cayenne and salt to taste. Adjust the consistency as desired by adding more water. Keep warm.

Bake the shrimp, uncovered, until pink throughout, 10 to 12 minutes. Serve the shrimp and sauce over the grits.

BRUNSWICK STEW

Serves 8

5 ounces ground beef

1 (15-ounce) can vegetable soup

1 (15-ounce) can tomato soup

1 (15-ounce) can lima beans

1 (15-ounce) can creamed corn

1 (11-ounce) can niblet corn

⅓ cup apple cider vinegar

⅓ cup Lillie's Q Smoky Sauce,
   or your favorite

1 (10-ounce) can Rotel tomatoes
   and green chiles

1¼ cups water, or as desired

Lillie's Q Hot Sauce or Louisiana
   hot sauce, as desired

2 pounds smoked pork, chopped

10 ounces smoked hot links, chopped

¾ pound pulled smoked chicken breast

Brown the ground beef in a large pot. Add the soups, lima beans, corns, cider vinegar, Smoky Sauce, Rotel, water, and hot sauce. Bring to a simmer and simmer for 1 hour. Add the smoked meats and cook just until hot.

Checkpoint Chicky Wings

The BBQ Shack

1613 E. Peoria St.
Paola, KS 66071
913-294-5908
http://www.thebbqshack.com

Rick Schoenberger is known in barbecue circles as "Shake." He is a competition barbecuer who made a successful transition from contestant to full-time pitmaster and restaurant proprietor. After winning a truckload of awards at barbecue contests, Rick started catering under the name Double Barrel BBQ Co. When his wife took calls for him back then, he was usually working on a catering job, so she'd tell the caller, "He's out in the shack."

After successful runs at catering, cooking at the local American Legion and VFW posts, and marketing his sauce and rub under the BBQ Shack name, Shake opened the restaurant in 2006. Two years later business was so brisk that he moved to the current location, with more seating and easier access. Guy Fieri paid a visit and aired it with positive raves on his Food Network *Diners, Drive-Ins and Dives* show.

The BBQ Shack has racked up impressive sales records in a small Kansas town that is a short commute from heavyweight barbecue competition in Kansas City. We have yet to catch Shake reading or quoting Shakespeare, but he has had that nickname since sixth grade, so he is surely no stranger to the works of the Bard!

The BBQ Shack is Mayberry Heaven to fans of the bygone *Andy Griffith Show* and *Mayberry RFD,* present company included. Andy, Barney, Goober, Aunt Bee, and other characters from the two popular shows would feel proud that the BBQ Shack honors their legacy with a collectors' treasure of Mayberry memorabilia and outstanding barbecue. Most menu items are named after a Mayberry character or place.

"Checkpoint Chicky" is the scene of Sheriff Barney Fife's speed trap. When Andy argued with Barney about his strict enforcement of the speed limit, Barney's classic reply was "Now, Andy, if you let them take 30, they'll take 35. If you let them take 35, they'll take 40," and so on. Same goes for Shake's wings. It's a good idea to make more than you think your guests will take. You can make the all-purpose rub with the recipe here, or you can order the BBQ Shack All-Purpose Barbeque Rub from Rick on the Internet. Get it and you will enjoy it!

"CHECKPOINT CHICKY" WINGS

Serves 4

¼ cup sugar

2 tablespoons onion salt

2 tablespoons garlic salt

2 tablespoons paprika

2 teaspoons chili powder

1 teaspoon black pepper

1 teaspoon lemon pepper

1 teaspoon rubbed sage

1 teaspoon dried basil

¼ teaspoon ground rosemary

¼ teaspoon cayenne

3 pounds chicken wings (about 15)

Canola oil or lard, for deep-frying

¼ cup barbecue sauce (optional)

To make the rub, combine the sugar, onion salt, garlic salt, paprika, chili powder, black pepper, lemon pepper, sage, basil, rosemary, and cayenne in an airtight container and blend well. Set aside until ready to use.

Rinse the wings with cold water and pat dry with paper towels. Cut into 3 sections, discarding the tips or saving them for another use.

Place the chicken wings in a large bowl or plastic tub large enough to permit mixing the wings and rub together. Sprinkle a liberal amount (1 to 2 ounces, or 2 to 4 tablespoons) of the rub in with the wings and mix by turning the wings over and over. You still want to see plenty of skin through the rub, so add the rub a little at a time. Place the wings on a smoker at 275°F for approximately 1½ hours, or until the wings reach 165°F on an instant-read thermometer. If you want a crispier skin on the finished wings, cool them down in the refrigerator for at least 1 hour or overnight.

Put the oil in your deep-fryer and preheat to 350°F (or put the oil in a deep pot and measure the oil temperature with a deep-frying thermometer). The fry basket in a turkey deep-fryer works great for these wings. Deep-fry the wings for 1½ to 2 minutes, until they brown and float to the top.

If you want hot wings or barbecue wings, put a dozen wings in a stainless-steel or ceramic bowl, pour the barbecue sauce over the wings, and toss and shake to coat with sauce.

Fried Cheese Stick Grits

Memphis Minnie's Barbeque Joint & Smoke House

576 Haight St.
San Francisco, CA 94117
415-864-PORK (7675)
http://www.memphisminnies.com

Memphis Minnie's is proof that "San Francisco barbecue" is *not* an oxymoron. Thanks to the late Bob Kantor, founder, and his hand-picked manager, Tom Campbell, you can feast on barbecue here that rivals America's best anywhere.

Bright colors on the walls and furniture evoke a nouveau-hippie feel instead of a Memphis barbecue joint, but it fits the neighborhood. You're in San Francisco's Lower Haight, after all.

Minnie's barbecue is cooked with real white oak in a Smoke Master pit named "Olivia." There is no mistaking it is real barbecue. And although it needs no sauce, we enjoy sampling Bob's South Carolina Mustard, North Carolina Vinegar, Texas Red Sauce, and Bee Izabob's Breath Spicy Hot Sauce, plus his chipotle mayo.

Minnie's fried cheese stick grits, pork rolls, collard greens, sweet potato chunks, coleslaw, mac and cheese, pit-smoked beans, corn bread muffins, and Smoky Mountain Wings are all delicious, and they go down just fine with the sake sampler or a frosty Anchor Steam beer.

Save room for banana pudding with whipped cream and vanilla wafers that equals any we've enjoyed in North Carolina, plus a slice of smoked pecan pie, and a fried peach pie as good as any we've had in Memphis.

Rest in peace, Bob. We wish Ben, Bob's wife, Gail, and the talented, dedicated staff the best in continuing Memphis Minnie's legacy at this remarkable barbecue joint.

Fried cheese grits are a best seller. You'll know why at first bite. Bob gave us the recipe with his signature southern-style generosity. His son, Ben, developed it.

FRIED CHEESE STICK GRITS

Serves 8 to 12

4 cups water

1 quart milk

2 cloves garlic, minced

5 cloves smoked garlic, mashed (recipe follows)

2 cups grits (not instant)

¾ pound sharp cheddar cheese

½ cup freshly grated Parmesan cheese

1 teaspoon salt

1 teaspoon black pepper

2 large eggs

3 tablespoons milk

1 cup cornmeal

1 cup corn flour

Canola oil, for deep-frying

Dipping sauce, salsa, or barbecue
  sauce, for serving

Bring the water, milk, and fresh and smoked garlic to a boil. Add the grits, stirring constantly, and simmer for 6 to 8 minutes. Remove from the heat and stir in the cheeses, salt, and pepper.

Pour the mixture evenly into a parchment-lined 9 by 13-inch pan and chill until very cold, 4 to 6 hours or overnight. Turn out, peel off the parchment, and cut into 1 by 1 by 4-inch sticks.

Combine and beat the eggs and milk in a small bowl. Combine the cornmeal and corn flour in a medium bowl. Coat the grit sticks in the egg wash and then in the cornmeal mixture. Place on a parchment-lined sheet pan and chill until ready to fry.

Put the oil in your deep-fryer and preheat to 370°F (or use a skillet and measure the temperature of the oil with a deep-frying thermometer). Fry the sticks for 3 to 5 minutes, until golden brown. Serve with your favorite dipping sauce, salsa, or barbecue sauce.

SMOKED GARLIC

½ cup extra-virgin olive oil

1 pound garlic cloves, peeled

Sea salt and black pepper

Preheat your smoker to 230° to 250°F.

Heat an ovenproof saucepan over medium-high heat. Starting the garlic on the stove saves roasting time. When it's hot, add the olive oil. Next, add the garlic cloves and season with salt and pepper. Let the cloves begin to caramelize, then put the pan in the preheated smoker.

Smoke-roast the garlic cloves for 1½ to 2 hours, until nicely browned. Let cool. This makes more than you'll need for the Fried Cheese Stick Grits, but you can store it in an airtight container in the refrigerator for up to a week and use it in a variety of dishes.

To make a garlic paste: When cool enough to handle easily, put the roasted garlic into a small bowl, mash with a fork, and add oil from the pan until a paste forms. This paste makes great garlic bread!

BBQ Egg Rolls and Cucumber Onion Slaw

Smokey D's BBQ

5055 NW 2nd St.
Des Moines, IA 50309
515-243-2747
http://www.smokeydsbbq.com

It's a good thing Iowa artist Grant Wood's sister, Nan, and his dentist, Dr. B. H. McKeeby, couldn't eat ribs at Smokey D's before posing for *American Gothic*. Their stoic daughter/father expressions would have given way to saucy-faced grins.

The mood is never somber at Smokey D's. Regulars know that the line moves quickly and it's worth the wait to fill up on barbecue ribs, smoked pulled chicken, sliced turkey, sliced brisket, burnt ends, pulled pork, baked beans, coleslaw, cucumber onion slaw, and other sides. At first bite, especially with the burnt ends and the ribs, you'll fully appreciate what happens when two championship pitmasters and their families team up to open a restaurant. This team has the added advantage that one member, Shad Kirton, is a chef. Darren and Sherry Warth, on the other

hand, needn't remind Shad and his wife, Angie, that their Smokey D's team won Grand Champion at the 2013 American Royal World Series of Barbecue. Shad and Angie's team, A Boy and His Barbecue, compete separately from Darren and Sherry and have won their fair share of big contests. At home in Des Moines, it's one big family, one big team, dedicated to serving you some of the best barbecue you'll ever eat.

The meat needs no sauce, but since three styles of Russ & Frank's BBQ Sauce are on the tables as the house sauce, why not try it? A little bit of the sweet, mild, tomato-based sauce is a nice complement to the ribs and brisket, and it's really good on fries. We like a dab of sassy on our pork and chicken.

Smokey D's has two other locations to accommodate downtown workers who don't have time to drive to the mother pit for lunch. The one on Locust is near the Des Moines Art Center's John and Mary Pappajohn Sculpture Garden, a downtown gem.

Thanks to Smokey D's for sharing these two delicious recipes with us, compliments of Chef Shad.

BBQ EGG ROLLS

Makes about 16

DRESSING

2 cups white balsamic vinegar

⅔ cup sugar

1½ tablespoons Smokin' Guns Hot Rub

1 teaspoon ground white pepper

1½ teaspoon celery seeds

FILLING

4 cups finely shredded cabbage

½ cup finely shredded carrots

½ cup finely julienned red onion

½ cup finely diced red bell pepper

1 bunch fresh cilantro, finely chopped

1 pound chopped barbecue pork (very small chop) or your favorite barbecued meat

Cornstarch, as needed

16 egg roll wrappers

Canola oil, for frying

Your favorite barbecue sauce, for serving

In a medium mixing bowl, combine the dressing ingredients, whisk well, and set aside.

In a large bowl, combine the cabbage, carrots, onion, red pepper, and cilantro and mix well. Add the dressing and toss to coat. Cover and refrigerate for at least 45 minutes. Add the pork and mix well.

Dust a work surface with cornstarch. Place one wrapper on the surface with points at 12, 3, 6, and 9 o'clock. Brush water on all edges of the wrapper to moisten. Place about ½ cup of drained filling in the center and spread the filling into a tube shape from left to right. The tube shape should be about 3½ inches long and 1½ inches wide.

Fold the bottom corner over the filling toward the top, stopping halfway between the filling and top corner. Fold the left and right corners in toward the center. Tightly seal the ends. Roll the egg roll toward the top corner to close. Dust the egg roll with cornstarch to keep it from sticking to the others. Repeat with the remaining filling and wrappers.

Heat oil in a deep fryer or deep pan to 365°F. Fry the egg rolls a few at a time until golden, 2 to 4 minutes.

Remove with a slotted spoon and transfer to a paper-towel-lined plate to drain. Serve with your favorite barbecue sauce.

CUCUMBER ONION SLAW

Serves 8 to 10

3 cups apple cider vinegar

1 cup sugar (see Note)

6 cucumbers, peel on, sliced ⅛ inch thick

1 medium red onion, finely julienned

In a small mixing bowl, whisk together the vinegar and sugar to make the dressing. Place the cucumbers and onion in a large bowl and toss to combine. Add the dressing and toss again. Cover and refrigerate for at least 2 hours before serving.

Note: Add more sugar if you like it sweeter. You can also add dried chiles, black pepper, and other veggies as desired.

Blue Cheese Bowl Appetizer

Ridgewood Barbecue

900 Elizabethton Hwy.
Bluff City, TN 37618
423-538-7543

ur good friend Fred Sauceman has sung the praises of Ridgewood for years. When Ardie was the official Curator of Sauces at the Southern Foodways Alliance symposium on barbecue, Fred readily volunteered to bring a fresh quart of Ridgewood Bar-B-Que Sauce. We can still picture Fred holding that jar carefully and reverently. He handed the jar to Ardie like it was a sacred object—which to many Ridgewood fans it is. All but a few drops of Grace Proffitt's famous sauce were consumed that night by enthusiastic symposium participants. We still have the empty jar. The remnants that went begging aren't safe to eat now, but the empty jar with the Ridgewood label is a treasure we cherish.

Besides our friendship with Fred, we have our own history with the Ridgewood. In 1984, when Ardie founded the Diddy-Wa-Diddy National Barbecue Sauce Contest, he wrote to Grace Proffitt and asked her to enter her sauce in the contest. Grace herself replied, with a nice letter, a newspaper article about the Ridgewood, and a bottle of sauce. We've been Ridgewood fans ever since! If you want to know more about Ridgewood, check out the DVD *Smoke in the Holler: The Saucy Story of Ridgewood Barbecue*.

Grace and one of her two sons, Terry, have since passed away. To the relief of thousands of Ridgewood fans who worried that the restaurant would close, Grace's surviving son, Larry, and his daughter, Lisa Peters, have stepped up to the pit. Larry, a pharmacist, owns Burgie Drugs in nearby Elizabethton, but he doesn't mind wearing two hats by helping Lisa and the twenty-seven Ridgewood staffers live up to the Ridgewood's reputation for quality.

Only two living persons know the Ridgewood sauce recipe—Larry and Lisa. It is committed to memory, true to the Proffitt tradition. That's no small task, as there are more than two dozen ingredients! You'll believe that when you taste it. We chuckle when reading the ingredients listed on the label: tomato catsup, salt, sugar, and spices.

Unlike most Tennessee barbecue joints, the Ridgewood serves hickory-smoked fresh ham instead of shoulders. You can taste the difference. With the generous portions of meat, homemade fries, slaw, and Grace's barbecue beans, you will not leave hungry.

is from pigs that made _Perfect_ Hogs of themselves

When you can't enjoy the Ridgewood's popular Blue Cheese Bowl appetizer in person, try ours. Just remember, there's none better than the original Ridgewood Blue Cheese Bowl. Saltine crackers are served with this at the Ridgewood. You can stick with that out of tradition, or add baby carrots, broccoli florets, celery sticks, and other munchy, crunchy dipping foods. This recipe also works well as a salad dressing.

BLUE CHEESE BOWL APPETIZER

Makes 2 cups

½ cup Danish or other blue cheese, crumbled

½ cup mayonnaise

½ cup dairy sour cream

¼ cup buttermilk

1 tablespoon Worcestershire sauce

2 teaspoons fresh lemon juice

1 teaspoon grated onion

1 large clove garlic, pressed

1 teaspoon Lawry's Seasoned Salt

Black pepper, to taste

In a medium bowl, combine all the ingredients and blend well. Cover and chill for at least an hour to allow the flavors to blend.

Rocky Mountain Oysters (aka RMOs)

Hoke's Genuine Pit BBQ

9134 W. 88th Ave.
Westminster, CO 80005
303-424-QPIT (7748)
http://hokesbbq.com

oke's opened in 1996 as a catering business, and the restaurant opened in 2002. The reason Hoke's barbecue is constantly good is that they stay true to their one mission to keep their barbecue genuine.

You understand why there's a line out the door when you slice into the tender prime meat with its smoke-concentrated beefy taste. We were impressed that it came with real beef juice for dipping and pureed horseradish—not the tamed creamy type—for adding another level of zip.

The thing we especially liked was the Rocky Mountain Oysters appetizer. No, they aren't oysters harvested from a fresh, cold-water mountain stream in the Colorado Rockies. Yes, they are what you think they are: bull testicles. They are rich and good! Some call them country caviar. Here's our version, compliments of our barbecue buddy Steve Holbrook, who also cooks up a mean batch of pig fries. If you can't find the breader at your local store, you can order online or substitute your own favorite breader. You can also order bull testicles online.

ROCKY MOUNTAIN OYSTERS (aka RMOS)

Serves 20 to 24

5 pounds frozen bull testicles

2 to 4 cups Atkinson's Flowering Onion Breader

Plenty of cold beer—Hey, it's a very hot job!

Morton's Hot Salt

Canola oil or lard, for deep-frying

To prep the golden nuggets: Thaw just enough to be able to skin them. While the testicles are still semi-frozen, slice them into coin shapes about 3/8 inch thick and then let them thaw completely.

In the meantime, put 1 cup of breader in a medium bowl and blend in enough beer to make a runny batter. Place 1 cup of dry breader in another medium bowl. If you run out of either the wet mixture or the dry batter, remix and refill the bowls as needed.

Use paper towels to dry the testicle coins, season them with Morton's Hot Salt to your liking, and then drop them into beer batter to cover. Lift, let drain slightly, then drop into dry batter to cover with a dry outer coating.

Put the oil in your deep-fryer and preheat to 350°F (or fill a skillet and use a deep-frying thermometer). Drop in the RMOs and fry until they become floating golden nuggets, 3 to 5 minutes, working in batches if necessary.

Fried Green Tomatoes

Williamson Bros. Bar-B-Q

1425 Roswell Rd.
Marietta, GA 30062
770-971-3201
http://realpagessites.com/williamsonbros

sk your taxi driver in metro Atlanta where to eat the best barbecue in town, and the odds are high that the reply will be "Williamson Brothers." The place has become very popular since Jack Williamson and his two sons, Danny and Larry, decided to move their Talladega, Alabama, restaurant to metropolitan Atlanta in 1989. They have since opened Williamson Bros. restaurants in Canton and Douglasville, Georgia. The menu is extensive enough to appeal to everyone who likes barbecue. People who don't especially like barbecue—unimaginable to us—will find enough delicious appetizers to make a feast, plus salmon, catfish, burgers, and hot dogs. A platter of Williamson Bros. barbecued pork ribs with a side of Brunswick stew, okra, and corn on the cob is a memorable feast. Start with a fried green tomato appetizer. Here's our version of the southern classic.

FRIED GREEN TOMATOES

Serves 6 to 8

4 to 6 medium green tomatoes

Salt and black pepper

2 cups all-purpose flour

2 cups cornmeal

2 cups cold milk

2 large eggs

2 tablespoons bacon grease,
   or more if desired

Slice the tomatoes ¼ to ½ inch thick. Season with salt and pepper to taste on both sides. Place the flour and cornmeal in separate shallow dishes for dredging. In a medium bowl, combine the milk and eggs, beating until incorporated. Place the bacon grease in a large skillet and heat over high heat. When the skillet is hot, dust each tomato slice with flour, then dip it into the egg wash, and then into the cornmeal. Fry some of the battered tomato slices for about 3 minutes, until golden on the bottom. Gently turn and fry the other side. Repeat with the remaining tomato slices.

B.B.'S
LAWNSIDE
BAR-B-Q

ABS   1395 TO 1850
ORT END   840
NG END   650

EAT   BY   THE   POUND
BEEF HAM PORK TURKEY   810
          OVER 20 LBS   795
                       765
SANDWICH BEEF   710
CHICKEN   WHOLE
             HALF   465

        DRINKS
G RC OR ICE TEA   120
POP IN CANS   75
STEWART   SODA   130

BEER   12 OZ 225
IMPORT 250   QUART 315

ST BRISKET

Texas Monthly

R WHITES

Main Dishes

With main dishes, eye appeal is important. Barbecue needn't be served on fine china, but it should be presented with care. Whether it's served on butcher paper, on a plastic plate, in a plastic basket or paper boat, or on a Styrofoam or paper plate, the food has to look good! Our good Texas buddy John Raven, PhB, has an opinion about the many barbecue joints in Texas and elsewhere that serve their barbecue on butcher paper. When John was a human rocket at chili contests, he was Daredevil Bad McFad. Today we call him Bad. Here's how Bad puts it as no one else can: "One problem I have with just about all the barbecue joints I have visited is that unforgivable butcher paper. I take my brisket to the table, and by the time I have cut one or two slices I am eating through the hole in the butcher paper and onto the top of a table that could use a good steam cleaning. I want a real plate, and I want a real fork. I carry a knife.

"The butcher paper serving that so many find so cute dates back to when minorities were not allowed in the barbecue joints. They were served at the back door and their food wrapped in butcher paper. Although I now qualify as a minority, I still want a plate or at least a clean tray."* John knows more about barbecue than anyone.

Beyond looks, the meat should be packed with smoked meat flavor and easy to chew. Ribs should be moist, tender, and done enough that they pull apart easily, but not so done that they fall off the bone. Pork should be moist and tender, not dry and stringy. Beef should also be tender and flavorful. House Park puts it best in their slogan: "Need no teef to eat my beef." The spices on the meat should complement the meat flavor, not overpower it. When it comes to sauce, we prefer ours on the side. Others like their meat basted and slathered with sauce before serving.

With a few exceptions, the dishes in this chapter reflect regional tastes and availability. You'll find beef in Texas, pork in the Carolinas, mutton in Kentucky, a little bit of bison in Colorado, and a variety of meats in the Midwest and elsewhere. We even threw in some fish and seafood from a couple of our favorite joints. Dig in!

*Quoted with permission from the book Bad is writing, *I Know More About Barbecue Than Anyone.*

Smoked Barbecue Beef Ribs

The County Line Bar-B-Q

6500 Bee Cave Road
Austin, TX 78746
512-327-1742
http://www.countyline.com

Is it legendary? We can go along with that. County Line Barbecue has been up on the hill since 1975. This is the original location. On the outside it looks like a Texas roadhouse.

The huge, meaty beef ribs, slow-smoked for 18 to 20 hours, are what put County Line on the map. When you're eating County Line beef ribs, you're going to want to "Get It All Over Ya!"—the trademark barbecue sauce, that is.

Although Country Line won't or can't divulge too many of their cooking secrets, they were eager to tell us how to smoke ribs at home. Trim some of the fat from the back side of the ribs before you put them on the smoker. An oak-wood fire is preferred for smoking at County Line, and that's our choice at home, too. Season the ribs all over with salt, freshly ground pepper, or perhaps a little garlic powder before placing them in the pit. We suggest seasoning with garlic salt and freshly ground black pepper. You don't need a hot fire; you do need to keep the ribs as far away

from the fire as possible. Ribs are not as tough as brisket, but they need to smoke for a long time. When we tested this recipe for beef ribs in a backyard smoker, it took 6 to 8 hours to cook a slab of ribs; 1 to 1½ hours per pound is a good rule of thumb to follow.

SMOKED BARBECUE BEEF RIBS

Serves 7 to 10

2 to 3 (5- to 7-pound) slabs beef back ribs

¼ cup garlic salt

3 tablespoons black pepper

Prepare a mesquite charcoal or oak-wood fire in your smoker; let burn for 1 hour or until the flames disappear. The temperature should be 200° to 225°F. Place the water pan in the smoker and fill it with water.

Season the ribs all over with the seasoning, sprinkling it on and not rubbing it in.

Place the ribs in the smoker and cover with the smoker lid; cook for 6 to 8 hours, until an instant-read thermometer registers 180°F or the ribs pull apart, adding wood and water as needed.

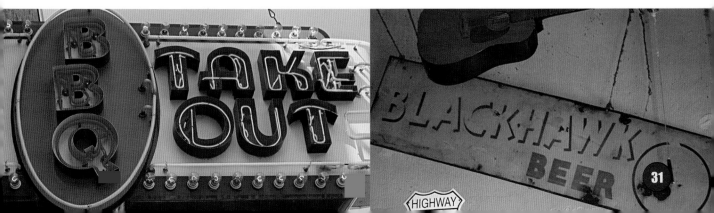

Barbecued Beef Shoulder Clod

Smitty's Market

208 S. Commerce St.
Lockhart, TX 78644
512-398-9344
http://www.smittysmarket.com

At Smitty's we like to park in the back and go in the back door and into the pit room, where you'll find one of the oldest barbecue pits in use in Texas and most likely in the entire United States. That's where you order your barbecue, and then you take your order into the dining room to get weighed and priced. That's also where you order your sides and drinks.

To sample a full feast of Smitty's barbecue, order one or two pork ribs, a slice of clod, a slice of brisket, a pork chop, and a smoked beef sausage link with pinto beans, soda crackers, raw onion slices, and dill pickle spears. It is served on butcher paper.

Smitty's has four pits plus a smoke room. The two pits on the old side were built in 1924, and the newer ones were built in 1972 and 1978. True to old-time tradition, the pits have no thermometers. It is a pitmaster thing.

John August Fullilove, pitmaster, is a son of owner Nina Schmidt Sells and Smitty's grandson. John's brother, James, manager of Smitty's Market, orchestrates pitmaster, restaurant, and meat-market operations to the traditional high standards customers expect at Smitty's.

BARBECUED BEEF SHOULDER CLOD

Serves 35 to 40

1 (18- to 22-pound) beef shoulder clod

Salt and black pepper

Season the shoulder clod all over with salt and pepper and place on an indirect fire built with post oak and heated to 400°F. Cover and cook for 4 to 8 hours, until tender.

Note: On a Weber Smokey Mountain, you'd probably have to cut the beef clod in half.

On a previous visit, John, a big, easygoing, "this is the way it is" type of person, told Paul the way it is when comparing beef brisket to beef shoulder clod. John said beef shoulder clod is better than brisket. Why? Beef clod has more marbling and therefore more flavor, and the yield for the clod is better. You lose at best 50 percent of brisket, where the shoulder clod will lose 40 to 45 percent, and it just tastes better.

When Paul asked John how long he cooks the clod and at what temperature, the answer put Paul into a mild state of shock. John said they cook at about 400°F for 4 to 8 hours, depending on how soon they need the meat. John explained that when you cook hot for a short time, it seals in the juices and you don't get the clods too smoky, and that's the way Smitty's prefers them. We can't argue with that.

Cooking Method

Cooper's Old Time Pit Bar-B-Que

505 W. Dallas St.
Llano, TX 78643
877-533-5553 or 325-247-5995 (for mail order)
http://www.coopersbbq.com

Cooper's is considered one of the meccas of barbecue, and we agree. The Cooper's in Llano has no real ties to the one in Junction (opposite page) except they were taught the same way. Cooper's in Llano is more rustic and has a little more ambience, but they are set up almost identically.

At one end of the parking lot is an enormous pile of mesquite logs. Next to that is the barbecue smokehouse with five old rectangular closed steel pits lined up in a row. At the pit closest to the door, customers choose their meat.

The barbecue at Cooper's is cooked cowboy style—that is, directly over smoldering hardwood coals. The logs are burned down to embers in a big enclosed fireplace, then transferred to the pits by wheelbarrow. The pitman shovels the coals under the meat. The brisket takes 6 to 8 hours and is outstanding, with the robust flavor of meat and smoke. Everything else is fabulous too: the huge pork chops, which are one of Cooper's signature items (hence the motto "Cooper's Old Time Pit Bar-B-Que, Home of the Big Chop"), the sirloin, the pork sausage, the chicken, the pork ribs, the goat, and on Tuesdays and Fridays, the beef ribs.

In its March 2001 issue, *Texas Monthly* stated that number three of the top fifty things that any good Texan should do before dying is to pick a piece from one of Cooper's Old Time Pit Bar-B-Que pits in Llano. Paul doesn't usually like mesquite-smoked meats, but he likes the way Cooper's cooks theirs, and he would have to agree with *Texas Monthly*. He'd also include the Cooper's in Junction.

BETTER THAN A $162 DUCK!

Cooper's Bar-B-Q & Grill
2423 N. Main St
Junction, TX 76849
325-446-8664

The first time Paul went to Cooper's in Junction, he and his friend, the late Stuart Carpenter, traveled there from Houston just to have some barbecue, not realizing or caring that it wasn't the famous Cooper's in Llano, Texas.

When they pulled into the parking lot, the view was amazing. In the back were fifty-some cords of mesquite stacked for aging (drying), a pit house that held five old rectangular pits with steel lids, and a 500-gallon fire barrel standing on its side with a 4-foot opening in it and a roaring fire burning away.

Paul and Stuart went inside, where displayed in the counter were samples of all the barbecue—brisket, ribs, two types of sausage (smoked and jalapeño), big thick pork chops, and cabrito (baby goat), as well as side dishes such as pinto beans, potato salad, and slaw. Their order went something like this: the point of that brisket, a link of smoked and jalapeño sausage, some ribs (the serving lady started

cutting off of the short end, but Paul and Stuart wanted them off the long end, so they just took all of them), and a couple of pork chops. They each also had beans and split an order of potato salad and slaw with two large drinks. The bill came to $85, and when they left, they ordered another $80 worth of barbecue to send to a friend in New York.

Paul and Stuart's trip to Cooper's in Junction always reminds Paul of the old country song "The $162 Duck," which is about a man with a duck who basically swindles a guy out of $162. Few people remember the song, but the analogy is this: The gasoline for the trip cost $77, and the lunch was $85, for a grand total of $162. But the analogy ends there, because there sure wasn't a swindle involved with Cooper's. Paul likes to tell people that the worst thing he can say is that he would go back, and he has been back four more times and if he is in the area he will go back again.

Tootsie's Mop

Snow's BBQ
516 Main St.
Lexington, TX 78947
979-773-4640
http://www.snowsbbq.com

erry and Kim Bexley own it. Tootsie Tomanetz is the pitmaster. So why call it Snow's? "As I understand it," a regular customer who was first in line early one Saturday morning told us, "the original owner had a full head of snow-white hair. I don't know his real name, but everybody called him 'Snow.'"

When fame comes to a place, crowds follow. That's what happened to Snow's when *Texas Monthly* magazine named it "Best Barbecue in Texas" in 2009. They open at eight in the morning and are sold out before noon. Tootsie and Kerry, and Tootsie's son, Hershey, fire up the pits with post oak for the brisket and oak for everything else at ten Friday night. Soon after, the meats go on, timed to be ready Saturday morning. Brisket, pork steak, pork ribs, sausage, and chicken: They smoke it to perfection. Snow would be proud of how Kerry, Kim, Tootsie, and Hershey are carrying on the Lexington tradition of excellence in barbecue.

Snow's is one of the few barbecue joints in America where you can get true barbecue for breakfast. We can't think of a better way to start the day!

Paul says Tootsie learned to cook like he did: a little of this and a little of that, tasting as you add ingredients you feel are needed. She told Paul her mop consists of water, salt, pepper, chopped onions, mustard powder, a pound of the cheapest margarine you can buy, a little Worcestershire sauce, and vinegar. Paul tasted her mop and came up with this rendition.

TOOTSIE'S MOP

Makes about 4½ cups

4 cups water

1 small yellow onion, chopped

8 tablespoons (1 stick) margarine

1½ teaspoons dry mustard

¾ teaspoon salt

¾ teaspoon finely ground black pepper

1 to 2 tablespoons
    Worcestershire sauce

½ cup white vinegar

Put the water and onion into a stockpot or Dutch oven and bring to a boil over medium-high heat. Lower the heat and simmer until the onion is opaque. Add the margarine, dry mustard, salt, pepper, Worcestershire, and vinegar and heat until the margarine has melted. Blend well, keep warm, and baste or mop meat as needed while cooking.

Beef Brisket

Head Country Bar-B-Q

1217 E. Prospect Ave.
Ponca City, OK 74601
888-762-1227 or 580-767-8304
(for mail order)
http://www.headcountry.com

ead Country Bar-B-Q sauces and rubs are famous throughout Oklahoma and beyond. They have built an impressive reputation and product line that is good for the Oklahoma economy as well as the many barbecue lovers who savor Head Country's signature flavors on their barbecue.

When Danny and Carey Head hired Paul Schatte from his career in school administration, Paul didn't waste any time getting busy with daily restaurant and sauce factory operations, getting acquainted with staff, and putting his leadership skills to work. He also soon became a fixture on the competition barbecue circuit, racking up one impressive win after another, competing as Head Country II. Today he is vice president and part owner.

Head Country's restaurant moved to the current location from the original smaller joint. With a capacity of seventy-five hungry people, they could still use some extra tables at the busiest times. Hickory-smoked sliced or chopped beef brisket, pork spareribs, pork shoulder, turkey, ham, chicken breast, and hot links are daily fare at Head Country. You can get barbecued baked beans, coleslaw, potato salad, baked potato,

french fries, chips, deviled egg, and jalapeño peppers on the side. Our favorite Head Country feast is beef brisket with barbecued beans, potato salad, coleslaw, and a deviled egg starter. You can't go wrong with any choices you make at Head Country, so don't cheat yourself out of grazing your way through the entire menu, one visit at a time, and choosing your own favorites.

Oklahoma is cattle country, so we are grateful that Paul gave us this award-winning Head Country beef brisket recipe.

BEEF BRISKET

Serves 18 to 20

1 (12- to 14-pound or larger) packer trim brisket aged 35 to 40 days

½ cup Head Country All-Purpose Championship Seasoning

1 (10-ounce) bottle Head Country Premium Marinade

1 (18-ounce) bottle Head Country Original Flavor, Hickory Smoke Flavor, or Hot Flavor Bar-B-Q Sauce

Prepare the brisket the night before you plan to cook it. There are two lean pieces of meat (the "flat" and the "deckle," or "point") sandwiched by fat. Separate the two lean pieces. Leave as much fat on the flat as you like; all of it is best in the cooking stage. The deckle should have as much fat trimmed off the surface as possible. The first time you trim out a brisket it may be difficult to find the two sections of muscle. If you have a good relationship with your local butcher, ask him to show you how to part the brisket. Most people just cook the flat, which is very good. You will be pleasantly surprised at the strong beef flavor the deckle has.

Once the two pieces are trimmed, season both with the Head Country seasoning. The flat portion can be seasoned very heavily, but the deckle should receive a light dusting of seasoning. The fat marbled in the deckle will have a salt flavor to it already. Seasoning this piece too heavily will give the meat a very salty taste. The flat can handle heavy seasoning because it will sweat a lot as it cooks.

After seasoning the meat, shake the bottle of marinade well before opening it. Drizzle some on both sides of the pieces of meat and massage it in. Place the seasoned meat in a plastic container and cover with a lid. Refrigerate it overnight.

The next day, remove the brisket from the refrigerator and allow it to warm up while you prepare the smoker. Build a fire that, when ready for cooking, will be 275°F. Seasoned pecan wood produces a good mild smoke flavor. Unseasoned wood or heavy-smoking wood will leave a creosote/smoky taste on the meat. Allow the fire to burn for 30 minutes.

Place the brisket flat in the smoker, fat side up. The deckle will not have a fat side. Push the muscle together rather than leaving it pulled or stretched out. Cook at 275°F for 3 hours. After 3 hours, check the temperature with an instant-read thermometer. Once the internal temperature reaches 160°F, remove the brisket from the smoker with a fork or heat-rated gloves and place the brisket fat side down on a double layer of aluminum foil cut large enough to seal the brisket tight. Pour ¼ cup of marinade over the top and seal the foil tightly. Do the same with the deckle piece, using a little less marinade. Return the brisket to the smoker and cook at 300°F for 3 to 3½ hours. When the internal temperature of the brisket reaches 200°F, remove the brisket from the smoker with heat-rated gloves. Open the foil and let the heat dissipate for 20 to 25 minutes. Remove the brisket from the foil and slice across the grain of both the flat and the deckle. Compare the taste of the pieces of beef. Serve with plenty of Head Country Bar-B-Q Sauce.

Smoked Beef Brisket

Franklin Barbecue

900 E. 11th St.
Austin, TX 78702
512-653-1187
http://franklinbarbecue.com

One of the qualities of what the late Murray Bowen described as a highly differentiated self is one who doesn't let praise or criticism influence his behavior. Pitmaster Aaron Franklin exemplifies that quality to a T. Franklin Barbecue is awash in praise and occasional criticism. The positive publicity has reached viral proportions, yet the occasional pundit will tell you that John Mueller's barbecue is better, and that that's where Aaron learned to barbecue. "I wish people would stop saying that," Aaron will say with a tired smile. "I was cashier at John's place, that's all." Maybe the persistence of the myth is as irritating as a fly in the pantry, but it has zero effect on Aaron's daily mission to produce the best barbecue possible in his custom-made, hand-built pits. Along with learning some stellar pitmaster skills by experimenting in his own backyard, Aaron learned to weld. He built or modified each pit at Franklin Barbecue, so he knows the hot spots and unique qualities of each. Unlike many pitmasters, he likes hot spots. When a hunk of meat needs more heat than the rest of the batch, he knows where to put it.

No wonder there's a long line of eager customers queued up outside hours before the doors open. They are only open for lunch, and they always sell out. If you're wondering if it's worth it, just ask several people standing in line. Many are regulars.

For the Full Franklin Experience, we recommend the brisket, ribs, sausage, pulled pork, turkey, and a Tipsy Texan sandwich with slaw, potato salad, and beans on the side. Customers rave about the espresso barbecue sauce, but Franklin meat needs no sauce. A sip of the sauce is good by itself, however. Unless you're sharing with friends, you'll have plenty to carry out and enjoy later. Also plan to take home a slice of Bourbon Banana, Pecan Key Lime, or Lemon Chess pie from Austin's favorite bakery, Cake & Spoon.

Aaron's wife, Stacy, is fully engaged in the business, and as soon as their infant daughter, Vivian, is teethed on rib bones, we hope she begins to learn the Franklin magic at the pit so the next generation will get to experience how true primal barbecue tastes.

Aaron generously shared this recipe with us. As he notes, cooking times and temperatures vary from brisket to brisket depending on marbling, breed, diet, and the use of growth hormones, as well as cooker type and its balance of convection versus radiant heat. We think that's a good excuse to practice until you get it Franklin-perfect.

SMOKED BEEF BRISKET

Serves 25 to 30

1 (12- to 15-pound) packer cut
   brisket with good marbling

2 tablespoons coarsely ground black pepper

2 tablespoons kosher salt

Trim the brisket fat down to ¼ to ⅜ inch. In a small bowl, combine the pepper and salt and mix well. Rub the brisket with the mixture. The idea is to not get too much seasoning—just enough to complement the brisket. Let rest at room temperature for about 1 hour.

Heat an offset cooker to 275°F and use a water pan. Place the brisket in the cooker fat side up with the point toward the fire. You might need to change the position depending on the type of cooker you're using, so use your best judgment. Maintain the fire at roughly 275°F. Every cooker is different; if you can hear the meat sizzling, it's too hot. Smoke for 6 to 8 hours, until the desired color is achieved (black like a Texas brisket!). Remove the brisket from the cooker and wrap tightly in butcher paper. Return it to the smoker and continue to maintain the fire until the meat starts to feel tender, 3 to 6 hours. It's ready when it's almost falling apart, but not quite! The internal temperature could be anywhere from 198° to 215°F. Let the brisket rest until it's cool enough to touch before slicing and serving.

Barbecue Brisket
with Pinto Beans

Black's Barbecue

215 N. Main St.
Lockhart, TX 78644
512-398-2712
http://www.blacksbbq.com

lack's is known as Texas's oldest barbecue restaurant continuously operated by the same family. It opened in 1932. Edgar and Norma Black, co-owners, are assisted by their sons, Kent and Terry, along with Shawn Lindsey and staff. Black's is a must stop when in Lockhart.

We especially recommend the sausages and brisket. Start with a big slice of brisket and a sample of each of the sausages: the original, which the Blacks have been making since 1932, plus the jalapeño/cheddar and the garlic sausage, which were introduced in 2003.

In addition to the brisket and pinto beans recipes, Kent Black graciously gave us the cooking procedure for their world-famous sausage.

Black's sausages are cooked in a rectangular pit with heavy lids, using indirect heat. They have a two-pit setup. The two pits share a common stack, or flue. They cook with post oak. Black's makes, stuffs, and hand-ties the sausages in small sausage rings, places them on sausage rods, and hangs them in the pits to smoke for 3 to 3½ hours at a low 175° to 200°F. We thank the Black family for sharing their recipes with us. Friendly Texas hospitality is a Black family tradition.

BARBECUED BRISKET

Serves 15

¼ cup salt

¼ cup coarsely ground black pepper

1 (9- to 10-pound) beef brisket

Prepare your pit or grill: An indirect-heat pit with a lid is preferred. We recommend using a hardwood such as post oak for heat and smoke. Some woods—mesquite and other types of oak—yield a strong, harsh flavor that is undesirable to many people. Try different hardwoods to suit your taste. Heat the pit or grill to 250° to 350°F. The lower the heat, the more smoke, the better the flavor.

Mix the salt and pepper together. Hand-rub the salt and pepper mix into the brisket. Place the brisket in the pit or grill and cook to the desired doneness, 8 to 12 hours. Serve with barbecue pinto beans.

PINTO BEANS

Serves 4 to 6

1 pound dried pinto beans, sorted for debris and washed

¼ pound salt pork, chopped

1 teaspoon black pepper

2 teaspoons paprika

2 teaspoons salt

1 teaspoon chili powder

Preheat your oven to 450°F. Place the beans in a large pot or cooker with a lid and cover with water. Add the salt pork, pepper, paprika, salt, and chili powder while stirring.

Cook, stirring occasionally and making sure they don't scorch, until the beans are soft, 3 to 4 hours. The beans can be served immediately or cooled and reheated the next day.

Note: You can also use a slow cooker and cook the beans for 5 hours on high heat or for 6 to 7 hours on low heat, stirring occasionally.

THE TEXAS CRUTCH

Legend has it that Paul Kirk coined the expression "Texas Crutch" when jesting with barbecue-contest cooks from Texas who routinely wrapped their meat in aluminum foil after smoking it for a while. Foiling meat betters your odds of getting tender barbecue. The juices steam-tenderize the meat.

In fairness to Texans, not all Texas pitmasters use the crutch, and it's used by cooks all over the country. It works. There's no right or wrong about it. Purists like Paul, however, say it makes "pot roast" out of briskets and butts. To Paul, it's not real, traditional barbecue.

We weaned ourselves from the crutch more than a decade ago. We like bark, and it's near impossible to get bark with the crutch. Nevertheless, you'll see some aluminum foil in some of our recipes, and we guarantee you'll like the result.

Barbecued Rib Eye

Ranch House BBQ & Steakhouse

10841 Kennedy Creek Rd. SW
Olympia, WA 98512
360-866-8704
http://www.ranchhousebbq.net

Amy Anderson and Melanie Tapia opened the Ranch House BBQ & Steakhouse in 2004. Amy, a graduate of Paul's pitmaster classes, brings years of world-championship barbecue cooking contest experience to Ranch House. Melanie, with her background in marketing and event planning, plus some impressive barbecue credentials as a competitor and founding member of the Southern California BBQ Association, brings complementary business expertise. Melanie worked for several large companies before starting her own event company in California. She hosted the first barbecue competition ever in Southern California and has organized more than twenty-five other contests. Among the twenty-five teams from four states at that first contest were heavy hitters Bad Byron of Bad Byron's Butt Rub, Mike Scrutchfield of Top Secret, and Amy Anderson's Smokin' Bullet from the Pacific Northwest. That's where Melanie and Amy met. In 2001 Melanie moved to Washington to assist in running Amy's catering business and now the restaurant. The people of Olympia and the many tourists who visit have good reason to celebrate the day Amy and Melanie met. They bring an exemplary commitment to excellence at the Ranch House BBQ & Steakhouse.

The original Ranch House was on the major highway to and from Lake Olympia, a great location. The red wooden shack with checkered curtains had the right aura and world-class barbecue. Word spread, and business was booming when, after 3½ years of growth and a pile of awards, a 100-foot-wide, 15-foot-high wall of mud and debris rumbled through the property, taking everything along with it. Ranch House BBQ was destroyed on the morning of Monday, December 3, 2007, when the mudslide swallowed up the water and septic systems, tore apart the restaurant and outbuildings, and destroyed the smokers that made Anderson's signature barbecue meats (and even the checkered curtains that made customers feel welcome).

Thanks to the owners' tenacity, with the help of overwhelming community support, Ranch House BBQ rose like the phoenix from the smoke and mud. Within 48 hours, a local hotel had offered use of its vacant restaurant space. Thankful for the opportunity to stay in business, Ranch House BBQ operated temporarily in the Governor Hotel until December 2008. A loan from the Small Business Administration made it possible to rebuild and reopen in a new building at the original location, to the delight of their fans.

Amy's original-recipe dry rub is applied to all Ranch House barbecued meats prior to smoking with apple and cherry wood from the Anderson family farm. Ranch House has been awarded "Best BBQ of South Sound" for several years in a row due to this winning combination of rub and smoke.

Ranch House BBQ offers a full range of championship barbecued ribs, brisket, pulled pork, and chicken, along with excellent charcoal-grilled steaks. One of its signature items is smoked rib eye steak. It is outstanding, especially if you order it medium-rare. Here, thanks to pitmaster Amy, is the recipe.

BARBECUED RIB EYE

Serves 1

PRIME RIB RUB

2 tablespoons sugar

2 tablespoons sea salt

1 tablespoon garlic powder

1 tablespoon paprika

2 teaspoons ground thyme

2 teaspoons ground oregano

2 teaspoons finely ground black pepper

1 teaspoon lemon pepper

1 teaspoon chipotle powder

RIB EYE

⅓ cup yellow mustard

1 whole beef rib eye (about 13 pounds)

Combine all the ingredients for the rub in an airtight container and store until ready to use, or up to 6 months.

Lightly brush the yellow mustard all over your rib eye. Then lightly sprinkle on the dry rub to coat the meat. Preheat your smoker to 225°F. Place the meat fat side up in the smoker and cook for approximately 1 hour. Let cool completely. Cut the meat into the desired steak size. Ranch House keeps it big—a full pound! Grill the steaks over hot coals to your desired doneness. Serve and enjoy.

BBQ HALLS OF FLAME & FAME

Goode Company Barbeque in Houston started the first Barbeque Hall of Flame. Then came the Kansas City Barbeque Society Hall of Flame, followed by an online hall of fame hosted by the North Carolina Barbecue Society. The National Barbecue Hall of Fame and Museum Committee, formed in Kansas City in 2003, disbursed their funds to local culinary schools and related charities in 2012 when the American Royal World Series of Barbecue assumed the assets and Web site of a virtual Hall of Fame in Iowa and installed a Barbecue Hall of Fame at the American Royal.

We applaud these noble efforts and would love to see all real or virtual barbecue halls of fame or flame grow into fully funded, continuously operated institutions. Unfortunately, though, they've been able to reach few, if any, individuals outside the barbecue network. It's OK to preach to the choir, but there's a lot of work yet to be done (and millions of dollars in funding to make it first class) to reach out to the general public and inspire a passion for barbecue throughout the land—a goal we heartily endorse.

To reach that goal the ultimate BBQ Hall of Fame would have to feature:

- **Interactive displays that tell the story of barbecue from thousands of years back to the present—the real history of barbecue as factually as it can be presented**
- **Several dining rooms featuring regional styles of barbecue**
- **National and international guest barbecue pitmasters each month, teaching classes and designing menus for the month—to truly appreciate barbecue you have to get it on your hands and into your belly**
- **Several indoor and outdoor demonstration kitchens equipped with the latest technology**
- **A large auditorium for presentations, movies, and documentaries related to barbecue**
- **A big hotel and conference center**
- **The ability to host four major invitational competitions each year— spring, summer, fall, winter**
- **An archive of barbecue-related books, newspapers, news clippings, videos, DVDs, CDs, tapes, photos, etc.**
- **A gift shop of barbecue memorabilia, grills, pits, books, gadgets, CDs, DVDs, sauces, rubs, posters, and more**

People have to experience barbecue to learn to love it. Can it happen? Yes! Will it happen? Maybe.

St. Louis Pork Steak

Charlotte's Rib BBQ

15467 Clayton Rd.
Ballwin, MO 63011
636-394-3332
http://www.charlottesribbbq.com

erb Schwarz was known in barbecue circles for his famous St. Louis restaurant, Charlotte's Rib, and for his many cooking and sauce contest awards, including a Grand Champion win at the American Royal, the World Series of Barbecue. Herb's barbecue handle was "Dr. Rollin' River," and his barbecue legacy is mighty, like the river that runs through St. Louis. After 25 successful years at Charlotte's Rib, Herb and his beloved wife, Pat, turned Charlotte's Rib over to their children. Today their daughter, Lisa, with co-owner Scott Brown, runs Charlotte's Rib, and their son, Joe, runs C. B. Joe's in Bon Terre, south of St. Louis.

One of Ardie's favorite memories of Herb is of sharing a barbecue tour of the best barbecue restaurants in St. Louis. The last stop was Char-

lotte's Rib. Ardie was so full of barbecue that he couldn't imagine eating another bite. Herb ordered ribs and a huge pork steak. As his guest, Ardie felt like he had to take at least a token bite and thank Herb for his hospitality. After a bite of rib and a bite of steak, he threw politeness to the wind and ate the whole thing. Charlotte's was the best barbecue on the tour!

We're proud to report that Lisa, Scott, and Joe learned their lessons well. Charlotte's Rib is still one of the best barbecue restaurants in America. Here, thanks to Lisa and Scott, is Dr. Rollin' River's Charlotte's Rib St. Louis Favorite Huge Hand-Cut Pork Steak.

ST. LOUIS PORK STEAK

Serves 8 (or 1 with a hearty appetite)

¼ cup canola oil

8 (¾-inch-thick) pork steaks

Seasoned salt

**Charlotte's Rib Mild Hickory
  or Spicy Southern Barbecue
  Sauce or your favorite sauce**

Set up and preheat your smoker to cook indirectly at 230° to 240°F. Meanwhile, heat the oil in a large skillet over high heat until hot. Sear each steak on both sides, about 3 minutes per side. Sprinkle seasoned salt to taste all over the steaks. Smoke for 3 to 4 hours, until fork-tender, then brush on Charlotte's Rib Mild Hickory or, for a little kicker, Charlotte's Rib Spicy Southern Barbecue Sauce to taste for a finishing touch. Then get ready for some of this world's greatest eatin'.

Rib Eye Steak

Louie Mueller Barbecue

206 W. 2nd St.
Taylor, TX 76574
512-352-6206
http://www.louiemuellerbarbecue.com

ueller has been a distinguished name in Texas barbecue since Louie Mueller first started selling barbecue in the alley behind his Taylor market in 1949. He moved to the present location in 1959.

The Mueller barbecue legacy continued through Louie's son, Bobby, and onward to Bobby's sons, Wayne and John, and daughter LeAnn. Bobby Mueller got a culinary star in his crown with a James Beard "America's Classic" Award in 2006, a rarity in barbecue circles.

After Bobby's death in 2008, Wayne continued the Louie Mueller tradition in Taylor. John and LeAnn are known for their barbecue in Austin.

Louie Mueller's exterior looks like a set from a Hollywood western. A weathered sign above the sidewalk roof reads "Louie Mueller Barbecue." You know the joint is open for business when a big American flag is waving from a pole stuck in the conduit pipe in the front sidewalk.

We like the people, the food, and the small-town, friendly feel of Louie Mueller. To us the joint feels like a shrine each time we open the screen door and step inside. It's a special place for sure—a stone, brick, and wood structure with tall ceilings, an assortment of tables and chairs, smoky walls, and a counter in the back for taking orders. A big doorway opens to a more recent addition, an annex converted from the adjacent corner building to handle the overflow from the main dining room. It has taken on the smoky

RIB EYE STEAK

Serves 4

4 (12-ounce) bone-in rib eye steaks

Coarsely ground black pepper

Salt

Set up your smoker with post oak or oak wood to cook indirectly at 375°F. Season the steaks all over with salt and pepper to taste. Place in the smoker and cook for 45 to 60 minutes or to the doneness you desire. Enjoy—this is a classic!

A standard introduction to the meats of Louie Mueller should include brisket, pork ribs, beef ribs, and the original sausage. If you like fiery sausage, try the jalapeño or chipotle.

As at many other Texas barbecue joints, the meat is served on butcher paper.

We have fond memories of the 12-ounce rib eye steak on the former menu. It was slow-smoked to medium-well instead of grilled hot and fast like a steakhouse steak. We're fans of the latter style as well, but there was something special about Louie Mueller's smoked rib eye seasoned with a simple mix of pepper and salt. It was good enough to make a vegetarian go into a temporary relapse. If Wayne ever returns it to the menu, treat yourself to one. Meanwhile, try our home-style version, but remember that there's no duplicating the atmosphere, aromas, and flavors on location at Louie Mueller Barbecue.

patina and has been installed with enough signs and other memorabilia from the mother building that a newcomer would assume the place has always been this big.

Taylor is our buddy John Raven's hometown, and John is no stranger to Louie Mueller. He told us, "Were I to recommend Louie Mueller's to a stranger, I would tell him it is a Texas tradition. It is as Texas as the state capital. Much of the 100-year-old building is still in its original condition. It is just a unique place. You need to go there even if you are a vegetarian."

Slaughterhouse Five Ribs

Joe's Kansas City Bar-B-Que and Catering

3002 W. 47th Ave.
Kansas City, KS 66103
913-722-3366
http://www.oklahomajoesbbq.com

The dream in sport barbecue is to go from grand champion pitmaster to successful barbecue restaurateur. Kansas City, Kansas, is where the dream came true for Joy and Jeff Stehney. After years of winning trophies and ribbons with their Slaughterhouse Five competition barbecue team, Joy and Jeff launched a barbecue restaurant business that has earned international fame. While the restaurant began as Oklahoma Joe's, in 2014 the name was changed to Joe's Kansas City Bar-B-Que to reflect their KC pride.

In their original location, they sell championship-contest-quality barbecue in a gas station. Yes, you can eat there and get gas. You'd best arrive ahead of or after the lunch and dinner rush, unless you don't mind standing in line for 30 to 45 minutes. Finding a vacant table by the time you get your order usually isn't a problem. Sometimes you'll share a table with strangers, but people aren't strangers for long when barbecue is on the table.

The walls are covered with sport barbecue photos, banners, and other memorabilia. Shelves next to the cash register feature trophies, gift baskets, sauces, and rubs for sale. A corrugated metal canopy over the order line displays a variety of T-shirts you can buy. The most popular says, "I can't believe my favorite barbecue place is in a gas station." Service at the order/pickup line is fast, friendly, and efficient. They want to help you and will honor special requests or substitutions.

Our favorites here are the ribs, but we also savor the beef, the Carolina pulled pork, and the burnt ends. The best sides are the rub-seasoned fries (one order easily serves two) and the spicy coleslaw. The ribs are pull-off-the-bone tender (as opposed to fall-off-the-bone) and flavorful, with the right kiss of smoke and seasonings. The brisket is lean, tender, and smoky—exactly as you'd want it if you were judging in a barbecue contest. The pulled pork is juicy, tender, and lightly seasoned. Spicy coleslaw is the perfect complement. The chicken is moist, flavorful, and pleasingly crispy on the outside. The Z-Man Sandwich, made with barbecue beef garnished with an onion ring, provolone cheese, and barbecue sauce, has become another of our favorites. Locally brewed Boulevard Wheat beer goes well with any of the Joe's cuisine, as do the soft drinks, water, or iced tea.

The locations in suburban Olathe and Leawood, nestled in busy shopping centers, are more upscale in décor but echo the home location with strategically placed corrugated roofing metal and walls adorned with barbecue-contest memorabilia.

Here's the secret to the outstanding ribs at Joe's Kansas City Bar-B-Que.

SLAUGHTERHOUSE FIVE RIBS

Serves 4 to 8

2 tablespoons granulated sugar

1 tablespoon light brown sugar

2 tablespoons Hungarian paprika

2 tablespoons Lawry's Seasoned Salt

1½ teaspoons chili powder

1½ teaspoons ground cumin

1 teaspoon granulated onion

1 teaspoon white pepper

1 teaspoon finely ground black pepper

2 (2½-pound) slabs spareribs

In a small bowl, combine the sugars, paprika, seasoned salt, chili powder, cumin, onion, white pepper, and black pepper and blend well. You can do this ahead of time, cover, and store in a cool, dark place until ready to use.

To prepare the ribs, remove the membrane from the back of the slabs and trim any excess fat. Season the slabs all over with all of the rub. Cover and let rest in the refrigerator for at least 2 hours or overnight.

Cook the ribs using the indirect method at 275°F. Jeff says that cooking the ribs at the higher temperature does two things: It renders the fat better, and you get more flavorful ribs. Cook the ribs for 5 to 6 hours, turning them every 2 hours.

The ribs are done when you can easily tear or pull two ribs apart.

RIB DOCTOR "MUSTGO"

Guy Simpson (aka Kansas City Rib Doctor) was visiting his sister in San Antonio, Texas, and told her that he would buy dinner every night. Martha (Kraatz) was thinking about his great offer. When she came back into the kitchen, she told Guy that that night they were having "Mustgo." Guy was thinking that this was some new food he had not heard about. He asked, "What is a 'Mustgo'?" Martha opened the refrigerator, looked at the food, and said, "This must go, and that must go!" Now you know the story of a "Mustgo!"

Memphis-Style Barbecued Ribs

Jack's Bar-B-Que

416 Broadway
Nashville, TN 37203
615-254-5715
http://www.jacksbarbque.com

Jack Cawthon is known as the "Bar-B-Que King of Nashville," and he has earned the title. He has been in the barbecue business for twenty years, catering and running a succession of Nashville restaurants. There's a popular Jack's in Nashville's historic Talbot's Corner, but Jack started Jack's Bar-B-Que on the corner of Broadway and 1st Avenue in a tiny concrete block building. Jack later renovated the building and added a patio overlooking Riverfront Park and Broadway.

The Broadway location couldn't be better. It's a few doors down Broadway from Tootsies Orchid Lounge, the famous honky-tonk where legendary Grand Ole Opry stars lingered in the radio show's Ryman-based heyday. Like Tootsies, Jack's enjoys an unobstructed view across Ryman Alley to the arched, stone-and-brick stage entrance of Nashville's famous Ryman Auditorium. After decades of minimal use, the rejuvenated auditorium began hosting performances again. Jack spruced up a former loading zone behind his place, set out tables, and kept doing what he does well in the kitchen.

Customers lately have recognized Lyle Lovett, Emmylou Harris, Merle Haggard, Lorrie Morgan, Garrison Keillor, and many others among the luminaries dashing toward those venerable steps. But seeing the occasional country star among the flow of stagehands, backup bands, and hit-maker wannabes aren't the only attraction at Jack's Bar-B-Que. Jack also serves fine plates of smoked pork and beef brisket.

The food is good—basic, flavorful, filling. Variety counts, too. In his formative years as a barbecue connoisseur, Jack couldn't settle on one idea. So he studied techniques for smoking Tennessee-

style pork shoulders, Texas-style beef brisket, St. Louis–style dry ribs, and sausage and chicken treatments drawn from his travels in the Carolinas, Georgia, and Kentucky. If you get a table on the back patio, kick back and enjoy the show. There's no playbill. You watch whoever happens down the alley—just as Jack does.

Jack serves some of the finest barbecue ribs in the South. Here is Jack's recipe.

MEMPHIS-STYLE BARBECUED RIBS

Serves 4 to 6

HAND RUB

2 tablespoons salt

1 tablespoon sugar

1 tablespoon paprika

¼ cup chili powder

1 tablespoon cayenne

¼ cup black pepper

2¾ pounds Curly's (aka St. Louis) spareribs

Using hickory wood, preheat an enclosed pit with a flat rack to 250°F. In a small bowl, combine the hand rub ingredients and mix well. Generously rub the mixture into the ribs. Place the ribs in the pit and cook them for approximately 4 hours. After the ribs are done, wrap them to keep them tender until serving.

Hogmatism: Specifically, the belief that pig barbecue—not beef, lamb, chicken, or other meats—is the only true barbecue. Generally, a set of rigid, narrow-minded beliefs about barbecue.

Glazed Barbecued Ribs

North Main BBQ

403 N. Main
Euless, TX 76039
817-267-7821 or 817-283-0884
http://www.northmainbbq.com

orth Main BBQ, "Home of the World's Best Ribs," was founded in 1981 by Hubert Green, Dollie Green, Ray Green, and Eddie Kelsey.

The all-you-can-eat lunch and dinner buffet includes award-winning ribs, chopped and sliced beef brisket, chicken breasts and quarters, pork shoulder, sausage, ranch beans, potato salad, coleslaw, plus raw onion slices, dill pickle chips, and pickled jalapeño peppers. Meats are hickory-smoked for 4 to 12 hours. If you want any drink other than iced tea, BYOB.

We love the story of how North Main got started. In the early 1980s the Greens owned and operated the very successful Green Trucking Company. When their trucks returned by late morning or early afternoon on Fridays, the employees would sit around and have a few Lone Stars and some iced tea, starting their Friday

night socializing early. One Friday Hubert decided to barbecue some ribs, which everybody enjoyed. As this Friday custom continued, the group grew and grew. Friends of friends showed up. Everyone would chip in money for the ribs, and eventually it went from two slabs to two cases of ribs. Figuring that this was a lot more fun than the trucking business, but not wanting to give up a good company, the Greens started the restaurant and kept the trucking company rolling. Now it was work, but it was also fun, and it was making money. They ran both businesses for a while. Eventually the barbecue won out.

One night while sitting out back enjoying the shade, Hubert was asked, "If you get more successful, are you going to open on Sunday?" Hubert calmly said, "No, I'll probably close on Saturday or maybe close for lunches!" That was Hubert's original feeling, but he later reconsidered, saying they needed to take care of the people getting out of church on Sundays.

Anybody in the restaurant business who sees North Main's buffet would say the buffet is set up backward, with the meat first. The Greens' answer: "No, it isn't." It's set up to give customers North Main's best barbecue, plus salads and beans if they want. And that's one reason they

have such good barbecue: The customer comes first and always will.

We are big fans of North Main's ribs. As to their "world's best ribs" boast: You decide. You can order the real North Main Secret Spice online. Our adaptation of the Greens' recipe makes more than you'll need for two slabs. You can store leftover spice in an airtight container for up to 6 months.

GLAZED BARBECUED RIBS

Serves 6 to 8

SECRET SPICE

Makes about 1½ cups

½ cup sugar

¼ cup seasoned salt

¼ cup garlic salt

3 tablespoons chili powder

1 tablespoon paprika

1 tablespoon finely ground black pepper

1 teaspoon cayenne

2 slabs St. Louis–style spareribs

FINISHING MOP AND GLAZE

¼ cup ketchup

¼ cup yellow mustard

¼ to ⅓ cup white vinegar

1 cup packed light brown sugar

To make the secret spice, combine all the ingredients in an airtight container and blend well. Store in a cool, dry place until ready to use or up to 6 months.

Preheat your smoker to 230° to 250°F. Season the ribs all over to taste with the secret spice. You can store the rest of the secret spice for up to 6 months. Place in your smoker and cook for 4 to 6 hours, or until done.

While the ribs are smoking, make the finishing mop and glaze. Combine the ingredients in a small saucepan over medium heat, stirring occasionally, and simmer for 15 minutes. Remove from the heat and cool to room temperature.

In the last 10 minutes of cooking time, mop the ribs all over with the finishing sauce. Remove from the smoker and let rest for 15 to 30 minutes. Slice and serve.

BBQ Rib Tips, Chicago Style

Honey 1 BBQ

2241 N. Western Ave.
Chicago, IL 60647
773-227-5130
http://www.honey1bbq.com

We go to Honey 1 for the rib tips. That's not to say we don't stay for the ribs, hot links, pulled pork, brisket, and chicken. We'll have a helping of each, please, but go heavy on the rib tips.

Although we like Mrs. Adams's sauce, we want sauce on the side so we can savor the full flavor of the meat with just a touch of sauce. You'll get it sauced "unless you say not to," as they advise on the menu. And if you're looking for the fries that come with your order: they're on the bottom, covered with meat. That's how it's done in many Chicago barbecue joints.

Honey 1 rib tips represent old-time Chicago aquarium smoked barbecue at its best. We've seen these cookers in Memphis and Minneapolis, but they reign in Chicago. No wonder, since they are made in Chicago. It takes skill and know-how to regulate temperatures in these cookers with the meat on a metal grid directly above the fire. Robert Adams and other Chicago pitmasters with roots in the American South have the skill and know-how.

Mr. Adams will tell you, "I came from Arkansas. We cooked with wood. We didn't have gas back then." At Honey 1, the meat is cooked with real wood to a perfect level of tenderness—firm and easy to chew. "THE SMOKE IS NO JOKE" is their motto. How about aluminum foil? "I don't cook with aluminum foil," Robert told us. "Once the meat is done, I'll wrap it in foil to keep it moist, but I don't cook with foil." We say amen to that!

When Robert saw the title of our book, he didn't hesitate to say, "*This* [Honey 1] is America's Best Barbecue!" We like his attitude. We applaud his pitmaster savvy and his barbecue. And you won't catch us arguing with Robert Adams. Pass the rib tips, please!

We had a great time working with a pitmaster of Mr. Adams's status. A crafty pitmaster, he told us what was in his recipes without really telling us, as in "You know, a little salt and pepper, some sugar, garlic, and onion, with some other spices." Here is what Chef Paul read into it.

RIB TIPS

Serves 4 to 6

RUB (ABOUT 1¼ CUPS)

½ cup granulated sugar

3 tablespoons salt

2 tablespoons black pepper

2 tablespoons dry mustard

2 tablespoons sweet paprika

1 tablespoon garlic powder

1 tablespoon onion powder

2 teaspoons dried basil

1 teaspoon cayenne

SAUCE (ABOUT 6 ¾ CUPS)

2 cups ketchup

2 cups red wine vinegar

2 cups water

1 cup packed light brown sugar

½ cup Worcestershire sauce

¼ cup prepared yellow mustard

2 tablespoons salt

2 tablespoons finely ground
black pepper

1 tablespoon garlic powder

1 tablespoon onion powder

2 teaspoons crushed red pepper

4 pounds rib tips

To make the rub, combine all the ingredients and blend well. Store in an airtight container in a cool, dark place until ready to use, for up to 6 months.

To make the sauce, combine all the ingredients in a saucepan over medium heat, stirring to dissolve all the sugar. Bring to a boil, then lower the heat and simmer for about 30 minutes. Cool to room temperature.

Set up your smoker to cook indirectly at 250°F. Season the rib tips all over with the barbecue rub. Place on the smoker and barbecue for 4 to 5 hours, until the ribs tear apart easily, basting with the sauce during the last 30 minutes of cooking.

Pigot:
An individual who is hogmatic, i.e., believes that the only true barbecue is pig barbecue; usually exhibits other hogmatic beliefs and behaviors.

Barbecue Pork Butt

17th Street Bar & Grill

32 N. 17th St.
Murphysboro, IL 62966
618-648-3722
http://www.17thstreetbarbecue.com

This is Mike Mills's home base and the birthplace of a barbecue dynasty. Mike is also the barbecue guru and partner in Blue Smoke restaurant in New York City.

Mike is humbly known as "The Legend." We assume it was due to his great success in the Memphis in May World Championship Barbecue Cooking Contest. For thirteen years he was the only person whose team won three times. His record was tied in 2006. Mike had said that if that happened he would come out of retirement and compete at Memphis in May again, but we think he has better sense than that. Mike is one of the most knowledgeable persons in barbecue, and he is not afraid to share his knowledge.

When Paul went to 17th Street, he was treated like a king (or a baron). Paul had some of Mike's outstanding ribs, brisket, chicken wings, and pulled pork. Then, while getting a tour of the kitchen, he saw a great meal being served, one he couldn't believe was intended for a single individual. Mike said, "That's what we call a 'pounder.'" Listed on the menu as a pound of pork shoulder, it's a pound-plus of pulled or chopped pork served with two side orders. Here Mike shares the recipe with us. You can order the Magic Dust from 17th Street's Web site.

Is Barbecue Better Than Sex?

Ardie and his barbecue buddies Phil and Cheryl Litman were on the bank of the Mississippi at Apple City Smokers chewing on some of the best baby back ribs any of them had ever tasted. Julia Rose Sampson, a Judge's Chairperson at Memphis in May that year, was with them, and Mike Mills and Pat Burke gave her a few ribs to try hot off the smoker. She began moaning and groaning and said that the ribs were better then sex. Cheryl, with her quick wit, responded immediately,

"All depends who you're having sex with or whose barbecue you're eating."

BARBECUE PORK BUTT

Makes 15 to 18 good-size sandwiches

1 (5- to 8-pound) pork butt

½ cup 17th Street Bar & Grill Magic Dust (page 60) or your own rub

MOPPING SAUCE

2 cups apple cider vinegar

½ cup water

2 tablespoons dark brown sugar

1 tablespoon canola oil

1 tablespoon sea salt

1 tablespoon chili powder

1 teaspoon cayenne

GLAZE

1 cup Apple City Barbecue Sauce (page 60)

PULLED PORK FINISHING SAUCE (OPTIONAL)

½ cup Apple City Barbecue Sauce

¼ cup apple cider vinegar

1 to 2 tablespoons 17th Street Bar & Grill Magic Dust

Pierce the pork butt all over with a dinner fork and season all over with the Magic Dust. Pierce it again to get the rub to penetrate, place the pork butt it in a pan, cover, and re-frigerate for 4 hours or overnight.

Remove the meat from the refrigerator and let it come to room temperature, about an hour. Heat your smoker to 230° to 250°F. Mike uses a combination of charcoal and apple wood, which gives the meat a sweeter taste. "Don't oversmoke the meat," cautions Mike. "Smoke should be an ingredient, not an overwhelming taste." Place the pork butt, fat side up, in the smoker and cook it indirectly for 8 to 12 hours, or until the internal temperature of the meat reaches 165° to 175°F on an instant-read thermometer if you're going to slice the meat, 185° to 195°F if you're going to pull the meat.

Right after you put the meat in the smoker, place the mopping sauce ingredients in a saucepan. Bring to a boil, stirring constantly to dissolve all the ingredients. Set aside to cool to room temperature.

After 1 to 1½ hours, start mopping the pork butt with the mopping sauce every 30 to 45 minutes, or as necessary. Turn and rotate the pork butt as necessary to avoid hot spots in your pit.

After 5 hours, check the internal temperature. The higher the internal temperature, the more tender the meat will be. When the internal temperature is where you want it for slicing, use a pastry brush to brush the pork butt with barbecue sauce and cook it for 10 to 15 minutes, repeating the process as many times as you like to glaze. Mike suggests only twice. Remove the pork butt from the smoker, place it on a cutting board, and let it rest, covered, for 15 to 20 minutes. Remove the bone and slice and serve with barbecue sauce on the side.

If you are going to pull or chop the pork butt, take it out of the smoker when the meat is in the higher temperature range, put it in a large pan, and let it rest, covered, for 15 to 20 minutes. Using heavy-duty dinner forks, pull the pork butt to shreds. Mix the finishing sauce ingredients and add half of this sauce to the pork. Blend it in, adding more as needed without overdoing it; you don't want the pork to be sloppy.

Make sandwiches with the sliced or pulled pork and finish with a swizzle of Apple City Barbecue Sauce or your favorite barbecue sauce.

Many thanks to Mike and Amy for sharing their recipes, which have been adapted and reprinted with permission from their book *Peace, Love, and Barbecue* (Rodale, © 2005 Mike Mills).

MAGIC DUST ®

Makes about 2½ cups

½ cup paprika

¼ cup kosher salt, finely ground

¼ cup sugar

2 tablespoons dry mustard

¼ cup chili powder

¼ cup ground cumin

2 tablespoons black pepper

¼ cup granulated garlic

2 tablespoons cayenne

Mix all the ingredients and store in a tightly covered container. You'll want to keep some in a shaker next to the grill or stove. Keeps indefinitely but won't last long.

APPLE CITY BARBECUE SAUCE

Makes 3 cups

1 cup ketchup (they use Hunt's)

½ cup seasoned rice vinegar

½ cup apple juice or cider

¼ cup apple cider vinegar

½ cup packed brown sugar

¼ cup soy sauce or Worcestershire sauce

2 teaspoons prepared yellow mustard

¾ teaspoon garlic powder

¼ teaspoon white pepper

¼ teaspoon cayenne

⅓ cup bacon bits, ground
  in a spice grinder

½ cup grated onion

Combine the ketchup, rice vinegar, apple juice, cider vinegar, brown sugar, soy sauce, mustard, garlic powder, white pepper, cayenne, and bacon bits in a large saucepan. Bring to a boil over medium-high heat. Stir in the onion. Reduce the heat and simmer, uncovered, for 10 to 15 minutes, until it thickens slightly. Stir often. Allow to cool, then pour into a glass jar. You can store the sauce in the refrigerator for up to 2 weeks.

Variation: To make this sauce a little hotter, add more cayenne to taste, another ¼ to ½ teaspoon. Be careful; a little cayenne goes a long way.

Q-Ban BBQ Sandwich

Back Door Barbecue

315 NW 23rd St.
Oklahoma City, OK 73103
405-525-7427
https://www.facebook.com/pages/
Back-Door-Barbecue/134661030025064

The front door of Back Door Barbecue is on busy 23rd Street. If you can find a metered parking spot nearby, go for it. Customers in the know, however, save their coins and park free in the back. Entering through the back door also gets you a bonus of walking along the hallway tribute to Texas barbecue, your first indication that this is Oklahoma barbecue with a Texas accent. The background music playlist is a mix of Texas swing reminiscent of the 1930s Cain Ballroom in Tulsa and country singer-songwriters and Oklahoma Red Dirt Music.

Order and pay at the counter. Find a place to sit. Your name will be called when your order is ready. Booths and tables line the walls. A long, tall communal dining table with stools along each side graces the middle, reminiscent of the old-time southern hospitality "my table, your table," where strangers are instant friends when there's good barbecue in front of them. A stranger/friend dining next to Ardie shared that his parents were such big fans of a place called Bad Brad's BBQ that they named him Brad.

Chef Kathryn Mathis has the perfect pedigree to make Back Door one of the best barbecue joints in America. A native of Guymon, in Texas County, Oklahoma, her panhandle proximity to the state of Texas made her no stranger to Texas foodways. Living in Austin for several years gave her first-hand encounters with iconic Texas joints such as Louie Mueller, Franklin's, and Salt Lick.

Her business partner, Chris Lower, is also a barbecue aficionado. They have spawned three other Oklahoma City originals: Big Truck Tacos, Mutt's Amazing Hot Dogs, and a wood-fired pizza place.

Instead of mesquite or post oak, pit boss Kenny Talley uses a hickory/fruit wood smoke combo that's so good even Texans love it. Kenny turns out remarkably delicious lean and juicy brisket, pulled pork, ribs, baloney, pork belly, and burnt ends with Back Door's Ponca City–made Cookshack FEC 750 pellet cooker, the largest available. Back Door's potato salad, slaw, fries, creamed corn, and other sides are beyond ordinary, as are the funky, delicious jar pie desserts.

Although Back Door's PB&J (pork, beef, and jalapeño) sandwich merits its popularity, we had a special take with the Q-Ban. Chef Kathryn is always thinking of ways to use their ingredients in new ways. With pulled pork, smoked ham, homemade pickles, homemade mustard and mayo already on hand, she reasoned, why not make a Q-Ban? Back Door's Cuban-style panini with smoky-spicy southern barbecue flavor notes is the best panini we've eaten, bar none. Here's how to build one when you're too far from the Back Door to get a real one. The prepping and cooking time required is worth it.

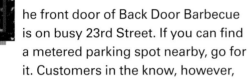

61

Q-BAN SANDWICH

Serves 1

1 ciabatta roll or any nice artisanal roll

1 to 2 ounces Mustard BBQ
   Sauce Mayo (recipe follows)

3 ounces Pulled Pork (recipe follows)

8 to 10 House-Made Dill
   Pickles (recipe follows)

2 slices Swiss cheese

3 ounces Smoked Ham (recipe follows)

Oil for the griddle

Preheat a griddle to 350°F. Slice the ciabatta roll in half lengthwise. Spread mustard BBQ sauce mayo on both sides. Layer the pulled pork, pickles, Swiss cheese, and ham on top in that order. Place the top on the sandwich. Lightly oil the griddle and place the sandwich on it, using a bacon press or a sandwich press to weigh the top down. Cook for 3 to 4 minutes, flip, and cook for another 3 to 4 minutes, until the cheese begins to melt. Cut the sandwich on the bias and serve.

Note: Back Door keeps the pulled pork and ham hot to help speed the melting of the cheese.

MUSTARD BBQ SAUCE

Makes about 2½ cups

½ cup apple cider vinegar

½ cup prepared yellow mustard

1½ tablespoons brown sugar

⅛ teaspoon black pepper

⅛ teaspoon cayenne

2 teaspoons chili powder

1 teaspoon Cholula hot sauce

1 cup plus 2 tablespoons soy sauce

Combine all the ingredients in a medium saucepan and bring to a boil over medium heat, stirring often. Remove from the heat, cool, and chill for at least 1 hour before serving.

Note: To make Mustard BBQ Sauce Mayo, mix 1 cup of Mustard BBQ Sauce with 2 cups of mayonnaise.

PULLED PORK

Serves 20 to 24

½ cup Memphis-Style Rub

1 (6- to 8-pound) pork butt

1 cup apple juice

Rub the rub all over the pork butt, wrap in plastic wrap, and refrigerate for at least 24 hours. Heat your cooker to 190°F. Place the pork butt in the cooker and smoke for 12 hours. Remove from the cooker, place on a large sheet of heavy-duty aluminum foil, and begin to wrap the foil upward. Pour the apple juice into the foil, wrap securely, using more foil as needed, and smoke for 2 more hours. Remove the meat from the cooker and place in a large pan. Unwrap the pork in the pan so you don't lose any of the juice. Use a fork to pull apart the meat and toss it with the juices.

HOUSE-MADE DILL PICKLES

Makes 4 to 6 pints

2 pounds Kirby cucumbers, sliced into "chips" about the thickness of a nickel

2 tablespoons chopped garlic

2 tablespoons kosher salt

2 tablespoons black pepper

2 tablespoons crushed red pepper

2 to 3 stems fresh dill

1½ cups water

1½ cups apple cider vinegar

Place the cucumbers, garlic, salt, black pepper, red pepper flakes, and dill in a heavy plastic bucket or a crock and set aside. Bring the water and vinegar to a hard boil, then pour over the cucumbers. Give it a little stir, put the lid on the container, and refrigerate for at least 48 hours before serving.

MEMPHIS-STYLE RUB (2½ CUPS)

1 cup kosher salt

½ cup granulated sugar

½ cup firmly packed brown sugar

3 tablespoons paprika

3 tablespoons chili powder

2 tablespoons onion powder

2 tablespoons garlic powder

2 tablespoons dry mustard

2 teaspoons ground oregano

2 teaspoons celery salt

2 tablespoons black pepper

2 teaspoons ground ginger

2 teaspoons coriander

2 teaspoons cayenne

Combine all the ingredients in a medium bowl and mix well. Store in an airtight container in a cool, dry place for up to 2 months.

SMOKED HAM

Serves 20 to 24

1 cup Memphis-Style Rub

1 (6- to 8-pound) picnic ham

1 cup apple juice

Heat your cooker to 190°F. Rub the rub all over the ham. Smoke for 10 hours. Remove the meat from the cooker, place it in a pan, and tent it with aluminum foil. Allow to rest for about 20 minutes. When the meat is cool enough to work with, use a fork to pull it apart. Stir in the apple juice and serve.

Bedlam Sandwich

Bedlam Bar-B-Q

610 NE 50th St.
Oklahoma City, OK 73105
405-528-7427
http://www.bedlambarbq.com

Bedlam Bar-B-Q is a shrine of sorts to Oklahoma's heritage and contentiousness. After years of being designated Indian Territory, Oklahoma was granted statehood in 1907. The Indian populace was not there by choice. President Andrew Jackson, in defiance of the U.S. Supreme Court, forced their migrations from indigenous lands. Many died along the way.

Prior to statehood, homesteaders of European descent cited the Homestead Act of 1862 as license for settling on land not designated for Indian use. When the Land Rush of 1899 happened, many "Sooners" who jumped the gun to stake homesteading claims found that "Boomers" had already beat them to the land by several years. With a diverse mix of Indians, settlers, cowboys, and politicians, Oklahoma is no stranger to rivalries.

The past aside, today's Oklahoma rivalries take place in sports arenas, especially football, basketball, and wrestling. Jeff and Cindy Watts, proprietors, hold court at Bedlam, where University of Oklahoma Sooners and Oklahoma State University Cowboys can celebrate their heritage, cheer for their respective teams, and break barbecue bones together. Jeff and Cindy make sure their rival customers get along with civility. What better way to do that than serving top-notch barbecue in a setting that pays tribute to both universities and to Oklahoma history.

We usually avoid chopped meat sandwiches, but when a joint puts its name on a sandwich, we have to try it. The Bedlam Sandwich is a barbecue microcosm of flavor; a blend of barbecued pulled pork, chicken, beef, and hot links does the job. Add a dash of sweet barbecue sauce and dig in.

THE BEDLAM SANDWICH

Serves 8

½ pound barbecued hot links, chopped

½ pound barbecued brisket, chopped (see page 38)

½ pound barbecued pulled pork, chopped (see page 201)

1 whole barbecued chicken, pulled and chopped

8 hamburger buns, buttered and toasted

1½ cups Bedlam Bar-B-Q sauce or your own favorite

In a Dutch oven, combine all the meats. Heat over low heat for 30 to 45 minutes, stirring occasionally. Divide the meat among the buns and top each with a dollop of sauce.

Badwich

Cherokee Strip BBQ

235 S. Perkins Rd.
Stillwater, OK 74074
405-377-2244
http://cherokeestripbbq.com

You've got to be good to survive in the barbecue business in Stillwater. You're sharing turf with the world-famous food emporium Eskimo Joe's, plus a smorgasbord of other dining options in this Oklahoma State University town known for avid OSU Cowboy fans and the home of Red Dirt Music. The saving grace is that barbecue fever is in every Oklahoman's DNA. It can't be satisfied with pizza, tacos, or burgers. It demands meats "hickory smoked to perfection," as pitmaster-owner Brett Brownlee puts it, "every day." That's a tall order. Brett is up to the challenge. He's a self-taught, trial-and-error pitmaster who learned the ropes well enough to prosper here with his wife and business partner, Erin, for more than a quarter century and counting.

You can't go wrong with any of Brett's barbecue—the ribs, brisket, pork loin, pulled pork, turkey breast, hot links, or Polish sausage will scratch your barbecue itch. But what really scratched our itch was the Badwich. This Cherokee Strip sandwich with chopped and sauced barbecue beef topped with a barbecue hot link sliced in half in a bun is aptly named as the signature sandwich in the home of "Oklahoma's Baddest BBQ." When you're too far away from Stillwater to stop by Brett Brownlee's Cherokee Strip, try our home-style version. It's so "Bad" you'll love it!

BADWICH

Serves 1

4 to 5 ounces hickory-smoked beef brisket, chopped (see page 40)

1 buttered and toasted bun

¼ pound hot link, sliced in half lengthwise

3 to 4 tablespoons of your favorite tomato-based barbecue sauce

Layer the brisket on the bottom half of the bun, top with the hot link, and add sauce and the top bun. Be "Bad" and enjoy!

SOME OF OUR FAVORITE SANDWICHES ON THE BARBECUE TRAIL

We're told that computer systems are built on simple binary, one/two, this/that, yes/no logic. When that logic grows exponentially into millions, billions, and trillions of binary-based applications, the world of cyberspace gets complicated. Not so with the sandwich, or so we'd think. Yet the simple concept of food between or atop slices of bread has infinite possibilities. When you think you've seen it all, along comes a new one. And we have yet to find one we don't like! Here's a selection of some of our favorites, with a couple of non-Q sandwiches we couldn't leave out.

EARL QUICK'S BAR-B-QUE – KANSAS CITY, KS
- Big E: a full pound of your choice of three barbecued meats in an 8-inch hoagie bun
- Bolo: a thick, round slice of hickory-smoked baloney, deep-fried, in a bun, with barbecue sauce

JOE'S KANSAS CITY BAR-B-QUE – KANSAS CITY, KS
- Brisket Z-Man: sliced smoked brisket, provolone cheese, two onion rings, a splash of barbecue sauce, in a buttered and grill-toasted kaiser roll

OKLAHOMA JOE'S BAR-B-QUE – BROKEN ARROW, OK
- Burnt Ends Z-Man: beef burnt ends, provolone cheese, two onion rings, a splash of barbecue sauce, in a kaiser roll

BIG BOB GIBSON'S PULLED CHICKEN AND WHITE SAUCE – MONROE, NORTH CAROLINA
- Pulled chicken, white sauce, and coleslaw in a toasted bun

FRANKLIN BARBECUE – AUSTIN, TX
- Tipsy Texan: post-oak-smoked tender brisket, sausage, and cabbage in a bun

CHEROKEE STRIP – STILLWATER, OK
- Badwich: blended barbecued beef and pork topped with a hot link in a bun

BACK DOOR BARBECUE – OKLAHOMA CITY, OK
- Q-Ban: pulled pork, smoked ham, Swiss cheese, homemade pickles, housemade mustard and mayo, in a ciabatta roll pressed and toasted on a hot, oiled griddle

THE HAPPY TOMATO – FERNANDINA BEACH, FL
- The Max: toasted bread, pimiento cheese, barbecued pulled pork, with barbecue sauce on the side

THE BBQ SHACK – PAOLA, KS
- Shack Attack: ½ pound each of three different barbecued meats topped with ½ pound of onion straws, with 1 pound of home-cut fries and four pickles on the side

JOHNNY'S BARBECUE – MISSION, KS
- The Remus: pimiento cheese, barbecued pulled pork, coleslaw, dill pickle chips, hickory barbecue sauce in a toasted bun

BEDLAM BAR-B-Q – OKLAHOMA CITY, OK
- Bedlam Sandwich: blend of barbecued pulled pork, chicken, beef, and hot links in a bun

DANNY EDWARDS BLVD BARBECUE – KANSAS CITY, MO
- Ol' Smoky: sauced burnt ends in a bun

TENDERLOIN GRILL – KANSAS CITY, MO
- Snoot Sandwich: boiled pig snoot, hot sauce, mustard, onion, and tomato in a bun
- Tenderger: grilled burger, deep-fried battered pork tenderloin, cheese, mustard, hot sauce, onion, and tomato

Barbecued Pork Steak
with Chunky Applesauce

Ironhorse Barbeque Company

2801 Hwy. 49 North
Paragould, AR 72451
870-239-9758
www.ironhorsebbq.us

Dave and Lynn Aronson started the Ironhorse Barbeque Co. in 1999, and it's a good example of what good food, good service, and great barbecue can do to build a business. Their slogan: "Our butts are smokin' for you."

Dave is a meat cutter, so he knows good meat and knows how and where to buy. He cuts all his own meat, grinds the burger meat, and makes the burgers. All the meat is fresh at Ironhorse, never frozen.

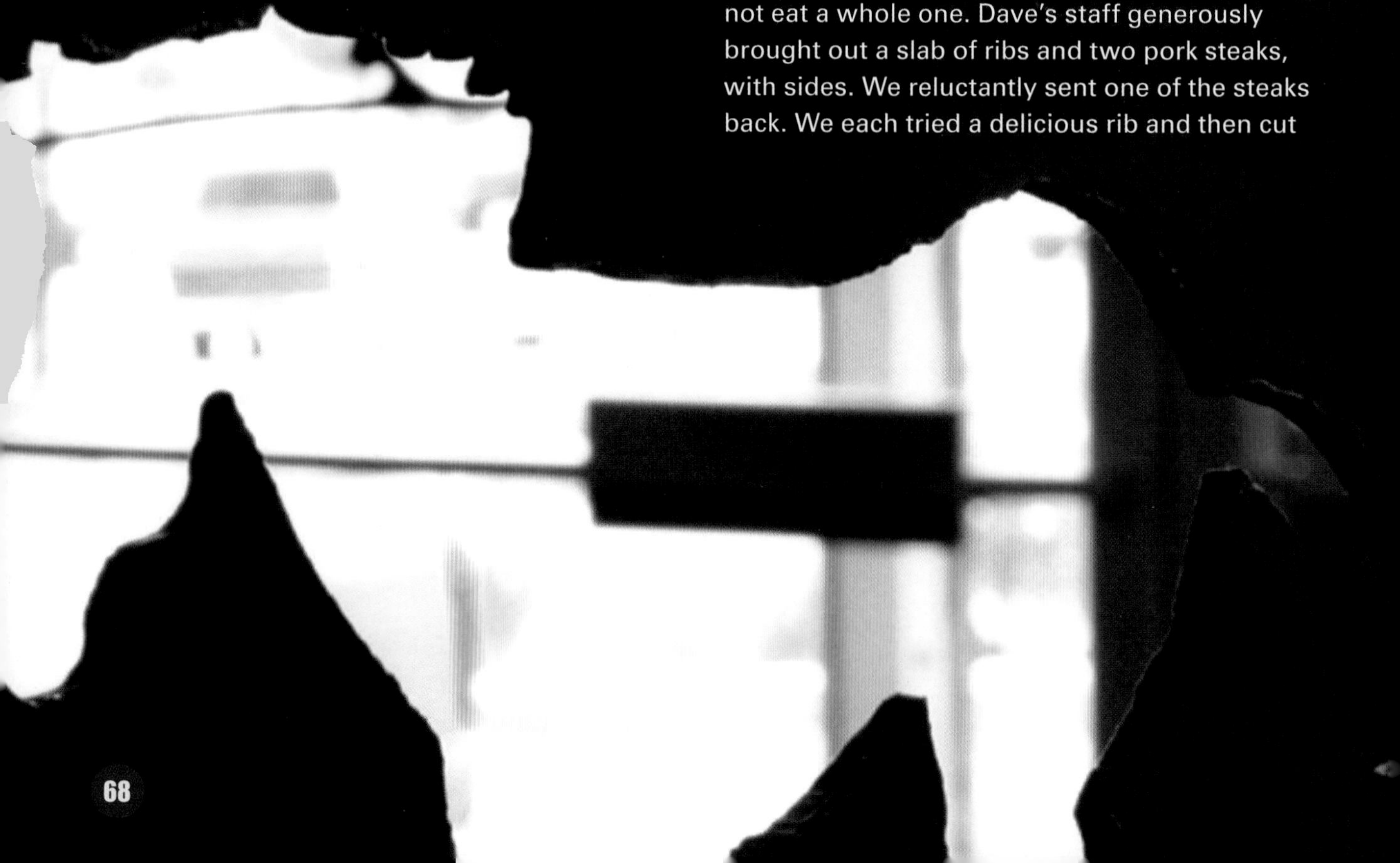

The original Ironhorse is a converted convenience store and gas station that is also Paragould's first and only motorcycle-themed restaurant. We sat down and asked to see Dave, and he came out and gave us the grand tour of his very clean kitchen. We told Dave we had heard great things about his pork steaks and asked to try one. In our barbecue travels, we had already had five meals that day, including four pig sandwiches, ribs and brisket, beans, and potato salad, so we were just going to taste his pork steak, not eat a whole one. Dave's staff generously brought out a slab of ribs and two pork steaks, with sides. We reluctantly sent one of the steaks back. We each tried a delicious rib and then cut

a small portion of pork steak (which was tender enough for a plastic fork), and it was great. That was all we thought we could eat since we had one more place to taste, but we sat and talked barbecue for another 30 minutes, and we ended up picking at that pork steak until it was gone. It was that good! Here is Dave's recipe. He slices his own steaks from a nice square-cut pork butt, and he uses a Southern Pride smoker.

BARBECUED PORK STEAK WITH CHUNKY APPLESAUCE

Serves 8

8 (1-inch or ½-inch) pork steaks (as tender as a mother's love)

Barbecue rub of your choice

CHUNKY APPLESAUCE

2 tablespoons canola oil

8 tablespoons (1 stick) butter

3 or 4 Granny Smith apples, peeled and cut into ¼-inch slices

1 cup raisins

1½ cups packed light brown sugar

½ cup Captain Morgan's spiced rum

Season your steaks on both sides with the rub. If you're using Ironhorse's seasoning, it's not real salty, so be generous with it. Cover the seasoned steaks with plastic wrap and refrigerate overnight.

Preheat your smoker to 225°F. The steaks need to be cooked low and slow with moist heat. A 1-inch steak takes about 6 hours to cook, and a ½-inch steak takes about 4 hours. When the steaks come off the smoker, they should be so tender you can cut them with a plastic fork. Place the steaks in a cooler or plastic container with a lid for 30 minutes before serving to allow them to steam and tenderize further.

While the steaks are resting, make the applesauce by placing the oil and butter in a large skillet over medium heat. When the butter melts, add the apple slices and cook until soft, 10 to 15 minutes. Add the raisins, brown sugar, and rum and cook over low heat until you get a chunky sauce consistency, about 30 minutes. Serve on the side with the pork steaks or pour it over them.

Pastrami

Bogart's Smokehouse

1627 South 9th St.
St. Louis, MO 63104
314-621-3107
http://bogartssmokehouse.com

Coincidental or not, Bogart's is located in a district of St. Louis that, in French, means "drunk" or "riotous." Antoine Pierre Soulard, namesake of the neighborhood, wasn't known for either. Humphrey Bogart, on the other hand, had a reputation for hard drinking. As far as we know, neither had a fondness for barbecue, but that's because they never had the opportunity to dine at Bogart's Smokehouse.

Pitmaster Skip Steele's barbecue career started at age 12, working in his grandfather's Memphis barbecue joint. After that he landed a job in a barbecue blues joint at age 17. "I like your food, and I want to work here," he told the owner. "Have you noticed that you're white?" the owner replied. "Yes, but I like your food and I'll do anything to work here, even clean the restrooms." "Have you ever seen our restrooms?" Skip was hired.

Three years later Skip was in charge of the kitchen. Later he got an agriculture degree at Iowa State, and after several years with the U.S. Department of Agriculture, he hired out as a steamboat captain. When he was eligible, he retired. As he was sprawled out on the driveway early into his retirement, his wife asked, "Are you going to spend your retirement getting drunk and smoking cigarettes?" "Sure, bring me another six-pack," he replied. Fortunately for the barbecue-loving masses, Skip got up from the driveway with a better idea. With business partners/managers Michael Macchi and Brian Scoggins, he created some of the best barbecue joints in America— Bogart's, Pappy's, and Adams, all excellent and all in St. Louis.

The last time we checked, Bogart's didn't have crème brûlée, but we believe Antoine would

MAD MADDIE'S ARTWORK

love the Ribs Brûlée, slathered with apricot preserves and gently torched. Instead of ham and eggs, Bogart could special-order pastrami and eggs. He would be cured of his old favorite at first bite! Everything else on the menu—brisket, prime rib, pulled pork, turkey, tri-tip, burnt ends, traditional sides, pork rinds, deviled egg potato salad, and four sweet, sour, spicy, or mild sauces—is carefully prepared and top-notch. Thus far, there are no St. Louis–style rib tips and pig snoot, but you won't leave wanting. Where else can you get pastrami in a barbecue restaurant? And never this good!

When Skip asked Chef Paul for help developing a special recipe for Bogart's pastrami, Chef Paul was glad to oblige. The mustard, coriander, black pepper, and hint of garlic make this signature pastrami extra special.

PASTRAMI

Makes enough for 16 to 20 sandwiches

1 (8- to 10-pound) corned beef

½ cup prepared yellow mustard

RUB

⅓ cup cracked or coarsely ground coriander

¼ cup coarsely ground black pepper

2 tablespoons light brown sugar

1 tablespoon granulated garlic

Soak the corned beef, covered, in water overnight in the refrigerator. This helps get rid of some of the salt.

Combine all of the rub ingredients and blend well.

Preheat your smoker to 250°F. Drain the corned beef and pat dry with paper towels. Using a pastry brush, paint the lean side of the brisket with the mustard and season with half of the rub. Turn the brisket over and repeat the process. Place the pastrami in the smoker and cook for about 1 hour per pound as a rule of thumb or until the internal temperature is 185° to 195°F.

Remove from the smoker and let rest, lightly covered with aluminum foil, for about 30 minutes. Enjoy.

Barbecued Pig Snoots

Smoki O's

1545 N. Broadway
St. Louis, MO 63102
314-621-8180

Smoki O's is a small barbecue joint just up from the football stadium area of St. Louis. In business since 1997, Smoki O's seats only about 10 customers, but takeout is also available. The side dishes here are homemade—and good. Their specialty is a pig snoot and rib tips combo. Because Paul grew up eating pig snoot sandwiches, he favors the snoots sans rib tips. Ardie likes the combo, a perfect combination of tender pork rib meat with crunchy snoot.

We regret that Kansas City has no joints with pig snoots that compare to Smoki O's pig snoots. We (especially Paul) consider ourselves fortunate that there's one joint in KC that serves pig snoots, thanks to Ashlee Ruhl, proprietor of the Tenderloin Grill on Southwest Boulevard, home of "Pig Snoot Heaven." Although Ashlee doesn't serve barbecue, and her snoots are a world away from Smoki O's in cooking method, we like to go

there for tenderloin sandwiches, burgers, and boiled snoots. Ardie hasn't made it through a whole snoot sandwich yet, even after downing a shot of Pig's Nose Scotch first. Paul downs them with gusto reminiscent of a New Yorker eating clams or oysters on the half shell. Ardie says they taste like bacon fat with barnyard rub. When he gets to the whiskers, he stops and orders a tenderloin sandwich or a cheeseburger.

Smoki O's snoots are different in that Otis doesn't cook the nostril, and by the time the snoots are smoked to a crisp and soaked in warm barbecue sauce, there is no hint of fat or barnyard flavors. You also won't find any bristly whiskers. Otis cooks them whole, then breaks them up. Smoki O's barbecue sauce, served warm, is a tomato base with a mix of sweet and sour.

Paul first met Otis and Earline Walker in New York City at the Big Apple Barbecue Block Party, which is an invitational, charitable barbecue party put on by Danny Meyers, owner of several restaurants and a major restaurateur in New York City. One of his restaurants is Blue Smoke. The whole city is welcome to come to the block party and buy samples of barbecue from as many as 10 invited barbecue pitmasters from around the country. Paul was invited as the Kansas City Baron of Barbecue, cooking certified Angus brisket. This was the birth of RUB—Righteous Urban BBQ—but that's another story. Otis was invited for his barbecued snoots and rib tips, the best in St. Louis.

Paul talked with Otis about his technique for smoking snoots. The recipe is at right. When you want rib tips with your snoots, try the Honey 1 recipe on page 57. Otis fries snoots until crisp and sells them as doggie treats.

BARBECUED PIG SNOOTS

Makes 12

12 pig snoots

Barbecue sauce

First, wash the snoots well with cold water, then slice them with a very sharp knife into strips about 2 inches wide. Place the strips in a large pot of water, bring it to a boil over medium-high heat, and boil for about an hour. The water will develop a white foam or skin, but don't worry—that's the fat cooking out of them. After they hard-boil for about an hour, rinse them off well with cold water.

Set up your grill to cook on low, direct heat (see page 215). If your grill will allow it, it's best to cook the snoots 12 to 14 inches from the coals. The snoots drip a lot of grease, and you have to watch them closely as they can flame up and be ruined in a brief moment if the coals are too close. If the coals are farther away, the flame-up just burns itself out without burning the snoots. If you can't keep the snoots far enough from the coals, just use a small amount of charcoal or briquettes to keep the heat low.

Grill the snoots, turning them often, until they crisp, 1½ to 2 hours. Don't put any sauce on them while they are cooking, but cover them with sauce as soon as you take them off the grill if they are to be eaten immediately. They keep well in the refrigerator and will immediately crisp up again if you don't put sauce on the ones you aren't eating immediately. Just take them out of the refrigerator and put them in the oven at 350°F for 15 to 20 minutes, uncovered. Top with sauce and serve.

Old-Fashioned Southern Pit Barbecue

The Dixie Pig

701 N. Sixth St.
Blytheville, AR 72315
970-763-4636

There's more than one Dixie Pig around the country, but this is the best and has no ties to any of the others. Back in 1923, when they started serving their genuine Old-Fashioned Southern Pit Sandwich in Blytheville, they were a big hit. For many years, people visited the Dixie Pig to enjoy their barbecue, and the Dixie Pig built a reputation that spread far and wide. Today it's run by Buddy "Pops" and Wanda and Bob Halsell, and they are still very proud of that reputation and continue to serve the same quality sandwich that made the Dixie Pig so well known, or as we would argue, famous. Their slogan: "When you feel piggish, come to the Dixie Pig for the best of old southern-style barbecue."

They cook pork butts on an old-fashioned southern barbecue pit, which is usually a concrete block and/or brick pit, 30 inches high and anywhere from 6 feet to 10 or more feet long, with a lid. It's fueled with charcoal and cooks using the direct method. Buddy said that they don't use any seasoning on their pork butt; they just cook and turn them for anywhere from 8 to 12 hours, depending on the size of the butts.

Since we were pacing ourselves when we visited the Dixie Pig (we planned to visit six other places), we had a small pig sandwich, cut in half. It was chopped pork butt, topped with a slaw with Dixie

Pig hot sauce on it. Paul can say without a doubt that that was some of the finest chopped pork he has ever put into his considerably large mouth. The slaw was lightly salted with vinegar on it, and the hot sauce had a slight sweet bite that complemented the meat. If you're anywhere near Blytheville and feeling piggish, don't forget the Dixie Pig.

This is a simple-looking recipe that might be a little challenging to execute, since it uses both the direct and indirect methods (see page 215). You'll need a charcoal fire that is at least 30 inches from the cooking grate, and you'll need a lid, so a pit is ideal.

OLD-FASHIONED SOUTHERN PIT BARBECUE

Serves 24 to 30

2 (6- to 8-pound) pork butts

Hamburger buns, for serving

Coleslaw, for serving

Hot sauce, for serving

Prepare a medium-hot charcoal fire 30 inches from the grates. Place the butts, fat side up, on the grill, cover, cook for 1 hour, and turn. Repeat every hour until the internal temperature of the meat reaches 180°F on a meat thermometer, 10 to 12 hours. Remove the meat from the pit. Remove the bone from the meat and place the butt on a cutting board. Use one or two French knives or cleavers to chop the pork into small pieces. Place some meat on half a hamburger bun, top with coleslaw and hot sauce, and serve.

BREAD IN THE 'CUE.S.A.

When we talk about "barbecue bread" or "Bunny bread" and you wonder, "What's that?!" here's the answer. A long-standing tradition in American barbecue joints is to serve cheap, mass-produced white bread with the barbecue. It serves two purposes. It is cheaper than whole wheat or multigrain breads, and the spongy texture soaks up excess fat and sauce.

In some Texas barbecue joints you can tell the locals from the tourists by their bread of choice. Locals choose the unleavened saltine crackers instead of bread. They're cheap, but they don't soak up the juices and sauce like bread. Southern joints will serve you corn bread and/or hushpuppies, but your sandwich will be on cheap white bread.

Garlic bread is a good accompaniment to barbecue. Here's a good garlic cheese spread recipe:

GARLIC CHEESE SPREAD

2 cups grated pecorino Romano

2 cups mayonnaise

2 tablespoons chopped fresh parsley

2 heads roasted garlic

2½ tablespoons lemon juice

Pinch of cayenne

Dash of hot red pepper sauce

Combine all the ingredients and blend well. The spread is also good on baked potatoes.

Burnt Ends Z-Man Sandwich

Oklahoma Joe's Bar-B-Que

333 W. Albany
Broken Arrow, OK 74012
918-355-0000
http://okjoes.com

Joe Don Davidson is one of the legendary success stories of modern barbecue history. He's a championship barbecue pitmaster and pit maker. He has exceptional barbecue restaurant savvy. He's a barbecue marketing genius. His slogan says it precisely in three words: "Joe knows barbecue."

In addition to his main restaurant in Broken Arrow, Joe has a venue inside Tulsa's famous Cain's Ballroom of the late Bob Wills and His Texas Playboys fame. Wills's Western swing band was so popular that they filled the ballroom even during Oklahoma's Dust Bowl days and the Great Depression.

The original Z-Man Sandwich was invented by Joe's friend and business associate, Jeff Stehney, in Kansas City. Jeff named the Z-Man after a radio sports show host and avid Oklahoma Joe's fan, Mike Zarrick. The original Z-Man Sandwich is a combo of sliced beef brisket, smoked provolone cheese, barbecue sauce, and two onion rings in a toasted kaiser roll. Turkey or pork can be substituted upon request. Although we're avid fans of the original, we believe Joe's Burnt Ends Z-Man elevates the sandwich to a stellar level of culinary excellence. Our first bite of this sandwich was at the end of four other stops at barbecue joints. As Chef Paul remarked, "It was an explosion of great flavors when it hit my taste buds." It is Joe's most popular sandwich in Broken Arrow and Tulsa. You'll know why at *your* first bite. You can make it from scratch in a little over 17 hours as detailed here, or you can let Joe do the work. It is worth the trip to Oklahoma.

BURNT ENDS Z-MAN SANDWICH

Serves 2

½ cup Cowtown All-Purpose Barbeque Seasoning or your favorite

½ cup Cowtown Steak & Grill Seasoning or your favorite

1 (10- to 12-pound) beef brisket, trimmed

1 cup Joe's Kansas City Bar-B-Que Sauce, or your favorite

2 kaiser rolls, sliced, buttered, and grill-toasted

2 slices smoked provolone cheese

2 onion rings

Preheat your smoker to 190°F. Combine the rub and steak seasoning and blend well. Season the brisket all over, saving some for later. Place in the smoker and cook until the internal temperature reaches 185°F, 10 to 12 hours.

Remove the brisket from the cooker. Cover loosely with aluminum foil and let rest for about 1 hour or until the brisket is cool enough to handle. Insert a sharp knife into the layer of fat that lies between the point and the flat. The flat is done. Wrap and store the flat for another use.

Increase the temperature of the smoker to 275°F. Trim the excess fat from the point and reseason with the rub mixture. Place the point in the smoker and barbecue for another 2 to 3 hours, until crispy. Remove the point from the cooker and cover lightly with foil for at least 1 hour. Do not try to cube the point while hot or it will fall apart. When cool, cut the point into ¾-inch cubes.

Preheat the oven to 350°F. Place the cubes in a large stainless steel bowl, pour the barbecue sauce over the cubes, and toss to coat. Pour onto a foil-covered sheet pan (for easy cleanup). Place in the oven for 8 to 10 minutes, until the barbecue sauce begins to caramelize.

To serve, place some burnt ends on each roll. Top with cheese and allow the cheese to melt on the hot meat. Top each with an onion ring and the top of the roll.

BBQ Pig Salad

Short Sugar's Drive-In

1328 S. Scales St.
Reidsville, NC 26992
336-342-7487
http://shortsugarsbar-b-q.com

You expect good food when you step inside a place as busy as Short Sugar's. People from all over have stories to tell about eating at Short Sugar's from their childhood, teen, and adult years. Our barbecue buddies David Bailey and Carl Rothrock, who grew up in this area, had shared so many fond memories of Short Sugar's that we had to try it. We were lucky and got a booth right away.

The place is an old drive-in. On one end is counter service; booths and table service are on the other end. Busy staffers, diners visiting and having a good time, and the familiar chop-chop-chop is what you'll hear. We got so conditioned to that sound that our mouths watered every time we heard it, and of course we ordered a chopped pork sandwich with hushpuppies and slaw. Every bite was delicious!

BBQ PIG SALAD

Serves 2

1 (10-ounce) bag prewashed salad greens of your choice

2 cups pulled or chopped barbecued pork shoulder (see page 201)

Salad dressing of your choice, homemade or store-bought

Put half the greens on each plate. Top with meat. Serve with dressings on the side.

We noticed that Short Sugar's, like many other barbecue joints, has a barbecue pig salad on the menu. B. B. Perrins in Decatur, Alabama, calls its barbecue pork salad "Pig in the Garden." We haven't tried either one yet, but in the interest of providing a public service to diet-conscious readers, here's a pig salad that's easy to make at home.

Barbecued Baloney

Mac's Barbeque

1030 W. Rogers Blvd.
Skiatook, OK 74070
918-396-4165

Some folks call barbecued baloney "Okie Steak." We've enjoyed some excellent barbecued baloney at Ozzies Bar & Grill on Monkey Island, Oklahoma, on the shore of the Grand Lake of the Cherokees. At Ozzies the King Kong of Hot Dogs is perfectly married to hickory smoke and Head Country Bar-B-Q Sauce. Starnes in Paducah, Kentucky (see page 80), also serves a great barbecued baloney sandwich. Matter of fact, hundreds of places in Oklahoma, Texas, Tennessee, Kansas City, and elsewhere serve barbecued baloney worth writing home about. Our favorite, however, is at Mac's in Skiatook.

We met Mike and Vickie McMillan, owners of Mac's Barbeque, on the barbecue contest trail several years ago. They won so many awards for their barbecue and sauce that they decided to open a barbecue joint. It's a small place, but they do a booming business, eat in or carry out, and they still manage to do some competing on the barbecue-contest circuit, especially now that daughter and son-in-law Holly and Adam Green are overseeing the restaurant.

All of Mac's barbecue is prize-winning quality—brisket, pork butt, ribs, and chicken. Mac's all-beef baloney stands above the crowd. Many places fry the baloney slices after smoking; Mac prefers it as it comes out of the smoker. If you can't make it to Skiatook (near Tulsa) soon, try barbecuing baloney at home. Here's how Mac does it.

BARBECUED BALONEY

Serves 6 to 8

1 (5-pound) stick all-beef baloney, cut in half lengthwise

Preheat your smoker to 225° to 250°F. Place the halved baloney in your smoker with no seasoning and smoke for 1 to 2 hours, until the outside is dark and crusty. Slice the baloney into ¼-inch-thick slices and serve on a bun.

Pulled Pork Sandwich

Starnes BBQ

1008 Joe Clifton Dr.
Paducah, KY 42001
270-444-9555

If you think you'll be more likely to get a seat at the counter by waiting three hours past noon, don't count on it. The counter stools at Starnes get warm as soon as the doors open at 11:00 a.m., and most days they stay warm until closing time.

Starnes offers a no-frills menu: hickory-smoked pulled pork, mutton, baloney. No ribs. However, if you skip Starnes because they don't serve ribs, you've missed one of the best barbecue restaurants on earth. Go to Paducah and eat at Starnes and we'll bet you a Moon Pie that you'll agree.

Starnes is definitely not the product of chic food marketing experts. It looks like a textbook example of how not to package a restaurant. It is small. The pit and supply rooms are bigger than the dining room. It seats maybe twenty people on stools that line the U-shaped counter, and there's room for two in each of the two little booths that cap the ends of the U. The walls are cinder block, painted green; plate-glass windows don't offer a scenic view, except the park on the other side of Joe Clifton Drive. It hasn't changed its 1950s-diner look since it opened in 1954, and the only idle days it has seen since then are Sundays and a few holidays. There's

a hodgepodge of Moon Pies, sauce, and snack foods filling shelves in the middle of the U, leaving enough space along the counter for the wait staff to serve your food and beverages. Formica countertop, linoleum tile floor, and a large framed gallery of past generations of Starnes proprietors lend atmosphere, but it's the food and the people that make it work. The wait staff and customers, mostly regulars and in-the-know travelers, give Starnes a friendly ambience that makes you feel welcome and glad to be there.

Sandwiches are served between two slices of white bread, toasted on one side. Inside, your order of pulled pork, mutton, ham, or sliced baloney will be slightly seasoned with a kiss of hickory smoke. The first time we ate at Starnes, the waitress asked if we wanted our sandwich "hot" or "mild." Mild was three shakes from the sauce bottle; hot was six shakes. The last time we ate there, the saucing was up to us. An abundance of the delicious hot tomato-vinegar-pepper sauce is within reach of all the customers, where they can shake it on as they wish. Ardie takes several bottles home and uses it on a variety of foods in addition to barbecue.

PULLED PORK SANDWICH

Serves 1

2 slices white sandwich bread

1 cup hickory-smoked tender moist pulled pork shoulder (see page 201)

Starnes Bar-B-Q Sauce as desired

Put the bread on a lightly greased hot grill or cast-iron skillet until lightly toasted on one side, less than 1 minute. Place one slice of bread, toasted side down, on a plate. Top the bread with meat. Add the other slice of bread, toasted side up. Press down firmly on the sandwich, then slice in half diagonally. Serve with sauce on the side.

Starnes barbecue is also sold downtown near the river at D Starnes at 108 Broadway. It has a separate owner and features some menu items not served at the original Starnes, such as soups, corn muffins, vinegar slaw, baked beans, and coconut cream pie, but the meat and sauce come from the original Starnes. It is also roomier, with counter and booth space to accommodate tourists and *Delta Queen* stopovers.

Even if you're dead set on getting ribs at a barbecue joint, give Starnes a try. After eating a Starnes sandwich, we think you'll exclaim, "No ribs? No problem!"

Pig in a Puppy

Kings Restaurant

405 E. New Bern Rd.
Kinston, NC 28504
800-332-6465
http://www.kingsbbq.com

Wilbur King, Jr., a true southern gentleman, family man, and Civil War buff, has a barbecue pedigree that is second to none. The King legacy began in the 1850s, when R. W. King opened a country store in Kinston. The country store tradition continued with R.W.'s son, Richard, whose son, Frank, opened a store in 1936 that became Kings Restaurant.

Our favorite swine dining experience at Kings is a cup of Brunswick stew appetizer, followed with a Pig in a Puppy and cold, sweet iced tea. There are times when you want wine or beer with your puppy, and you can get that at Kings as well. You can order a hog heavenly feast from Kings, delivered fast and easy via the Carolina Oink

Express. Get the works in a Pig Out Party Pack, or smaller portions of chopped pork, sausage, country ham, center sliced ham, chitlins, collard greens, black-eyed peas, hushpuppies, delicious Brunswick stew, coleslaw, potato salad, pecan, apple, chocolate chip, or sweet potato pie, and—most important for making your own Pig in a Puppy—Kings's own hushpuppy mix and the famous sauce we have savored for years, Kings Delight BBQ Sauce. The sauce is classic eastern North Carolina vinegar with some signature ingredients that make it stand above the crowd. We like it on everything short of ice cream! If you can't make it to Kings, you can call their toll-free line or order online.

How did Wilbur King, Jr., get the idea for the Pig in a Puppy? He told us that one day when business was slow in the restaurant (had to be between lunch and dinner, as Kings is a popular, busy restaurant), he was messing around in the kitchen. He dropped some hushpuppy mix in the shape of a hot dog bun into the deep-fryer and fried it until crisp and golden on the outside. When he removed it and let it cool a bit, he

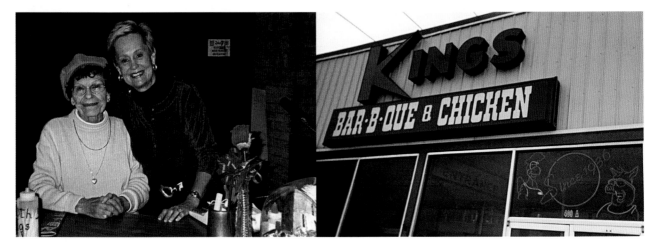

sliced it in half. Some of the mix was uncooked and soft, so he scooped it out and filled the cavity with chopped pork, sauce, and coleslaw. The Pig in a Puppy was born!

Wilbur mixes large amounts for the hungry crowd at Kings, and it's hard to put an exact formula on this because the cornmeal mix varies depending on the corn crop and what company makes it. Wilbur uses a white corn hushpuppy mix from Lakeside Mills, and you can order it from Oink Express. Thanks to Wilbur, inventor of the Pig in a Puppy, here's a home-version recipe.

PIG IN A PUPPY

Makes 4

2 cups self-rising white cornmeal

1 medium onion, minced

1 teaspoon salt

1 teaspoon finely ground black pepper

1 large egg, beaten

¾ cup milk or buttermilk

Canola, peanut, or vegetable oil, for deep-frying

1 cup chopped barbecue pork butt (see page 59)

½ cup Kings Delight BBQ Sauce

1 cup coleslaw (see recipes in Chapter 3)

To make the hushpuppy batter, mix the cornmeal mix, onion, salt, and pepper together in a large bowl until well combined. Stir in the egg and milk to form a thick, moist batter. Let the batter rest for 30 to 45 minutes to allow the self-rising mix to work.

Fill your deep-fryer with enough oil for the hushpuppies to float and heat the oil to 350°F (or use a deep pot and measure the oil temperature with a deep-frying thermometer). If you'd rather make traditional hushpuppies, use a teaspoon or scoop to drop batter by teaspoons into the oil. Fry until the puppies turn golden brown and float to the top, turning the puppies once so that they brown evenly on both sides. Drain on paper towels.

For pigs in a puppy, mold a large piece of batter into a round ball, lay the ball in one palm, and use your other hand to gently flatten the ball into a thin oblong shape (think flat football) the size of a hot dog bun. Dampen your free hand and move the batter to the dampened hand so it will slide off the dampened hand into the oil. Move your hand as close to the oil as is safe and let the puppy slide off into the hot oil. Cook for about 4 minutes, or until the outside is crisp and golden, turning the puppy once for more even browning. Remove from the fryer, drain, and let cool.

When the puppy is cool, slice it in half. If it didn't cook completely through, you may want to scoop out some of the doughy part and discard it. Fill the puppy with chopped pork, sprinkle with sauce, top with coleslaw, sandwich it, and serve. It's a delicious plate of "Southern Goodness" that you'll not soon forget!

Barbecue Hash

Maurice's Gourmet Barbeque

1600 Charleston Hwy. West
West Columbia, SC 29169
800-MAURICE (628-7423) (to order)

aurice Bessinger's legendary Piggie Park Barbeque is known worldwide. The recipe for his Gourmet Blend BBQ Sauce was given to him by his father. Maurice also learned cooking and restaurant management from his father. According to the company story, it took Maurice 55 years to build the Piggie Park chain and the Flying Pig Express into the "largest barbeque operation in the country."

The original Piggie Park sports a huge Confederate battle flag on a pole in the parking lot. Inside, in addition to great food and friendly service, you'll find religious and political pamphlets and a book written by Maurice, *Defending My Heritage.*

On the walls you'll see framed photos of Maurice with famous dignitaries and entertainers. If Maurice got the same admonition from his parents that we did—"Never discuss politics or religion with friends or strangers"—he didn't heed it. Fortunately our parents didn't forbid eating barbecue where the owner's views on politics and religion are freely dispensed!

When you sit down to enjoy a pulled pork sandwich or a slab of ribs with Carolina Gold BBQ Sauce, your mind won't be on politics or religion, just good food. The mustard-based sauce is said

to have been inspired by a reference to mustard seed in a biblical passage.

A dish the Piggie Park is famous for and that's found all over South Carolina is barbecue hash. Here's our recipe.

BARBECUE HASH

Serves 6 to 8

2 pounds barbecued pork
  shoulder (see page 201)

¼ cup white vinegar

2 tablespoons light brown sugar

1 tablespoon rubbed sage

2 teaspoons ground ginger

1 cup diced onion

8 tablespoons (1 stick) unsalted butter

Salt and black pepper

Cooked rice, for serving

Cube the meat and place it in a heavy cast-iron pot or a Dutch oven with enough water to cover. Add the vinegar, brown sugar, sage, and ginger. Simmer over medium-low heat until the meat falls apart, about 1½ hours, adding water as needed. Transfer the meat to another pan, add the onion to the pot, and bring to a gentle boil. When the meat is cool enough, remove and discard any connective tissue, veins, bone fragments, etc., and pull the meat into small bits. Return the meat to the pot and add the butter. Continue stirring and cooking to combine the meat and onion. Season with salt and pepper to taste. Serve over rice.

Pit Ham

Clark's Outpost BBQ

101 N. Hwy. 377
Tioga, TX 76271
800-932-5051 or 940-437-2414
http://www.clarksoutpost.com

lark's Outpost was founded by Warren Clark in 1974. It's known for genuine slow-smoked Texas barbecue. Barbecue historian Dr. Howard Taylor told us we had to stop at Clark's Outpost, and we're glad he insisted. The main thing that got Paul's attention was the smoked ham—something dear to his heart and that most barbecue joints don't do. He prefers the good old bone-in cured ham but will take a PIT ham (one that is partially internally trimmed) next.

Clark's has some of the best ham in the universe, and it's really easy to do. It just takes a lot of patience. Here's how Clark's does it.

PIT HAM

1 (12- to 14-pound) PIT ham

Prepare a hickory fire in your smoker and heat it to 190°F. Place the ham in the smoker and smoke it for 18 hours. Let rest for 30 minutes; then slice and serve.

Hash on Rice with Carolina Coleslaw

Melvin's Legendary Bar-B-Que

538 Folly Rd.
Charleston, SC 29412
888-MELVINS (635-8467)
or 843-762-0511
http://www.melvinsbbq.com

Melvin Bessinger of Charleston, South Carolina, is the elder brother of Maurice Bessinger of West Columbia, South Carolina (see page 84). Each has attained fame in his own right for many years of selling millions of pounds of tender pork barbecue with a mustard-based sauce to a barbecue consumer public that keeps coming back. We won't take sides. We like both!

The South Carolina Bessinger barbecue legacy began with Melvin and Maurice's father, Big Joe Bessinger. Big Joe was born in 1891 in Orangeburg, South Carolina. His lifelong career was in farming, but his legacy was the barbecue sauce he invented and the interest in the barbecue restaurant industry that he inspired in his sons. Big Joe invented a mustard-based barbecue sauce in 1933. He called it the Golden Secret Recipe BBQ Sauce. Melvin, age 10 at the time, learned the secret recipe from Big Joe. Big Joe opened the Holly Hill Café in 1939 and later the Eat at Joe's café with Melvin when Melvin came home from World War II.

Melvin Bessinger's impressive restaurant career portfolio includes not only founding Eat at Joe's with his dad but also founding Piggy Park Drive-Ins, Bessinger's BBQ & Burgers, and Melvin's Legendary Bar-B-Que. Melvin retired to the family farm after 71 years in the restaurant business, but his two Melvin's Bar-B-Que restaurants are still going strong, serving barbecued Carolina pork hams, pork ribs, and smoked chicken—all with the famous Golden Secret Recipe BBQ Sauce. The menu also includes much-acclaimed burgers, onion rings, hash on rice, collard greens, lima beans, fried okra, mac and cheese, corn on the cob, baked beans, sweet potato soufflé, and fries.

If you hanker for a taste of Melvin's barbecue, you can order ribs, pulled pork, chicken, and a variety of mustard-based sauces online. We recommend starting with the original 1933 Golden Secret Recipe BBQ Sauce before trying the newer varieties. You can barbecue your own fresh ham until tender enough to be pulled by hand and then serve it with Melvin's original sauce. Save enough for making hash on rice, a South Carolina tradition. We don't have Melvin's secret recipe, but we think you'll like our version here, and we threw in a recipe for homemade Carolina coleslaw to go with it.

HASH ON RICE

Serves 6

1 medium sweet onion, minced

2 tablespoons canola oil

4 pounds barbecued fresh
    ham, chopped

Salt and black pepper

2 cups water

2 cups mustard-based barbecue sauce

4 medium russet potatoes,
    peeled and chopped

2 cups long-grain white rice, cooked
    according to package instructions

In a large soup pot over medium heat, sauté the onion in the oil until soft, 3 to 5 minutes. Add the meat and salt and pepper to taste; stir the meat with the onion until mixed. Sauté for 6 minutes. Add the water and the barbecue sauce and bring to a boil; then turn the heat down to low and simmer for 10 minutes. Add the potatoes and simmer until tender, 15 to 20 minutes. Serve over hot rice.

CAROLINA COLESLAW

Serves 10 to 12

1 large head green cabbage
    (about 3 pounds), shredded

3 to 4 celery stalks, diced

1 medium Spanish onion, diced

1 small green bell pepper,
    seeded and diced

3 medium carrots, grated

2 cups sugar

½ cup white vinegar

½ cup apple cider vinegar

½ cup olive oil

1 teaspoon celery seeds

1 teaspoon kosher salt

In a large bowl, combine all the vegetables and mix in the sugar. Set aside. Combine the vinegars, olive oil, celery seeds, and salt in a medium saucepan, bring to a boil, and pour over the cabbage mixture. Toss to coat all the ingredients. Cover and chill overnight before serving.

A Southern Barbecue

Loaded Pork-Stuffed Potato

Curtis's BBQ

40 Old Depot Rd.
Putney, VT 05346
802-387-5474
http://www.curtisbbqvt.com

You have to admire Curtis Tuff. There he is, a barbecue pitmaster in rural Vermont, where New England cuisine runs more along the lines of fresh baked bread from King Arthur Flour; dairy-fresh butters and cheeses, including the world's best goat cheese; Grade A Vermont maple syrup; fresh microbrews from Harpoon, Long Trail, Magic Hat, Otter Creek, Rock Art, or Trout River; plus fabulous fresh seafood from the nearby coastal waters of Maine.

There is reason to believe, however, that barbecue is indigenous to Vermont and other New England states. Some think Native Americans in the area engaged in some form of barbecue cooking prior to the arrival and settlement of Europeans. Be that as it may, Curtis Tuff certainly deserves credit for his key role in introducing modern-day New Englanders to real barbecue over the past four decades. His customers rave about the quality of Curtis's ribs, chicken, sauce, stuffed potatoes, potato salad, coleslaw, macaroni, baked beans, sweet yams, corn on the cob, corn muffins, and homemade root beer.

Christine Tuff, co-owner of Curtis's BBQ and Curtis's wife, also plays a key role in the success of the restaurant. Curtis and Christine's daughter, Sarah, and son-in-law, Chris Parker, run a second Curtis's BBQ in Chester, Vermont. They learned the cooking techniques, recipes, and business from Curtis and Christine. For a masterly online introduction to Curtis and his cuisine, go to our barbecue buddy Mark Dolan's Barbecue Pilgrim Web site and click on the Curtis stories: www.bbqpilgrim.com.

Chris Parker told us the story of how Christine Tuff invented their popular stuffed potatoes: "According to Christine, it started as a way to use up the meat that fell off the rib bones and was not usable for much else. So she tried it as a snack and thought that she had struck gold, and some 20 years later we can't make these fast enough to keep up with the demand."

LOADED PORK-STUFFED POTATO

Makes 1 potato

1 (9-ounce) Idaho baking potato

Pat of butter (optional)

6 ounces chopped barbecued
   pork butt (see page 59)

3 ounces Vermont cheddar cheese

2 tablespoons sour cream

1 tablespoon bacon bits

¼ cup sliced mushrooms,
   or more to taste

Curtis's own award-winning Southern
   Style Bar-B-Q Sauce (we like the Spicy)

1 tablespoon dried chives

Using hardwood, such as hard maple or oak, preheat the grill to 250°F. Grill the potato for about 1 hour over indirect heat, or until it is soft when you squeeze it. Remove the potato from the grill, cut the potato open, and add the pat of butter. Fill the potato with the chopped pork, then top with the cheese, sour cream, bacon bits, mushrooms, barbecue sauce to taste, and chives. Grab a fork and maybe a friend, because you may need help eating all of this!

Bar-B-Q Spaghetti

The Bar-B-Q Shop

1782 Madison Ave.
Memphis, TN 38104
877-DSAUCES (372-8237)
or 901-272-1277
http://www.dancingpigs.com

From the atmosphere to the friendly service and the outstanding food, the Bar-B-Q Shop is a place that makes you feel good. No wonder it's a Memphis favorite! Dark red walls, lots of wood, and subdued but sufficient lighting give the place a warm, inviting feel. If you're faced with a wait, and you're starving, see if there is a place for you at the bar. The last time we were there that's exactly what we did, and it was our honor to be served by Mrs. Hazelteen Vernon

herself—a kind, strong, beautiful, and dignified lady. Competence, friendliness, and dedication to serving customers with care must run in the family, because Frank and Eric Vernon are the same way.

Once you've dined at the Bar-B-Q Shop, you'll be back. Graze your way through the menu. Ribs come wet or dry. Try both. The pork sandwiches are some of the best we've ever eaten. Get barbecued beans on the side. You'll order those beans at each visit! And you have to try the Bar-B-Q Spaghetti, a Memphis classic. Although the recipe here is available online from the Bar-B-Q Shop, it's a must-have dish for any book about American barbecue. Bobby Flay also featured this recipe on a Food Network show on barbecue specialties. Since we're so partial to the way the Vernon family cooks and serves this dish, here's the recipe.

BAR-B-Q SPAGHETTI

Serves 6 to 8

1 cup chopped onion

¾ cup chopped green bell pepper

1 pint Dancing Pigs Original
    Bar-B-Q Sauce

1 cup sugar

2 tablespoons liquid smoke

½ cup cooking oil

Pinch of salt

1 pound spaghetti, prepared according to
    package directions, rinsed, and drained

Chopped barbecued pork shoulder,
    for serving (see page 201)

In a large skillet, combine the onion, green pepper, barbecue sauce, sugar, liquid smoke, oil, and salt. Cook for 30 minutes, stirring occasionally. Pour the sauce over the cooked spaghetti and stir. Top with pork shoulder and serve hot.

WHERE ARE THE BARBECUE POLICE?

Kansas City artist and cartoonist Charlie Podrebarac has created many classic "Cowtown" cartoons with a barbecue theme. One of our favorites is titled "Most Cowtowners Travel Well. Others. . . ." Pictured is a backyard cook, dressed in chef gear, standing at a grill. There are two hot dogs on the grill and one hot dog skewered on a grill fork. The chef is holding the skewered dog upward. He says, "Who wants some Bar-B-Q?" The "other" Cowtowner, dressed in red with "K.C." on his chest and a righteous scowl on his face, is pointing at the hot dog. He says, "If I want 'Barbecue,' I'll go to Kansas City and order some. That, sir, is a grilled wiener!"

Some people hold to strict differences between barbecuing and grilling. Barbecue is slow and low. Grilling is hot and fast. We accept and understand the difference, but backyard cooking is as American as apple pie. If some Americans want to call a backyard hot dog party or a hamburger or steak party a barbecue—gas grill or charcoal grill—we're OK with that. The accepted term has evolved from cookout to barbecue.

The U.S. government, on the other hand, has defined barbecue in a way that leaves no room for grillers or cooking with gas. Here's the government definition:

Barbecued meats, such as product labeled "Beef Barbecue" or "Barbecued Pork," shall be cooked by the direct action of dry heat resulting from the burning of hard wood or the hot coals therefrom for a sufficient period to assume the usual characteristics of a barbecued article, which include the formation of a brown crust on the surface and the rendering of surface fat. The product may be basted with a sauce during the cooking process. The weight of barbecued meat shall not exceed 70 percent of the weight of the fresh uncooked meat.*

It is our understanding that federal regulations are, in effect, laws. If this is so, the federal government is not enforcing the law as it applies to barbecue. There are restaurants, for example, that label any item with barbecue sauce on it "barbecue": pizza, burgers, oven-baked ribs or beef or chicken, slathered with barbecue sauce and sold as barbecue. Where are the Barbecue Police? We have yet to see or hear of any. We hope we never read a newspaper headline that reads like this: "Local man arrested in backyard by FBI. Grilled burgers and called them 'barbecue.'"

---

*Code of Federal Regulations, Title 9, Chapter III, Part 319, Subpart C, Section 319.80, revised: 1/1/1985

Smoked Garlic Sausage

Meyer's Elgin Smokehouse

188 Hwy. 290
Elgin, TX 78621
800-MRS-OINK (677-6465)
or 512-281-3331
http://www.cuetopiatexas.com

Meyer's is billed as "The Capital of 'Cue-Topia, Texas,'" which, according to R. G. Meyer, is "the perfect state of barbecue." A strong case can be made for naming the Elgin-Lockhart area a barbecue capital. Although we have our favorites, you can't go wrong in your search for great barbecue in this legendary section of lower central Texas.

Our good barbecue buddy John Raven told us that for a Texas commercial product today he likes Meyer's sausage out of Elgin. John keeps some Meyer's hot sauce in his cupboard, too, just waiting for the right moment.

We didn't even try to get an original sausage recipe from Meyer's or any other sausage kings in Elgin. Although the recipe we're sharing with you makes darned good sausage, the easiest way to get a taste of true Texas smokehouse sausage is to go to Elgin in person or online. Make sure you allow enough time to prepare the casings the night before.

SMOKED GARLIC SAUSAGE

Serves 12 to 24

4 yards hog casings

Apple cider vinegar

4 pounds pork butt with fat

2 pounds boneless beef chuck
  or round with fat

1 large onion, minced

6 cloves garlic, minced

2 tablespoons minced fresh sage

1 tablespoon salt

1 tablespoon black pepper

2 tablespoons crushed red pepper

1 teaspoon cayenne

Vegetable oil

The day before you plan to stuff the sausage, rinse the sausage casings inside and out under cold water. Prepare a solution of 1 cup water to 1 capful of cider vinegar. Soak the casings in the solution overnight.

In a meat grinder, coarsely grind the meats and place in a large bowl. Thoroughly mix in the onion, garlic, sage, salt, black pepper, crushed red pepper, and cayenne. Refrigerate overnight. Stuff the casings to 1 inch thick and 5 inches long and tie off. They can be refrigerated for 3 days or frozen for 6 months at this point.

Prepare a smoker with oak or mesquite and preheat to 225°F. Rub the sausages with just a little vegetable oil. Don't overdo it or they'll get messy and then turn to mush. Smoke the sausages for 2 hours or until the skin looks ready to pop.

Beef PB (Polish Boy) Deluxe

Mt. Pleasant BBQ

12825 Kinsman
Cleveland, OH 44120
216-561-8722

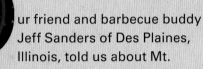

Our friend and barbecue buddy Jeff Sanders of Des Plaines, Illinois, told us about Mt. Pleasant BBQ. Jeff is the inventor and CEO of Roadhouse Bar-B-Que Sauces, Inc., and every sauce he makes is on our faves list. He found Mt. Pleasant BBQ while promoting his sauces one fine day in Cleveland.

Before we found out about Mt. Pleasant BBQ, we thought Cleveland was mostly a rock-and-roll rib burner town—home of the Rock and Roll Hall of Fame and Museum and site of the annual Memorial Day weekend Great American Rib Cook-Off & Music Festival. Thanks to Wayne Whitmore and "BuddyRoadhouse," Jeff's handle on the Roadfood.com forum, we've added "great barbecue" to what we think about Cleveland.

Jeff, knowing that we're regulars at Arthur Bryant's, told us that "Mt. Pleasant BBQ is a classic in terms of location and ambience." He went on to say, "The interior makes Arthur Bryant's look like a four-star restaurant in Paris!" That's just the kind of environment we like! You go to Mt. Pleasant BBQ for the food—barbecued ribs, pulled pork sandwiches, fresh-cut skin-on fries, mac and cheese, collard greens, and barbecue beans. If you're not hungry for barbecue (imagine that!), Wayne also has fried fish and fried chicken on the menu. But we agree with Jeff that what brings down the house is Mt. Pleasant's Beef PB (Polish Boy) Deluxe! As Jeff says, it's "an unholy mess that is pure pleasure to eat!" We put together a home version, but the best way to get a Mt. Pleasant BBQ PB Deluxe is to buy one from proprietor Wayne Whitmore.

BBQ PB (POLISH BOY) DELUXE

Serves 1

½ cup barbecue sauce

1 clove garlic, pressed

1 (6-ounce) beef kielbasa

1 standard hot dog bun

1 cup barbecued pulled pork butt (see page 59)

1 cup creamy coleslaw (see page 143)

1 handful fresh-cut fries (see page 130)

Combine the barbecue sauce and pressed garlic. Cover and refrigerate overnight.

Lightly oil your grill rack and prepare a charcoal grill for direct-heat cooking over medium-hot coals. Grill the kielbasa, turning once, until sizzling and grill marks appear, about 4 minutes. On a dinner plate, put the kielbasa in the bun; add pulled pork; top with coleslaw and then fries. Sprinkle sauce on to taste. Enjoy the messy feast!

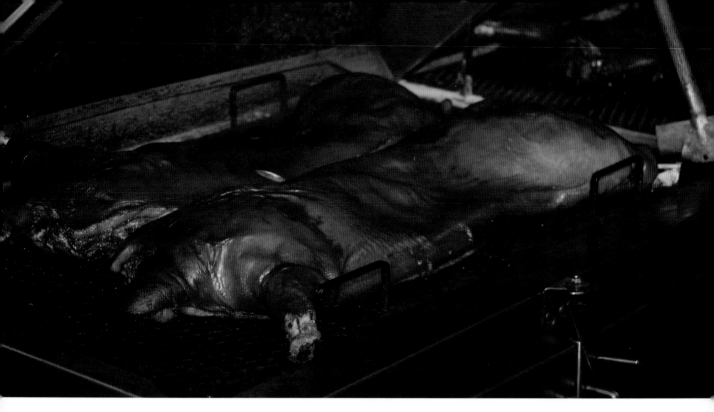

Barbecued Whole Hog

The Pit

328 W. Davie St.
Raleigh, NC 27601
919-890-4500
http://www.thepit-raleigh.com

True to original head pitmaster Ed Mitchell's high standards, The Pit will serve you some of the finest pit-cooked whole hog you've ever tasted. Hogs raised free-range without growth hormones and antibiotics plus old southern pitmaster techniques are the secret. The Pit's creative side dishes, made from fresh, local ingredients, from farm to table, are also outstanding.

Although The Pit is a white-tablecloth restaurant, the food is pure down-home eastern North Carolina style. From the chopped whole hog accented with vinegar and pepper sauce to the Brunswick stew, the skillet-blackened Brussels sprouts tossed with a touch of prepared mustard, fried green tomatoes, hand-cut fries over chopped barbecue pork, juicy tender beef brisket, pork jowl bacon bruschetta, barbecue chicken wings, barbecue chicken, home-style beans, collard greens, coleslaw, and made-from-scratch hush puppies and biscuits with sweetened butter, it's all good. We've heard that The Pit's fried chicken rivals Gus's in Tennessee. Of course, don't miss the banana pudding for dessert.

Thanks to Sandi, Patrick, and Lynn Ford, our friends at Ford's Foods in Raleigh, for updating The Pit for us and taking some pictures. No doubt they were too polite to sneak in some of their own classic Bone Suckin' Sauce (one of our favorites), but it must have been tempting. There were no complaints about The Pit's eastern and western North Carolina–style sauces, however. Patrick is

a big fan of The Pit's pork jowl bacon bruschetta, which he describes as "insanely good, like *foie gras* of bacon."

Local brews and a full array of cocktails are available. Diners can sit at the new bar and watch kitchen staff chop barbecue and fill orders.

Meanwhile, Ed Mitchell's dedication to teaching and preserving the art and science of cooking barbecued whole hogs and other southern delicacies continues throughout the United States and worldwide.

When Ed was at The Pit, here's what he shared with us about the proper way to barbecue a whole hog. You can get a dressed and butterflied or split hog from a butcher or hog supplier.

The Pit's barbecue pits are 74 inches long, about 6 feet wide, made with fire brick on the inside and decorative bricks on the outside. You can adapt this recipe to your own pit.

BARBECUED WHOLE HOG

Serves 90 to 100

1 (150-pound) dressed hog, butterflied or split

Salt and black pepper

1 gallon pepper vinegar sauce

Open the pit and take out the grate. Bank about 40 pounds of charcoal around the inside walls of the pit in a big circle. Pour two large chimneys of hot coals around the outside of the charcoal ring. Preheat the pit to about 250°F.

Trim any excess fat from the inside of the hog and season the inside all over with salt and pepper. Put the grate back over the charcoal and top with the hog, close the lid, and cook overnight. With a meat thermometer, check the temperature of the hog in the hams and shoulders. The temperature should be at least 165°F, but most prefer 185° to 195°F. Serve with the sauce.

Rib Gumbo

B. B. Perrins Barbecue aka Sports Grille

601 Holly St. Northeast
Decatur, AL 35601
256-355-1045

Our longtime friend and expert barbecue buddy Ron "Sheepdog" Harwell, PhB, introduced us to B. B. Perrins Barbecue. Ron lives in Decatur and has been a regular customer at B. B. Perrins since his friend and owner Benny Perrin first opened for business in 1988. The original menu featured a rib sandwich or pork sandwich with Golden Flake potato chips, Coca-Cola, and white bread: University of Alabama stadium–style manna for Crimson Tide fans.

Ron says they should add "Family" to the name, "Because during any given meal you choose to dine with Benny, his wife, Courtney, and daughter, Mary Caitlin, there are sure to be families enjoying various entrées on the menu."

The "sports grille" theme reflects Benny's impressive sports career. He was a two-sport All-American in high school. After graduating from Decatur High School, he played on the legendary Paul "Bear" Bryant's last two national championship football teams in 1978 and 1979. After Alabama he racked up an impressive four-year stint in the National Football League with the St. Louis Cardinals.

Benny's B. B. Perrins Sports Grille has been serving consistently good food for more than a quarter century. Although the decor is sports-themed, specifically college football, with a predominant Alabama Roll Tide motif, don't expect the usual game nosh cuisine here. The menu is all southern barbecue. The smoked pork ribs, pulled pork, and tenderloin are rubbed with Benny's homemade blends and served with Grandaddy Perrin's "secret sauce," a sweet, tomato-based recipe tweaked through the years by the Perrin family. And in this part of the country, no chicken plate would be complete without a signature white sauce. Pat's slaw, jailhouse slaw, potato salad, baked beans, or corn on the cob is a perfect complement to the meat dishes. The barbecue salads are a daily big hit, but what caught our eye and palate is the local favorite, Rib Gumbo. Benny was gracious enough to share his award-winning legendary recipe with his friends—enjoy!

AWARD-WINNING LEGENDARY B. B. PERRINS RIB GUMBO

Serves 10 to 12

2 cups dehydrated onion

7 quarts cold water

4 cups diced onion

8 cups diced green bell pepper

8 cups diced celery

½ cup chopped or jarred fresh garlic

½ cup Cajun seasoning

10 bay leaves

1 (16-ounce) jar beef base paste

1 #10 (6-pound, 6-ounce) can tomatoes, drained

1 (12- to 16-ounce) bag frozen okra

3 cups cornstarch

2 pounds boneless smoked rib meat, straight out of the smoker

Cooked rice, for serving

Place the dehydrated onion in a small bowl, cover with hot water, and let hydrate for about 15 minutes. In a large slow cooker, combine the rehydrated onion, 6 quarts of the cold water, onion, green pepper, celery, garlic, Cajun seasoning, bay leaves, and beef base paste. Bring to a boil over medium-high heat and cook for about 20 minutes. Add the tomatoes and okra, bring to a boil, and cook for another 20 minutes.

In a bowl, mix the cornstarch with the remaining 1 quart cold water until smooth. Slowly add the mixture to the gumbo and cook until the gumbo thickens. Then add the meat and stir to combine. Serve over a bed of rice and enjoy.

Tamales and Beans

McClard's Bar-B-Q

505 Albert Pike
Hot Springs, AR 71901
866-622-5273 or 501-623-9665
http://www.mcclards.com

When you stop at McClard's for barbecue, you're walking into more than 75 years of barbecue history. In 1928, the Westside Tourist Court became Westside Bar-B-Q with *cabrito*, baby goat, as its star menu attraction. In 1942, McClard's moved into its current location—a whitewashed stucco building—and became McClard's Bar-B-Q.

If you get a chance, go to McClard's Web site and read about its history. The story of how Mc-Clard's legendary barbecue sauce came into the restaurant's possession is like something you see or hear of only in the movies. The story goes like this: a customer was staying at the Westside for two months and couldn't afford to pay the $10 he owed; he asked them if they would accept instead a recipe for "the world's greatest bar-b-que sauce." They tried the traveler's sauce, and now everybody knows about the world-famous McClard's Bar-B-Q Sauce.

Fourth-generation McClards now run the kitchen, with some outstanding numbers. Each week they serve 7,000 pounds of mouthwatering hickory-smoked beef, pork, and ribs, along with 250 gallons of spicy barbecue beans, 250 gallons of coleslaw, 3,000 hand-rolled hot tamales, and 3,000 pounds of fresh-cut potatoes french-fried to perfection. The number that intrigues us most is the handmade tamales—that's more than 400 a day!

Tamales are nontraditional barbecue fare, but they turn up at barbecue joints in the Mississippi Delta, Memphis, and Hot Springs. We call McClard's barbecue tamales with beans upscale barbecue. They are a pleasant change at a barbecue restaurant. Making them isn't rocket science, but it is a bit of a fiddle, and it takes some practice to learn how to wrap them. You may put just about any good-tasting filling in your tamales that you want, but McClard's filling of finely ground barbecued meat is different.

We strongly suggest that you make your fillings on one day and do the wrapping and filling the next. Tamales require a lot of handwork, but these barbecue tamales are worth it! Here is our version thanks to some tips from owner Scott McClard.

TAMALES AND BEANS

Makes 20 to 24 tamales

CHILI BEANS

1 pound dried pinto beans

1½ cups chopped onion

4 cloves garlic, minced

1 to 2 tablespoons chili powder

1 (6-ounce) can tomato paste

Pinch of black pepper

TAMALE DOUGH

4 cups white masa harina

3 cups warm beef or chicken stock

2 cups lard

FILLING

2½ pounds barbecued brisket (see page 42), chopped

2½ pounds barbecued pork butt (see page 59), chopped or pulled

¼ cup barbecue seasoning of your choice

1 to 2 cups barbecue sauce of your choice

Wash and rinse the beans well, pick over, and drain. Place in a large kettle and cover with water. Bring to a boil over high heat. Remove from the heat and set aside for 1 hour. Drain the water and add fresh water to cover the beans. Add the onion, garlic, chili powder, tomato paste, and pepper to the beans. Bring to a boil over high heat. Reduce the heat and simmer, covered, until the beans are tender, 45 minutes to 1 hour. Taste and adjust the seasonings, adding salt if necessary.

To make the tamale dough, put the masa harina in a large bowl and reconstitute by adding warmed stock. Beat with a wooden spoon until the dough is thick but smooth. Add a little more stock if necessary, but be sure to keep the mixture firm.

In another large bowl, beat the lard with a mixer fitted with a paddle until it is very fluffy, 3 to 4 minutes. Continue to beat at medium speed and add the masa a little at a time until well combined. The texture should remain light and fluffy. To see if the mixture is mixed well, drop a teaspoon of the dough into a glass of water. If it floats, it's ready. If not, beat it some more. Cover and allow to rest for at least 30 minutes before using.

While the masa is resting, prepare the filling. In a large bowl, combine the beef, pork, and barbecue seasoning and blend well. Place the mixture in a food processor and process to an almost smooth paste, adding barbecue sauce as needed. You can also use a meat grinder to grind it to an almost fine paste. Cover and refrigerate until ready to use.

McClard's tamales are hand-rolled, bigger than most other tamales—5½ to 6 inches long. Spread about ¼ cup of masa dough over a sheet of parchment paper (6 to 8 inches long) and place 3 to 4 ounces of the filling in the center of the masa. Roll the paper lengthwise to seal in the barbecue mixture and tie together on each end with butcher's twine. Repeat with the remaining masa.

Fill a large pot with water and bring to a boil, then reduce to a simmer. Drop the tamales in and boil for 30 to 45 minutes.

To serve, take the tamales out of the parchment paper and top with chili beans.

Smoked Glazed Fresh Pork Ham

Danny's Place

902 S. Canal St.
Carlsbad, NM 88220
505-885-8739
http://www.dannysbbq.com

Paul has known Danny and Carolyn Gaulden for more than a decade. Their new digs are a far cry from their original barbecue. On August 1, 1975, Danny and Carolyn opened a Dairy Queen/Barbecue. It was the only one in the whole world. It was also a thorn in the side of the DQ people. It was legal since Danny had one of the original franchise contracts with DQ, and it was permitted, but word started to spread about this Dairy Queen that sold fantastic barbecue. That was the start of a lot of problems. There was too much publicity, and other franchisees wanted to do the same but couldn't. The Barbecue Maverick was the one and only.

There was a lot of pressure on the Gauldens to stop serving barbecue, and it went on until February 2004. Push came to shove, and the decision was made to stop serving a $1.50 sundae and start serving $5.00 hand-cut barbecued brisket sandwiches. They shut down and remodeled and have never looked back. And now the world around Carlsbad, New Mexico, has a new barbecue joint: Danny's Place!

Here's how Danny smokes a fresh ham. His glaze is great for ribs and ham. Serve it with some of Danny's Potato Salad (page 138).

SMOKED GLAZED FRESH PORK HAM

Serves 10 to 12

1 (8-pound) fresh pork ham

⅓ cup of your favorite basic rub

Danny's Rib and Pork Finishing Glaze (recipe follows)

Remove the rind or the skin (this lets the smoke penetrate more), but leave the fat intact. Put a basic rub on it. If you don't have one handy, some salt, pepper, and a little garlic will work just fine. Cook low and slow at 225° to 250°F and keep the smoke going fairly often. Barbecue until the internal temperature of the meat reaches 160° to 175°F. The higher the internal temperature, the drier the ham will be. Remember, this isn't as lean as a pork loin, but not as fat as a Boston butt. It's in the middle. This process makes it more tender if you bring it up easy. About 30 minutes before it's done, baste a couple of times with the rib glaze here or your favorite barbecue sauce.

DANNY'S RIB AND PORK FINISHING GLAZE

Makes ½ cup

¾ cup packed light brown sugar

¼ to ⅓ cup yellow mustard

2 tablespoons apple cider vinegar

Mix all the ingredients in a small saucepan and bring to a simmer. Let cool until you're ready to baste the ribs or pork. The glaze should be at least thick enough to coat a spoon. If the glaze is too thick, add more vinegar or some beer. Apply to the ribs or roast the very second they come off the pit or grill. Or put on a coat of the glaze about 2 minutes before removing the ribs or roast and then another as soon as they are off the pit or grill.

Barbecued Mutton Ribs

Southside Market & Barbeque

1212 Hwy. 290
Elgin, TX 78621
877-487-8015 or 512-285-3407
http://www.southsidemarket.com

outhside Market in Elgin, which was named the Sausage Capital of Texas in 1995, is a must-stop when you're making your way through the hill country of Texas. A little more than 1.5 million pounds of hot sausage is made annually in Elgin (pronounced "EL-gun"). Elgin sausage is also known by its more affectionate names, Texas Hot Gut and Elgin Hot Guts.

Fresh beef and pork seasoned with secret herbs and spices make Southside Market's sausage unique. Produced since 1882, the original "hot" was toned down in the 1970s to appeal to a broader base of consumers. Forget about getting the original recipe for Southside Market's Texas Hot Gut. It's a trade secret.

When you get in line to order a link of Hot Gut and some brisket, don't pass up the mutton. If you think you don't like mutton, you haven't eaten mutton at Southside Market. Bryan Bracewell, third-generation owner, insists that the mutton is actually lamb, but we say what we've tasted there is mutton and we're sticking to it.

Here is Paul's version of the mutton ribs at Southside Market.

BARBECUED MUTTON RIBS

Serves 6 to 8

¼ cup kosher salt

¼ cup coarsely ground black pepper

¼ cup paprika

2 tablespoons chili powder

2 tablespoons ground cumin

2 tablespoons granulated garlic

1 tablespoon cayenne

2 mutton breast (ribs), trimmed

Preheat your smoker to 375°F. Combine the salt, pepper, paprika, chili powder, cumin, garlic, and cayenne and blend well.

Sprinkle the mutton breast all over with the rub and rub it in. Place on your smoker and cook indirectly for 4 to 5 hours,w until done, turning every 1½ hours. The ribs are done when you can take two side-by-side ribs and tear them apart easily.

NAPA VALLEY MILK FED
LAMB SHANK

1190 LB

ALLEY MILK FED
BONE LAMB CHOP

490

Barbecued Rack of Lamb

Daisy May's BBQ USA

623 W. 46th St. at 11th Ave.
New York, NY 10036
212-977-1500
http://www.daisymaysbbq.com

Chef Adam Perry Lang probably has the best pedigree of any chef we have run across in all of barbecue. He has proven himself in some of the greatest fine dining restaurants in the world and is now creating some of America's best barbecue at Daisy May's BBQ USA. If you can't make it down to the restaurant, and you're out and about in New York City, try one of the mobile barbecue carts located around the city.

The selections at Daisy May's are quite extensive. They include Texas chopped brisket and Carolina pulled pork sandwiches, chicken and rib combinations, and a thorough selection of soulful side dishes. Daisy May's BBQ is a deliciously different way to entertain. The barbecued rack of lamb is a perfect example of that difference.

BARBECUED RACK OF LAMB

Serves 6

MARINADE

2 tablespoons Worcestershire sauce

½ cup chopped sweet onion

10 cloves garlic, chopped

**1 tablespoon fresh thyme
leaves (about 10 sprigs)**

**1 tablespoon fresh rosemary
leaves (about 10 sprigs)**

1 tablespoon ancho chile powder

1 tablespoon black pepper

1 tablespoon crushed red pepper

¼ cup water

LAMB

2 (8-bone) racks American lamb

SPICE BLEND

½ cup smoked paprika

2 tablespoons chili powder

2 tablespoons garlic salt

1 tablespoon lemon pepper

GLAZE

¼ cup honey

½ cup barbecue sauce of your choice

1 clove garlic, grated

½ jalapeño pepper, grated

Salt

To make the marinade, puree the Worcestershire sauce, onion, garlic, thyme, rosemary, ancho chile powder, pepper, crushed red pepper, and water in a blender. Set aside until ready to use.

Trim off as much fat from the lamb as possible, leaving the fat and meat in between the rib bones intact. Place the lamb racks in a resealable plastic bag large enough to hold them and pour in the marinade. Seal the bag and shake it around a little to coat the lamb with the marinade. Refrigerate for 3 to 4 hours, or overnight.

Preheat a barbecue to 275°F, using oak wood. Remove the racks of lamb from the refrigerator and wipe off most of the marinade with paper towels; it's OK to leave some on.

In a small bowl, combine the spice blend ingredients and sprinkle it all over the racks until the meat is thoroughly coated.

Place the seasoned lamb racks bone side down in the barbecue and cook over indirect heat until the meat registers 125°F on an instant-read thermometer, about 1 hour and 15 minutes. While the lamb is cooking, combine the glaze ingredients. Remove the meat and coat with the glaze. Return the lamb to the barbecue and continue to cook for 20 minutes. Remove, wrap in plastic, and allow to rest for about 5 minutes. Cut into individual chops and season each chop individually with salt.

Butterflied Leg of Lamb with Caramelized Onion BBQ Sauce

Dinosaur Bar-B-Que

246 W. Willow St.
Syracuse, NY 13202
888-476-1662 ext. 211 or 315-476-4937
http://www.dinosaurbarbque.com

Dinosaur Bar-B-Que is a genuine honky-tonk rib joint, and in Paul's humble opinion it is "the rock 'n' roll biker bar and bar-b-que of the millennium." There are now eight Dinosaur restaurants in several East Coast cities, and also in Chicago, but the original is in Syracuse. All are popular and busy. You'll know why from your first visit—and you'll be back!

John Stage, pitmaster-founder, with two biker friends, Dino and Mike, started the Dinosaur tradition in 1983 with a cut-in-half 55-gallon-drum pit in Syracuse. They got the idea while full of "rotgut grub and beer." It still felt like a good idea the next day. They were traveling to biker events anyway. They fancied themselves good cooks. Why not sell barbecue and make some money on the road? They took their barbecue on the road for the next five years, showing up at East Coast fairs, festivals, and motorcycle shows. By 1988 John's reputation for great barbecue was established and he was tired of selling it on the road, so he opened a takeout joint in downtown Syracuse. By 1990 he had a sit-down restaurant with waitresses and a full-service bar and thousands of fans. The momentum roars on like a full-throttle hog on a highway.

Inspiration for the name came from two sources: Dino's name and a Hank Williams, Jr., song about the sad transition of his favorite honky-tonk, Dinosaur, to a disco. The business name has evolved from Dinosaur Productions to Dinosaur Concessions and finally to Dinosaur Bar-B-Que in 1985, when John and Mike came up with the recipe for Dinosaur's famous sauce.

The early fare was grilled meats with Italian accents—such as barbecue-sauced Delmonico sandwiches. Then, thanks to a customer at a Hagerstown, Maryland, gig, John had a barbecue epiphany. In so many words this southern gentleman politely told John the food was good, but it wasn't barbecue. He told John about the barbecue method of cooking as done down South. John took the man seriously, and then he took to the road on a barbecue pilgrimage to Virginia, North Carolina, Tennessee, and Mississippi. He saw, he asked questions, he took notes, and he ate. Last stop: Memphis. By then John was hardcore passionate about real barbecue and bringing it home to New York. Thank you, Mr. Southern Gentleman, whatever your real name is.

continued on page 106

BUTTERFLIED LEG OF LAMB
WITH CARAMELIZED ONION BBQ SAUCE

Serves 6 to 8

MARINADE

1 cup plain yogurt

Grated zest of 1 lemon

½ cup fresh lemon juice

1 tablespoon olive oil

**4 scallions, white and
green parts, sliced**

6 cloves garlic, chopped

¼ cup chopped fresh mint leaves

2 tablespoons dried thyme

2 tablespoons black pepper

1 tablespoon ground cumin

1 tablespoon kosher salt

LAMB

**1 leg of lamb, boned by a butcher
(4 to 5 pounds boneless)**

Salt and black pepper

SAUCE

2 tablespoons butter

**1 large onion, thinly cut into
half-moon slices**

**Pinch each of kosher salt
and black pepper**

Pinch of sugar

1 cup chicken broth or stock

1 tablespoon Dijon mustard

**1 cup Dinosaur Bar-B-Que
Sensuous Slathering Sauce**

1 teaspoon ground cumin

3 tablespoons chopped fresh mint

Whirl all the marinade ingredients together in a food processor. Prick the lamb all over with a fork and nestle it in a large nonreactive bowl. Spoon the marinade onto the meat and slather it around until the meat is well coated. Cover and marinate in the fridge for 6 to 8 hours or overnight.

Prepare a hot coal bed and mound the coals on one side of the grill. Preheat it to 325° to 350°F. When you're ready to cook, scrape off all the marinade and pat the meat dry. Season the lamb with salt and pepper. Lay the lamb, boned side down, directly over the coals. Sear it for 4 minutes. Flip it over and sear the other side for 3 to 4 minutes. Slide the meat away from the coals to cook it with indirect heat. Cover the grill, check to make sure the heat is 325° to 350°F inside, and roast for 50 to 60 minutes, or until the internal temperature of the meat reaches 145° to 150°F on an instant-read thermometer. Remove the meat from the grill and let it rest for 15 minutes before carving.

Start the sauce cooking while the meat roasts. Drop the butter into a saucepan and melt over low heat. Add the onion, season with salt and pepper, and add a pinch of sugar. Cook slowly, stirring every now and then, until deeply caramelized, 5 to 7 minutes. Add the broth, mustard, barbecue sauce, cumin, and any meat juices. Fold in the mint at the end. Keep warm over low heat until ready to serve.

Carve the lamb across the grain (watch for grain changes) into ¼-inch slices. Retain all the juices from slicing, then stir them into your sauce. Top the lamb with the sauce and serve.

continued from page 104

Today's Dinosaur restaurants are owned by George Soros and offer a full line of barbecue meats and other great eats—with outstanding beverage choices as well. Their starters, called "Palate Igniters," include catfish or spicy shrimp boil, chicken wings, fried green tomatoes, and deviled eggs, some with several size and flavor options. Pulled pork, spareribs, brisket, and chicken are the featured barbecue meats. Grilled steaks and chicken, plus specialty sandwiches such as pulled pork with mushrooms or melted cheese, Cuban-style seasonings, a tasty variety of burgers, with sides of beans, fresh-cut fries, salads, mac and cheese, chili, mashed potatoes and gravy—all that and more round out Dinosaur's barbecopia of a menu. All of that great food, plus bands such as Naughty Lil' Pig Show, Silent Fury, Dark Hollow, Greezy Wheels w/ Penny Jo, Legendary Jones Gang, and Turnip Stampede give substance and meaning to why Paul calls Dinosaur "the rock 'n' roll biker bar and bar-b-que of the millennium."

Paul has been a Dinosaur diner several times in Syracuse and New York City, once when he was preannounced and treated like royalty, and other times unannounced, to get the food that everyone else gets. As expected, he got the same great barbecue on each visit. He has concluded that Dinosaur barbecue is really as good as John has always told him. And everyone gets the royal treatment at Dinosaur.

Paul has asked for the rib recipe and cooking procedure several times, and they agreed to give both "tomorrow." Tomorrow hasn't come yet, but Dinosaur did share this fantastic leg of lamb recipe from the fun and fabulous *Dinosaur Bar-B-Que—An American Roadhouse* cookbook John wrote with Nancy Radke.

Lamb Ribs

Jack Stack Barbecue

13441 Holmes Rd.
Kansas City, MO 64145
816-942-9141
http://www.jackstackkc.com

The Fiorella family has had a major presence in the Kansas City barbecue scene for more than half a century. Russ Fiorella got the family tradition going when he opened the Smoke Stack Barbecue restaurant in 1957. The original building on Prospect Avenue stands vacant and weather-worn today, sporting realtor signs instead of a working smokestack and signs advertising slab specials. Russ's first son, Jack, opened today's famous Jack Stack in Martin City with his wife, Delores, in 1974. Their success with an expanded menu of hickory-grilled steaks and seafood in addition to a complete menu of barbecue meats led to the opening of three more restaurants in Kansas City, each with a popular following of local fans and tourists. They also run a busy online sales business, shipping barbecue and Jack Stack sauces and seasonings nationwide.

We like all four locations, but our favorite, perhaps out of nostalgia, is the Holmes Road store. It is a big wooden structure reminiscent of the Prospect Avenue original. Inside the decor could be described as Ozark Victorian. Some walls are like weathered barn lumber. Others are covered with fancy wallpaper of Victorian design. Framed vintage photos, farm implements, and other memorabilia adorn the walls. It feels warm and welcome and puts you in a good mood for feasting and fun.

Jack Stack is one of the few barbecue restaurants in Kansas City that offers lamb ribs. With Jack's method of cooking them there's no gamy flavor. Be sure to try them on your next visit.

The nice thing about lamb ribs is that they can be barbecued or grilled. Here is our rendition of Jack's lamb ribs. You can order some of Jack's barbecue rub to be more authentic.

LAMB RIBS

Serves 4

4 slabs Denver lamb ribs (6 to 7 bones each), trimmed

1 tablespoon onion salt

1 tablespoon garlic salt

1 tablespoon dried parsley

2 teaspoons herbes de Provence

1 teaspoon black pepper

1 teaspoon kosher salt

Olive oil

To prep the ribs, trim any excess fat and remove the membrane from the back of the ribs. Combine the onion salt, garlic salt, parsley, herbes de Provence, pepper, and salt and blend well. Rub the ribs with olive oil and season all over. Place on a plate, cover, and let rest for 30 to 60 minutes.

To grill the ribs, cook over medium coals (see page 221) for 45 to 60 minutes, turning every 10 to 15 minutes and taking care not to burn them. To barbecue the ribs, cook with indirect heat for 1½ to 2 hours, turning every 45 minutes. Serve with Jack Stack sauce or your favorite barbecue sauce on the side.

Panfried Chicken Livers

Jack Stack Barbecue

13441 Holmes Rd.
Kansas City, MO 64145
816-942-9141
http://www.jackstackkc.com

Jack Stack gave us several recipes, including Jack Stack Lamb Ribs (page 107) and Jack Stack Cheesy Potato Bake (page 133). To our regret, the fabulous panfried chicken livers that were once served at the original Jack Stack on Holmes Road are no longer on the menu. However, Jack Fiorella and his son-in-law, Case Dorman, were kind enough to share the recipe with us. Now you can enjoy them at home.

PANFRIED CHICKEN LIVERS

Serves 6

HORSERADISH SAUCE

¾ cup mayonnaise

¼ cup drained prepared horseradish

1 tablespoon dried parsley

CHICKEN LIVERS

1 pound fresh chicken livers

1 cup all-purpose flour

3 tablespoons cornmeal

2 tablespoons cornstarch

2 tablespoons Lawry's Seasoned Salt

1 tablespoon baking powder

1½ teaspoons dried parsley

2 teaspoons onion powder

1 teaspoon black pepper, or to taste

1 quart whole milk

Vegetable oil, for frying

To make the Horseradish Sauce, combine the mayonnaise, horseradish, and parsley in a small bowl and mix thoroughly. Cover and refrigerate until needed.

Clean and rinse the livers and pat dry. In a large bowl, thoroughly mix ½ cup of the flour with the cornmeal, cornstarch, seasoned salt, baking powder, parsley, onion powder, and pepper. Add the milk to this mixture and mix with a wire whisk until well combined.

Heat ¼ inch of vegetable oil in a large skillet until sizzling, about 325°F. Thoroughly coat the livers in the remaining ½ cup flour and shake off the excess. Dredge the floured livers in the batter and place half of them in the oil, one at a time, being careful not to crowd them. Cook the livers for 5 to 7 minutes, until golden brown, turning once halfway through. Remove the livers from the oil and drain them on paper towels. Repeat with any remaining livers, adding more oil as needed. Serve with Horseradish Sauce.

Barbecue Turkey Breast

Buckingham's Smokehouse Bar-B-Q

3804 Buttonwood Dr.
Columbia, MO 65201
573-449-7782

This Buckingham's is halfway between Kansas City and St. Louis, Missouri, and a must-stop when driving on I-70. The original Columbia Buckingham's opened in 1998 and was an old drive-in restaurant. The new Buckingham's is out in the suburbs of Columbia, and it's a little more difficult to find than the original. True, you can't just turn off of I-70 and go a block and a half anymore, but it's worth the extra drive.

The owner, Mark Brown, spent about 24 years as a roadie for the groups Pink Floyd, AC/DC, and Fleetwood Mac. When he decided it was time to get off the road, he hooked up with David Campbell of Springfield, Missouri, the founder of Buckingham's Smokehouse Bar-B-Q, where he honed his passion for great barbecue.

One of Paul's favorite things other than Buckingham's ribs is a pulled turkey sandwich. Yes, a pulled turkey sandwich: different but very good. Here's a recipe you can try at home.

BARBECUE TURKEY BREAST

Serves 20 to 24

1 (9- to 12-pound) boneless 3-lobe turkey breast with skin on

Salt and black pepper

¼ cup Buckingham's barbecue seasoning or your own rub

40 to 48 slices white bread

Sliced pickles, for serving

Sliced onions, for serving

Barbecue sauce, for serving

Season the turkey breast with the salt, pepper, and barbecue seasoning. Preheat your smoker to 230°F, place the turkey in the smoker, and cook for about 4 hours, until the internal temperature of the turkey reaches 170°F on an instant-read thermometer when inserted in the center or thickest part of the turkey. Remove the turkey from the smoker and let rest for 15 to 30 minutes.

Remove the skin from the turkey and discard. Put the turkey in a baking pan or dish large enough to hold it. Using two heavy-duty dinner forks, shred the turkey breast. Serve on white bread or a bun with pickles and sliced onion, with barbecue sauce on the side.

Pulled
Slicec
Slicec
Smok
Smok
2 M

Mashe
freshly wh

Mom's
chunky ma

Steak
thick cut p

e Spa
ain Be
ain Bis
Ribs

wl of mix
Salad
Salad

ITEI
Sandw
Entree
Salad
rs Pla

EVE

Barbecued Bison Ribs

Big Papa's BBQ

6265 E. Evans Ave., Unit 1
Denver, CO 80222
303-300-4499
http://www.bbqdenver.com

n 2003, when Frank Alfonso moved from his hometown in North Florida to Denver, he decided to venture into the barbecue business. "When you're a southern boy, barbecue is in your DNA," he told us. He designed Big Papa's with good food and fast service in mind but didn't compromise on the traditional slow and low method of cooking barbecue. Frank adapted well to his new environment by putting an item not likely to be seen in North Florida or Alabama on the menu.

At Big Papa's you order your food at the cashier counter, pay for it, get seated, and soon your order is brought to the table. Since it isn't everywhere that you can get barbecued bison ribs, we highly recommend you try them at Big Papa's. We don't know how they compare to the bison ribs at the Fort, which our barbecue buddy Dr. Ira Salmon in New York City told us about, but we're pretty sure he would be just as enthusiastic about Big Papa's ribs.

Here's the basic technique for barbecuing bison ribs that Frank shared with us. A Memphis-style tomato-based, tangy barbecue finishing sauce is recommended.

Thanks to Denverite Adrian Miller, barbecue buddy and Southern Foodways Alliance member, for telling us about Big Papa's. Thanks also to Ardie's friend Linda Ray, of Littleton, for the photos and menu.

SMOKED OVER SPLIT HICKORY

	Lite with 1 side	Entreé with 2 sides	Just the Ribs 1/2 Slab *no side included*	Full Slab
	10.75	16.99	9.99	18.99
	10.99	16.99	11.99	21.99
	9.99	15.99	9.99	18.99
	12.49	18.99	11.49	21.99

SALADS

omato wedges and cheddar	2.25
nders served on a bed of greens with tomato wedges and cheddar	8.45
moked meat on a large bed of greens with tomato wedges and cheddar	8.45

OR THE NON-SMOKERS

et served on top a moist french bread hoagie	6.99
ts served with your choice of two sides and hush puppies	9.85
nders served on a bed of greens with tomato wedges and cheddar	8.45
chicken tenders served with your choice of two sides	8.95

BIG PAPA'S
B·B·Q

6265 E. EVANS AVE., UNIT 1
Denver, Colorado 80222
303.300.4499

12652 W. KEN CARYL AVE.
Littleton, Colorado 80127
720.922.3233

TO GO
WE DELIVER

CATERING AVAILABLE!
*Ask for details

FEED THE FAMILY

BP Picnic (serves 3-4)
$28.95
*from $7.25 per Person

1/2 Slab of St. Louis Style or Baby Bac
1/2 Chicken and 1/2 lb. of any third Me
1/2 Pint of BBQ Beans and Cole Slaw
1/2 lb. of Steak Fries

BP Picnic (serves 6-8)
$57.90
*from $7.25 per Person

Full Slab of St. Louis Style or Baby Ba
Whole Chicken and 1 lb. of any third M
One Pint of BBQ Beans and Cole Slaw
1 lb. of Steak Fries

Wings by the Pound

1 lb: 5.99	2 lbs: 11.99	3 lbs: 17.99	5 lbs: 2

STARTERS

Fried Catfish Nuggets (10 Piece)
Wings (One Whole Pound)
1/2 lb of Baby Back Rib Tips served on a bed of fries

DESSERTS

Brownie a chocolate brownie with chunks of Ghirardelli™ Chocolate
Banana Pudding creamy pudding with fresh bananas an ͡la wafers
BP Homemade Cobbler a bed of fruit with a flaky crumb topping

---

BARBECUED BISON RIBS

Serves 7

1 slab bison ribs (about 7 ribs per slab)

Dry rub of your choice

Barbecue sauce of your choice

Sprinkle the ribs lightly with the rub. Preheat your grill to 225°F and cook the ribs, using indirect heat, for about 4 hours. Remove the ribs from the pit, slather with sauce, and grill both sides directly over hot coals just long enough to crisp the outside. Serve immediately.

Spatchcock Chicken

B's Barbecue

Hwy. 43 North—751 B's Barbecue Rd.
Greenville, NC 27834
http://www.ncbbqsociety.com/trail_
pages/bs_bbq_large.html

B's is the only barbecue joint we know of that has a road named after it (and one of the few with no phone). B comes from the nickname of the founder, William "B" McLawhorn, who opened B's in 1978. We knew B's reputation for great barbecue, and after our friend Carl Rothrock gave it high marks, we knew for sure we had to eat at B's. Carl lives in Greenville and knows B's well.

As we expected, B's looks like two roadside shacks—one for serving, dining, and carryout and another for the barbecue pits. The restaurant shack used to be a country store, but it works fine as a barbecue joint—friendly, with a good feel to it. If you can't find seating in the spacious, dimly lit inside, there are picnic tables outside. For customers on the run—and there are many—B's does a brisk business at the carryout window.

B's has four big steel box pits with lids. Each pit has a side door for adding coals that are fired up outside the pits in big containers. Two pits are about 5 by 15 feet. The two smaller ones, used for cooking the chickens, are about 4 by 8 feet.

William's daughter, Peggy McLawhorn, and her three daughters—Tammy Godley, Donna

McLawhorn, and Judy Drach—run B's today and do a fine job of it. Pitman Dexter Sherrod cooks the meat the same way it's always been done at B's. That means hardwood charcoal for heat and smoke, with hours of slow and low in the pit. That goes for B's moist, tender, and flavorful whole hog and B's famous chicken, too. B's sauce is the typical eastern North Carolina cider vinegar and peppers with B's special accent. Each dining table sports a Crown Royal whiskey bottle that contains B's sauce. It's one of the best ideas for recycling we've seen.

As for the sauce recipe, we're told that the only way you can get it is to marry into the family.

When Carl told Judy that she might expect to get a proposal, she said that she "married for love the first time, but this time it would be for money." Single millionaires should consider taking a trip to Greenville. Matter of fact, everyone who loves barbecue should plan a trip to Greenville. B's barbecue is worth it!

Don't choose between whole hog and chicken at B's. Have both. But get there well before 2 p.m. if you expect to eat. It's a busy place, with cars and trucks filling the parking lot and parked along the highway. Carl raved about the chicken, and we see why. Each order is a half chicken. This recipe is our version.

SPATCHCOCK CHICKEN

Serves 4

EAST CAROLINA BASTING SAUCE

3 cups cider vinegar

2 tablespoons black pepper

2 tablespoons sea or kosher salt

2 tablespoons packed brown sugar (optional)

1 tablespoon cayenne

1 large whole fryer chicken

Preheat your pit or grill to 230° to 250°F. Combine all of the basting sauce ingredients and whisk to blend.

Remove the giblets from the bird, along with any fat. Rinse the chicken inside and out with cold water. Pat the chicken inside and out with paper towels to dry it. Put the chicken on a cutting board, breast side down with the tail pointing away from you. Pull the chicken to an upright position on its neck end. With a sharp knife, cut down the right or left side of the backbone, through the thigh joint, which is just gristle, then go down the backbone, cutting through the rib bones. Be careful to keep to the backbone, not the breast bone. Repeat the process on the other side of the backbone.

Open the chicken, breast or skin side down, with the breast end pointing toward you. In the middle of the breast you'll see the keel bone. Some people call it the breast bone, but it's the keel bone. At the top of the keel bone, in the center, there is a white piece of gristle about the size of a quarter; with your knife, cut straight down the center of the gristle.

Place your thumbs on either side of the cut, and with your fingers under the keel bone or your fingers on the skin side of the breast, push down with your thumbs and up with your fingers and the keel bone will pop up; you can then pull the keel bone and attached gristle out. Turn the chicken over and press on the breast, flattening the chicken out. Season with pepper and salt. Place the chicken on your pit or grill skin side up and cook indirectly for 3 to 4 hours, depending on the size of the chicken, until the internal temperature in the thighs are 165°F or higher. Do not turn the chicken. Baste the open side of the chicken with the sauce at 1½ hours and baste the skin side every 30 minutes until done.

Smoked Catfish

Stevenson Bar-B-Que

114 S. Ash
Paul's Valley, OK 73075
405-238-2040

Velmer Stevenson serves great barbecue. Our barbecue buddy Russ Sifers first told us about Velmer, and after eating Velmer's barbecue and catfish, we heartily agree. Residents in nearby Duncan can now enjoy Velmer's good eats at his Big Steve's BBQ & Catfish. Stevenson family members continue to help out, including Velmer's son, Herman, and niece, LaDonna. Russ did such a good job with his Stevenson profile that we've blended his words with ours for this new write-up.

Stevenson Bar-B-Que is located in a former Braum's Ice Cream building in Paul's Valley, Oklahoma, about an hour south of Oklahoma City, just off I-35 at Exit 72. The inside isn't fancy: red-and-white checkered plastic tablecloths, plenty of paper napkins. The barbecue and the friendly service are more important than décor, and that's what we like about Stevenson's.

Velmer Stevenson, also known as "Big Steve," is on duty, greeting everyone. He is a large man with large, gentle hands and a salt-and-pepper beard. His smile is infectious, and his brown eyes sparkle with pride over his food. He is friendly and laid back. As Russ said, "Each time I speak with Mr. Stevenson I leave feeling happy about the world in general and barbecue in particular."

Velmer's smoker is a custom-made, five-door cylinder about the size of a van with an offset firebox. The doors open with a pulley system, and the entire rig rolls out for hauling to the car wash every two weeks. He fires up the pit with pecan and hickory.

Stevenson's serves ribs, brisket, pork steak, hot and Polish links, chicken, chopped beef, and fried catfish. Velmer uses his own dry rub and baste. His vinegary mild and hot sauces are true to his mother, Willie Mae's, Louisiana influence. The hot sauce is sincerely hot and spicy. The smoked/sauced chicken is lean, moist, and tender. The ribs, lightly rubbed, are tender, lean, moist, and flavorful.

The barbecued steak is a big slice of pork shoulder almost 2 inches thick, fork-tender and moist with a kiss of smoke and rub. Velmer has a saying, "If you can't cut it with a plastic knife and fork, it's yours free." The Stevenson motto: "It's tender as a mother's love." The brisket is also tender, moist, and flavorful, with a splash of hot sauce. The hot link is standard fare, and the chopped beef is a little like tender burnt ends.

Stevenson's fries are fresh cut, served hot, and not greasy. The beans are large and cooked in a gray gravy somewhat like Texas ranch beans, though Texas beans tend to have a red gravy instead. The coleslaw is homemade, fresh, crisp, and quite good.

Stevenson's bread pudding and banana pudding are Texas recipes made from scratch by Velmer's wife, Laverne. The banana pudding has fresh chunks of bananas and is creamy but not too rich. The bread pudding is warm, sweet, and such a hit that it is now available frozen in several big-box stores.

Velmer talked with Russ about offering smoked catfish. He's still talking, but after eating his fried catfish, we see why he's sticking with it. Nevertheless, he left Russ with a craving for smoked catfish, one of our favorites too. Velmer hasn't shared his smoked catfish recipe yet, but we think this one would do the trick!

SMOKED CATFISH

Serves 6

6 (13- to 15-ounce) head-on whole catfish

½ cup canola oil

2 cups dry barbecue rub

Preheat your smoker to 225° to 250°F. Wash the fish inside and out thoroughly with cold water. Pat dry and then lightly oil the fish with the canola oil. Rub the fish inside and out with a medium to heavy amount of the rub. Place the fish on a screen, baking sheet, or smoker rack sprayed with nonstick cooking spray. Make sure you have a medium-thick amount of smoke in your cooker; then place the fish in the smoker and smoke for 45 to 75 minutes, until the fish is opaque and the flesh is just beginning to flake. Watch it carefully. It is better to cook, test, and then finish cooking rather than overcook it.

SMOKED FISH: IT'S BARBECUE

Some of our friends in the barbecue community think smoked fish isn't real barbecue. We beg to differ. Smoked fish is one of the earliest barbecue delicacies known to humankind.

We'll never know what our ancestors cooked at the first barbecue—fish, fowl, or four-legged animal—but if the ubiquitous engravings of Indians smoking fish on green sapling grates over flaming smoky logs is reliable documentation, smoked fish was on the menu at early barbecues.

Although smoked fish shacks aren't as plentiful today as in the past, many can still be found across America. Thanks to our friend Meathead in Chicago, we were introduced to the James Beard Award–winning Calumet Fisheries smoke shack. They have been in the fish-smoking business since 1948. Calumet doesn't ship, and you can't dine in. On cold days, you can dine in your car. On warmer days people dine outside like tailgaters.

Fritz's, "Kansas City's Oldest Smokehouse," established in 1927, offers take-home smoked salmon fillet, tomato-basil fillet, or peppered salmon fillet.

Ron Lockhart, a Boca Raton, Florida, barbecue buddy, is one of the most knowledgeable and enthusiastic smoked fish aficionados we know. Ron and his wife take annual smoked fish road trips to the UP of Michigan; Door County, Wisconsin; and northern Minnesota. Their stops include:

- **Charlie's Smokehouse, Ellison Bay, WI**
- **Gustafson's Smoked Fish and Beef Jerky, Brevort, MI**
- **Manley's Fish Market, Saint Ignace, MI**
- **Krueger's Fish Market, Mackinaw City, MI**
- **King's Fish Market, Moran, MI**
- **Carlson's Fishery, Leland, MI**
- **Bearcat's Fish House, Algoma, WI**
- **Northern Waters Smokehaus, Duluth, MN**
- **Russ Kendall's Smokehouse, Knife River, MN**

Ron said, "At each place I stopped they'd show me their smoking method, which always turned out to be a large box with a washbasin on the bottom with a few maple logs smoldering." Ron, in search of chubs (aka ciscoes), enjoyed smoked whitefish and "outrageously delicious" lake trout in Michigan and Wisconsin. He finally found smoked chubs at Russ Kendall's in Minnesota, operated by Gordy Kendall, Russ's son. He noted, "They're lightly smoked, naturally oily, and bursting with flavor." The freshly caught chubs are put in plain salt brine overnight and smoked the next day. "Heaven! His lake trout were unlike anything I've ever eaten. Again, locally caught, brined and smoked. They, too, have an oily flesh that makes them a perfect candidate for the smokehouse."

Ron would rather eat smoked fish than ribs or brisket. At home in South Florida he smokes ocean fish using methods he learned in Wisconsin, Michigan, and Minnesota. After soaking in a brining solution for 2 to 4 hours, they rinse and start smoking the fish at very low temperatures to slowly permeate the fish with smoke. After at least 2 hours at 120° F or less, they crank the temperature up to 170° F to finish the smoking process. Ron bought an electric smoker for ease of temperature control. The smokehouse masters controlled temperatures by leaving the door ajar. "No thermometers here! Over years of cooking they've got the method down pat!"

Thanks and a tip of our hats to Meathead and Ron for inspiring us to put this smoked fish homage in the book. Meathead's Web site, amazingribs.com, is the world's go-to virtual place for a barbecue treasure house of reliable information and recipes.

Smoked Salmon

Arapahoe Café & Bonnie Q BBQ

626 Lake Dillon Dr.
Dillon, CO 80435
970-468-0873 or 970-468-7533
http://www.arapahoecafe.com

The reservoir that flooded the original location of Dillon, Colorado, is named after the town. Lake Dillon, huge and very deep, is Denver's primary source of water.

The most important landmark building that was moved from old Dillon to higher ground is the Arapahoe Café & Pub, owned and operated by Doug Pierce and family. Outside and in, the building shouts friendly informal Rocky Mountain ambience.

Arapahoe's full-service breakfast, lunch, and dinner menu features home-style cuisine that is widely known as the best good eats in the Rockies. They say to be sure to "Ask us what Doug's been smokin'." We can testify that whatever Doug's been smokin' will not disappoint you. Doug's award-winning barbecued pork spareribs are spot on, up there with the best we've ever eaten.

Doug's barbecue is so popular that he, with partner Julie Willing, known as "Da Boss," opened a new Bonnie Q BBQ Roadhouse Room & Catering Company, named after Doug's daughter, Bonnie. The roadhouse is a perfect setting for parties and special occasions, with ample room for eating, dancing, and celebrating. Vintage barbecue signs and memorabilia add a perfect accent to the scene.

OUR BARBECUE IS SO GOOD

The Bonnie Q team has competed in Kansas City Barbeque Society (KCBS) sanctioned contests in Frisco and Dillon for more than two decades, bringing home numerous awards. Their competition barbecue expertise stands out in what they serve in the café, roadhouse, and catering gigs. It rocks!

When Doug Pierce develops a recipe, you can count on it being remarkably good. When we asked him to demonstrate his culinary talents with one of his smoked salmon recipes, we knew it would be Doug-tested and yield fantastic results. It can be served as is with crackers, cream cheese, and pepper jelly or tossed into a salad with a light vinaigrette. You can scramble it with eggs, spinach, cheese, and tomato. It is also good lightly tossed with mayonnaise, diced onion, and celery as you would do if making tuna salad. Let your imagination go!

IT'LL MAKE YOUR BIG TOE WIGGLE!

**Doug Pierce,
Bonnie Q BBQ, Dillon, CO**

SMOKED SALMON

Serves 6 to 8

CURE

1 pound brown sugar

½ cup maple sugar

¾ cup kosher salt

1½ teaspoons black pepper

½ cup lemon juice (concentrate is OK)

½ cup grapefruit juice

¼ cup molasses

½ cup Triple Sec

1 (4- to 5-pound) whole side of salmon

Combine all the cure ingredients in a medium bowl and mix well.

Place the salmon with the skin side down in a stainless-steel pan or porcelain baking dish. Pour the cure evenly over the salmon. Refrigerate for 6 hours, turn over, and refrigerate for an additional 6 hours. Remove the salmon from the cure (which can be discarded or reused, if kept refrigerated, for up to 1 week).

Heat your cooker to 250°F. Smoke the salmon for approximately 2 hours, until the thick portion of the salmon begins to flake. Very gently remove the salmon, lifting it from underneath, and place on a sheet pan. A long spatula may be helpful.

Beer-Battered Cod with Tartar Sauce, and Marinated Chicken

Smoky Jon's #1 BBQ

2310 Packers Ave.
Madison, WI 53704
608-249-RIBS (7427)
http://www.smokyjons.com

hen most people think of Madison, Wisconsin, cheeseheads, brats, and beer come to mind. Barbecue aficionados familiar with Madison add "Smoky Jon's."

Smoky Jon Olson, avid hunter and "Madison's All-Time BBQ King," has been serving tender smoky barbecue to the citizens of and visitors to Madison for more than 30 years. Now and then he leaves the restaurant in the capable hands of pitmaster Joel Latham and staff while he networks with fellow barbecuers at contests and National Barbecue Association conferences. That's how we met him.

We like Smoky Jon and his barbecue, but since we haven't tried it for a while, we decided to ask Ardie's friends Ron and Mary Buchholz and their son Geof to pay a visit to Smoky Jon's "inhognito" and give us this candid report.

continued on page 122

BEER-BATTERED COD WITH TARTAR SAUCE

Serves 6 to 8

TARTAR SAUCE

1 cup mayonnaise

1 tablespoon Dijon mustard

1 scallion, white and green parts, minced

1½ teaspoons fresh lemon juice

2 tablespoons minced dilled gherkins

1 tablespoon minced drained capers

2 tablespoons snipped fresh parsley

Pinch each of salt and black pepper

COD

Cooking oil, for deep-frying
   (about 1 quart)

1 cup all-purpose flour

¼ cup cornstarch

½ teaspoon salt

1 large egg, lightly beaten

1 cup beer, or as needed

2 pounds cod, haddock, or hake
   fillets, cut into approximately
   1½ by 3-inch pieces

Combine all the tartar sauce ingredients in a small bowl. Cover and refrigerate. Preheat the oven to 200°F. Cover a baking sheet with paper towels and top with a wire rack. In a medium pot or a deep-fryer, heat about 3 inches of oil to 365°F (use a deep-frying thermometer if you're using a pot).

Meanwhile, mix the flour and cornstarch with the ½ teaspoon salt. Whisk in the egg. Slowly add the beer while whisking just until the ingredients are incorporated.

Dip the fish pieces in the batter and place on a plate or the wire rack you will be using to drain the fried fish. If you have some batter left over, you can dip the fish in the batter again after the first coat of batter dries on the fish awaiting frying.

Place the fish pieces, two at a time, in the oil. Cook until the fish is done and the crust is lightly golden, about 4 minutes for ¾-inch-thick fillets. Remove the fish with tongs and put on the rack to drain. Sprinkle salt over the hot fish and put the baking sheet in the oven while you cook the other batches. Serve with the tartar sauce.

MARINATED CHICKEN

Serves 24

¾ cup Whirl liquid butter
  substitute or drawn butter*

3½ ounces Smoky Jon's Flavor
  Magic Gourmet All Purpose
  Seasoning or rub of your choice

24 (5-ounce) boneless skinless
  chicken breasts

In a small bowl, combine the Whirl or drawn butter and the Flavor Magic and blend well.

Place the chicken breasts in a large, deep pan. Pour the Whirl mixture over the chicken breasts. Evenly coat the chicken all over with the paste. Cover the pan with plastic wrap and marinate for at least 2 hours or overnight in the refrigerator.

Grill over hot charcoal (see page 218) just until done. Makes an awesome chicken sandwich on a bun or in a combo with ribs. This recipe makes a lot, but it freezes well.

*To make drawn butter, melt 2 sticks of butter over medium heat in a small saucepan. Bring it to a low boil and boil until the milk solids in the butter separate and sink to the bottom of the pan. Watch carefully so it doesn't burn. Spoon off the clarified butter and use ¾ cup in the recipe.

continued from page 120

The exterior of Smoky Jon's leaves no doubt that you're looking at a barbecue joint. Neon and painted signs, with pigs, ribs, and barbecue in a bun, will definitely get your attention. Inside, Smoky Jon's "has a rustic North Woods look with pine log walls, rough-cut knotty-pine trim, knotty-pine tongue/groove plank ceilings, and deep burgundy brick paver-type quarry tile floors," as Ron describes it. Awards, a string of small lighted pigs, banners, a Wisconsin "No. 1 BBQ" vanity plate, and other memorabilia add to the feel of the joint.

Is Smoky Jon good enough to wear the barbecue king title? Yes! The marinated barbecued chicken is a house favorite and won't disappoint. The ribs have just the right kiss of smoke, or "smoky undertone" as Ron aptly puts it, and are tender, juicy, and delicious. If you like naked ribs, as we do, ask for sauce on the side or your ribs will be served slathered with Smoky Jon's sauce. It's good stuff, mind you. We just like to decide how much sauce to enjoy with our ribs. The pulled pork sandwich is served with sauce

on the side. It's good enough to stand alone, but a touch of Smoky Jon's sharp, tangy barbecue sauce lends a nice complement.

What also catches our attention at Smoky Jon's is the beer-battered cod. As longtime beer-battered Minnesota walleye pike fans, we knew Smoky Jon would make us equally enthusiastic about his cod, and he did! The dinner comes with four pieces of cod, two sides, and a dinner roll with butter. Put some tartar sauce on the lightly coated, seasoned battered fish cooked to tender flakiness and enjoy. Any of the sides go well with it—creamy coleslaw, spicy barbecue baked beans, spicy buttered corn, applesauce, fries, and side salad. We agree with Ron that the best of all the sides, however, is the barbecue baked beans.

Smoky Jon's priority is to serve great barbecue in a welcoming setting with friendly service. He delivers that and throws in a moist, rich, flavorful Chocolate Cherry Bundt Cake for dessert. It is the only dessert on the menu, but it's worth

saving room for a few bites. Order one slice with enough forks for everyone at the table. Our hats are off to Smoky Jon Olson and pitmaster Joel Latham. We thank them for the two recipes.

Barbecue Shrimp

Gridley's Fine Bar-B-Q

6842 Stage Rd.
Bartlett, TN 38134
901-377-8055

imes have changed since the days when we made a point of dining at Gridley's on Summer Avenue during the Memphis in May World Championship Barbecue Cooking Contest. Our feast at Gridley's was capped by a visit to Graceland to pay our respects to the King. Back then Gridley's wait staff wore bow ties and gold jackets. Gridley's was synonymous with Memphis barbecue, and the only sauce packed in a clever cardboard briefcase for Memphis tourism and convention promotions was Gridley's, founded by the late Clyde Gridley. We thought that Gridley's heyday had come and gone, but thanks to Jamie and Doug Walker, we can now say that Gridley's is alive and well and as good as or better than it ever was. Today's Gridley's is farther from Graceland, but the drive to the new smaller Gridley's is worth the adventure.

Jamie and Doug Walker bought Gridley's from Dr. and Mrs. William Coley, who were looking for a buyer at the same time Jamie and Doug were looking for a business to offset losses in their manufacturing company due to competition from China and Mexico. They needed a career change, and since they are one of the hardest/smartest-working barbecue joint couples we've ever met, barbecue lovers are the better for it.

Gridley's walls are decorated with Memphis and Elvis memorabilia, plus some photos of former

BARBECUE SHRIMP

Serves 4

2 pounds large shrimp

¼ cup Gridley's Shrimp Seasoning

¼ cup liquid margarine

Preheat your oven to 300°F. Put the shrimp in a shallow baking pan. Sprinkle the seasoning mix on the shrimp and pour the liquid margarine on top. Bake for 3 to 5 minutes, then turn the shrimp over and cook for another 3 to 5 minutes. Be careful not to overcook, or the shrimp will be rubbery. Serve immediately, letting people peel their own shrimp at the table.

CAJUN BARBECUE SHRIMP

Serves 4

2 pounds large shrimp

BARBECUE SAUCE

½ pound (2 sticks) butter

¼ cup olive oil

½ cup beer (not dark)

¼ cup Heinz chili sauce

3 tablespoons fresh lemon juice

2 tablespoons Worcestershire sauce

2 cloves garlic, peeled

2 to 3 bay leaves, finely crushed

½ teaspoon dried thyme

Pinch of crushed rosemary
   or rosemary leaves

1 teaspoon dried oregano

¼ teaspoon white pepper

½ teaspoon black pepper

1 teaspoon cayenne

2 teaspoons paprika

2 teaspoons hot pepper sauce

Rinse, peel, and devein the shrimp. Combine all the sauce ingredients in a big pan and simmer gently for about 10 minutes. Cool the sauce to room temperature, then add the washed and cleaned shrimp. Marinate overnight in the refrigerator.

Cook the shrimp on the stove over high heat, stirring just until all the shrimp turn pink, 3 to 4 minutes.

Serve with chunks of crusty French bread to soak up the sauce, a green salad, and lots of napkins. Shrimp must be eaten with your fingers to get the whole experience.

Gridley's restaurants. Service is fast and friendly. Bow ties and gold jackets just wouldn't fit the new decor, so we didn't miss that relic of bygone days. The barbecue shrimp (not truly barbecue, as everyone knows), ribs, and pulled pork sandwich with slaw are every bit as great as we enjoyed at the former Memphis Gridley's. Jamie and Doug own and operate another Gridley's in Conway, Arkansas. Congratulations and thanks to Jamie and Doug Walker. Surely the Clyde Gridley family would be proud that their legacy continues!

To get the true Gridley's flavor, you have to have the real sauce and seasonings. Thank goodness that's possible! Call Gridley's to put in your order for sauce (mild or hot), Gridley's Rib Rub, and Gridley's Shrimp Seasoning. When you can't go to Gridley's and you yearn for its shrimp at home, try the recipe here. If you're out of Gridley's Shrimp Seasoning, try Paul's Cajun BBQ Shrimp, the recipe here, to get you by until the next shipment of Gridley's seasonings arrives.

Sides & Condiments

Sides should be outstanding. Since the average adult stomach can hold only a quart of food and beverages at one sitting, it makes sense to be fussy with your ounces.

Our side dish and condiment standards are not complicated. Aside from looking good and tasting great, we want them to be a good match with the meat. To illustrate with some extreme examples, it won't work to garnish barbecued spareribs with pickled herring. Serving New England clam chowder with barbecued brisket is also not a good idea. Maybe that's why most joints seem to serve beans, slaw, and potato salad, though a few feature more creative options such as **BBQ Corn Bread (page 155).**

In this chapter, we've chosen side dishes and condiments worthy of sharing plate space with the best barbecue in America or elsewhere. Enjoy!

Jo Jos

Ted's 19th Hole Bar-B-Que

2814 E. 38th St.
Minneapolis, MN 55406
612-721-2023

olf is an eighteen-hole game. The "nineteenth hole" is a refreshment place, usually a clubhouse. Thanks to the late legendary pitmaster and pro golfer Ted Cook, the 19th Hole is also a refreshing barbecue joint.

Ted's neighborhood is poised for change. On our last visit, in fact, next door a sign in a cracked glass storefront window proclaimed, "There's Hope Outreach Mission." At a nearby gas station you prepay the clerk stationed behind thick bulletproof glass, and a few tattoo parlors and beer joints echo the past, but coffee shops and ethnic eateries hint of a promising future.

Moses Quartey is a Minneapolin by way of Ghana. He came to the University of Minnesota for graduate studies in microbiology and biochemistry. To make ends meet, Moses took a job at Ted's, then owned by mother and son Priscilla and Mike Davis. Moses found a higher calling, and now he owns Ted's. Moses, like Priscilla and Mike before him, prepares and cooks the barbecue exactly as Ted did starting in 1968. He has also kept Priscilla's soul foods on the menu. "We've been doing the same thing for 40 years, over and over again," Moses told us.

Ted's is carryout only. The menu is on the wall behind the white Formica order counter. Framed pictures of menu items adorn another wall. When you're ready, look up to the window, and, like a hungry traveler seeking manna from heaven, tell Moses what you want.

What Ted's lacks in comforts it makes up in food and friendly service. We liked the pork ribs best—spares, lightly rubbed, slow smoked with apple, cherry, and hickory in a genuine custom-

OUR RIBS ARE TENDER AS A MOTHER'S LOVE

Moses Quartey, Ted's 19th Hole, Minneapolis, MN

built barbecue pit that is grandfathered from Minneapolis's strict smoke-emission codes. Like the original Famous Dave's in nearby Calhoun Square and the Cozy Corner pit in Memphis, Ted's pit is enclosed with sliding glass walls and a chimney hood that vents from the center. Some pitmasters call it an "aquarium pit." Moses can check the meat without losing heat and smoke. Ted's grandmother's tomato-based tangy sweet sauce with a touch of allspice lends a tasty complement to the barbecue.

For a totally soulful barbecue feast, add beef ribs, sliced barbecue beef, pulled pork, chicken, rib tips, and all the sides—collard greens, red beans and rice, black-eyed peas, baked beans, potato salad, coleslaw, corn muffins. Take home some made-from-scratch 19th Hole peach cobbler and sweet potato pie for a post-feast treat. But most of all, do not leave Ted's without your Jo Jos! Moses Quartey told us how to make them: "Leave the skins on. Wash them up. Cut them up, and deep-fry them." Here's the full recipe.

JO JOS

Serves

4 to 6 russet potatoes, scrubbed but not peeled

Canola oil, for deep-frying

Salt

Pat the potatoes dry;, slice them into ⅛-inch-thick rounds or 2½-inch-long wedges about ½ inch wide. Heat the oil in your deep-fryer to 350° to 360°F (or use a deep pot and measure the oil temperature with a deep-frying thermometer). Place the potato rounds or wedges in the hot oil and fry until golden brown. Carefully remove them from the hot oil and drain them. Season with salt to taste and serve.

Famous Fresh-Cut Fries

Arthur Bryant's Barbeque

1727 Brooklyn Ave.
Kansas City, MO 64127
816-231-1123
http://www.arthurbryantsbbq.com

There's nothing fancy about this famous "world-class restaurant." The late Mr. Bryant called it simply "a greasehouse." The walls are adorned with framed photos and testimonies by famous and wanna-be-famous customers. There's also a framed portrait of Arthur Bryant and an enlarged cartoon by Lee Judge, a local political cartoonist. The cartoon features Saint Peter and Mr. Bryant at the Pearly Gates. Saint Peter wants to know, "Did you bring sauce?" Arthur Bryant's sauces can be purchased at the restaurant, in supermarkets throughout KC, or online.

The menu features barbecued brisket sandwiches, pork spareribs, turkey, chicken, ham, beans, coleslaw, and fries. Arthur Bryant's fries are a favorite, and they are a welcome exception to the ubiquitous precut frozen majority sold at other places. Bryant's fries pair well with all barbecued meats on the menu. Dip them or douse them with Arthur Bryant's Original sauce or Sweet Heat for extra pleasure. Here's how they do it.

FAMOUS FRESH-CUT FRIES

Serves 4

4 pounds pure lard, such as Armour, or as needed

4 large russet potatoes, washed but not peeled and cut into 5/16-inch french fries or as desired

Salt

Heat the lard to 325°F in a deep-fryer. You could use any frying shortening such as Crisco or a canola oil instead of lard, but you'll lose flavor. Divide the fries into about 8 batches and blanch each batch for about 3 minutes in the hot oil. Drain each batch on paper towels or a wire rack. For best results, put the blanched fries in a cooler until all of the batches are done.

To finish the fries, heat the oil to 375°F. Drop the blanched fries into the hot oil in batches and cook for 4 to 5 minutes, until they are as crisp as you want. Season to taste with salt. The result is a sweet, crispy-outside/soft-inside mound of fries fit for royalty.

SANDWICHES			MEAT TRAYS
BEEF	5⁴⁵	RIB LONG END 5⁷⁵	ANY COMBO OF
HAM	5⁴⁵	RIB SHORT END 6⁷⁵	BEEF, PORK, CHICKEN
PORK	5⁴⁵	1/2 CHICKEN 4⁹⁵	HAM, SAUSAGE, PORK
TURKEY	5⁴⁵	SAUSAGE 5²⁵	SERVED BY THE POUND
			MEAT TO GO BY THE
COMBO - ANY 2 MEATS			WHOLE SLAB PORK RIBS

NEW
AUTHUR BRYANT'S
RICH & SPICY BBQ SAUCE
NOW
AVAILABLE AT YOUR TABLE
OR TAKE A PINT HOME
$2.65

SIDE ORDER			DRINK
ARTHUR'S FRIES 1⁷⁵ WITH SAND ⁸⁵			COKE LEMON
BAKED BEANS 1⁵⁰ PT 2⁷⁵ QT 5⁰⁰			DIET COKE RED CREAM
PICKLES 4			SPRITE ICE TE
			SM ⁹⁵ MED1¹⁵ LARGE
ARTHUR'S LEGENDARY SAUCES			BEER
PT 2⁵ QT 4 ⁶⁵			PITCHER 4²⁵ MU

PORK RIBLET
SANDWICH
$5.95

WHAT IS THE GREASEHOUSE UNIVERSITY?

The late Arthur Bryant appreciated the fame his barbecue joint attracted, but it never went to his head. Pleased and amused would be the more accurate description. "It's just a greasehouse," he would say.

The Greasehouse University owes its name to Arthur Bryant. It has no physical campus. It has no uniform curriculum. But it's real. It's the barbecue school of hard knocks. Master of Barbecue and Doctor of Barbecue Philosophy degrees are awarded by the university in cooperation with the Kansas City Barbeque Society.

Our hope is that someday there will be an actual Greasehouse University campus.

North Carolina–Style Boiled Potatoes

Stephenson's Bar-B-Q

11964 NC 50 Hwy.
North Willow Spring, NC 27592
919-894-4530

o us an important measure of the character of a community is the quality of its barbecue. Thanks to Stephenson's Bar-B-Q, Willow Spring gets high marks on character, even though the restaurant is 10 miles from downtown. A journey to this rural agricultural area for swine dining is worth your dime.

Founder Paul Stephenson started out as a farmer. He got the inspiration to go into the barbecue business when he figured out that the hogs he was selling to other pitmasters were getting a higher monetary yield as ribs and sandwiches than he was getting from selling the whole animal for someone else to cook. His value-added bulb lit up. Eventually Paul learned how to barbecue, and he made the transition from farmer to pitmaster. Paul and his wife, Ann, managed to raise two boys, Andy and Wayne, thanks to the popularity of the barbecue. The business was also a good venue for teaching and learning business skills, pitmaster skills, and the value of hard work and customer service.

Stephenson's accommodates crowds of hungry customers in a country-style setting. Try the chopped pork ribs, but be sure to get potatoes too. You won't get boiled potatoes on the side at any barbecue joint except in eastern North Carolina, where "barbecued potatoes" are standard fare. Our version, with a mix of red and white unpeeled new potatoes, is different from Stephenson's, but it's true to the eastern North Carolina boiled potato tradition. We like it so much that it's routine fare at home and when we entertain. A delicious variation is to smash the cooked potatoes and add butter and shredded cheese.

NORTH CAROLINA–STYLE BOILED POTATOES

Serves 6 to 8

1 cup apple cider vinegar

1 teaspoon hot sauce, preferably Texas Pete

1 teaspoon kosher salt

1 teaspoon crushed black pepper

1 teaspoon crushed red pepper

3 pounds small new potatoes, red and white

8 tablespoons (1 stick) unsalted butter, melted

Salt and black pepper

Put the vinegar, hot sauce, salt, black pepper, and red pepper in a jar. Screw on the lid and shake the jar to mix the ingredients. Set aside.

Cover the potatoes with cold water. Add the vinegar sauce. Bring to a boil and simmer until tender, 45 to 60 minutes. Drain. Top with melted butter and season with salt and pepper to taste. Serve immediately.

Cheesy Potato Bake

Jack Stack Barbecue

13441 Holmes Rd.
Kansas City, MO 64145
816-942-9141
http://www.jackstackkc.com

ack Stack gave us several recipes, including its lamb ribs (page 107) and the chicken livers (page 108) it used to serve at its Holmes Road location. These cheesy potatoes are one of our all-time favorites, and we have yet to meet anyone who doesn't like them. You can purchase aged cheddar cheese sauce at the grocery store or online. Enjoy!

CHEESY POTATO BAKE

Serves 6 to 8

2½ cups heavy cream

1 cup aged cheddar cheese sauce

1 cup freshly grated Parmesan cheese

½ cup freshly grated cheddar cheese

½ cup freshly grated Jack cheese

2 tablespoons minced garlic

2 teaspoons onion powder

½ teaspoon garlic salt

2 teaspoons black pepper

2 teaspoons kosher salt

2½ pounds red potatoes

Minced fresh parsley, for garnish

Preheat the oven to 375°F. In a large bowl, combine the heavy cream, cheese sauce, cheeses, garlic, onion powder, garlic salt, black pepper, and kosher salt and mix well.

Wash and cut the potatoes into ⅛-inch-thick slices and place immediately into the sauce mixture. Mix by hand to coat all the surfaces of the sliced potatoes. Place the mixture in a 9 by 13-inch baking dish and cover tightly with aluminum foil. Bake for about 1 hour. Uncover and bake for 20 to 30 minutes longer, until the top is golden brown. Let cool, garnish with parsley, and serve.

Vanized Potato

Van's Pig Stands

717 E. Highland
Shawnee, OK 74804
405-273-0000
http://www.pigstands.com

Van's Pig Stands are in the mainstream of American barbecue history, so we couldn't leave them out of the story. "Van" is the nickname of the founder, the late Leroy F. Vandegrift. Today Van's son, Jerry Vandegrift, is the owner, president, and "Head Hog" of the Van's Pig Stands enterprise. Jerry's son Jev is area manager for the Shawnee stores and for retail barbecue sauce sales. They own Pig Stands in Shawnee, Moore, Norman, and Oklahoma City.

We're partial to Van's Shawnee location, due to its history as the oldest barbecue restaurant in Oklahoma owned and operated by the same family. It has been there since 1935. We also like the atmosphere, the service, and the excellent Pig Sandwich® common to all Van's Pig Stands.

Another fun retro perk about the Shawnee joint is the return of the Charcoal Room in the basement. Go down there and have a feast.

Start with the chicken liver appetizer. With your charcoal-grilled rib eye or Kansas City strip, get the house salad and Vanized Potato. Save room for key lime pie, pecan pie, or another of the seven delicious dessert choices. You'll want to make some return trips for a rib dinner, brisket dinner, charcoaled tuna, or poached salmon.

With the closing of many original Pig Stands in Texas, we can thank the Vandegrift family for keeping the Pig Stands tradition alive. The first Pig Stand opened in Dallas in 1921, brainchild of Jesse G. Kirby. That's when transportation by private auto was really beginning to take off, and Kirby noticed that people liked their cars so much they were reluctant to get out, even to eat. So Kirby invented drive-ins. You ordered from your car, had your food delivered to your car, and stayed inside the car to eat. Model Ts and other 1920s cars had running boards to make it easier to get in and out. Pig Stand servers—preteen or early-teen boys dressed in white shirts, white hats, and black bow ties—would hop onto the running board to take customers' orders. Thus they were nicknamed "carhops."

Besides being the first drive-in restaurant, Pig Stands have been credited with several other restaurant firsts in their Texas birthplace. Here's the complete list:

First drive-in restaurants

First curb service with carhops

First drive-through service

First restaurants to use neon signs

First restaurants to use fluorescent lighting

First restaurants to use air-conditioning

Invented Texas Toast

Invented onion rings

Invented chicken-fried steak sandwich

Today's Van's Pig Stands in Oklahoma have added another invention: the twice-baked potato. Predicting how much food a barbecue joint will sell on any given day is always a guess, as it was at Van's Pig Stand in the late 1940s. Instead of having to tell customers who ordered a baked potato that they were sold out, the Vandegrifts started erring on the side of too many instead of too few. Throwing out the extras bothered Grandmother Thelma Vandegrift, so she set her mind to figuring out how to avoid all that waste. And thus the twice-baked potato was born. Here is Van's recipe. For best results, prepare the potatoes at least 24 hours before serving.

VANIZED POTATO

Serves 6 to 8

5 pounds Idaho baking potatoes

½ yellow onion, diced

½ pound bacon, diced

½ cup Milnot or other evaporated milk

1½ teaspoons salt

½ teaspoon black pepper

Garlic spread or garlic butter, for serving

Preheat the oven to 400°F. Wash the potatoes and place them directly on a rack in the middle of the oven for at least 1 hour, until soft when pricked or squeezed.

While the potatoes are baking, put the onion and bacon in a small saucepan over medium-low heat and cook, stirring regularly to prevent sticking, until the onions are translucent, 3 to 5 minutes. Remove from the heat and set aside.

Remove the potatoes from the oven. Cut off one side of each potato, keeping your knife as close to the skin as possible, so you don't remove any of the potato inside. Then, using a spoon, remove the potato flesh from inside the skin and place in a large mixing bowl, being careful not to pierce the skin with the spoon. Reserve the skins.

Add the milk, salt, pepper, bacon, and onions, including the bacon drippings, to the mixing bowl with the potato flesh and mix thoroughly until you have a smooth mashed potato consistency. Then, using a pastry bag or a gallon-size food storage bag with a corner cut off, squeeze the potato mixture back into the potato skins. Cover the potatoes and place in the refrigerator to chill for a few hours or overnight.

When ready to serve, place the potatoes on a sheet pan and cook in a 350°F oven for 20 to 30 minutes, until golden brown on top. Serve with a side of garlic spread or garlic butter.

Grilled Potato Salad

Burn Co. Barbecue

1738 S. Boston Ave.
Tulsa, OK 74119
918-574-2777
https://www.facebook.com/Burncobbq

ay "Make me happy" to the person taking your order in most barbecue joints and you'll get a puzzled look. "Are you flirting? Do you think you're in a certain fast food burger joint? Do I look like a therapist?"

At Burn Co. they will know exactly what you want. You'll soon be feasting on a Happy Plate with more than 3 pounds of superb barbecue meats and unbelievably delicious sides. If you're solo, get a to-go container. The Happy Plate is enough for several meals.

When the doors open at 10:30 in the morning, hungry customers are queued up, ready to enter and order. Soon the tables are full and the line is still out the door. Burn Co. fans line up day after day, eager to share in the feast before it's sold out.

Co-owner cousins Adam Myers and Robby Corcoran, friends since childhood, opened Burn Co. in January 2011. Adam was sales manager at Tulsa's Hasty-Bake Charcoal Ovens Company. Robby was weary of managing ho-hum, sous vide chain restaurants. No more precooked frozen vacuum-packed boiler-bag food for Robby. Burn Co. serves real barbecue prepared fresh every day, cooked with fire and smoke the old-fashioned way.

When Burn Co. outgrew the original location on 11th Street, it moved to bigger digs downtown and added twelve new Hasty-Bakes to the original eight to meet surging customer demand. Every item on Burn Co.'s menu is cooked in a Hasty-Bake. For home cooks the new Burn Co. offers fresh meat for sale from a refrigerated display case. Head butcher Craig Kus is ready to take your order, cut to your specifications.

Burn Co. turns out an amazing variety of barbecue and side dishes—pulled pork, spareribs, chicken, fatties, hot links, sausage, smoked sliced shawarma, beef verde with flour tortillas, sandwich varieties, mac and cheese, beans, grilled potato salad, and more. Adam and Robby like to experiment with new recipes, so be prepared for a surprise menu item now and then. It's all fantastic!

Burn Co. exemplifies why Hasty-Bake has earned a popular niche in the barbecue cooker industry since 1948. Our friend Phil Litman, for example, says there are two things he will not part with until the Grim Reaper takes him: his Hasty-Bake and his Golden Retrievers. "Crazy as it may sound, but I swear there is no other smoker or grill device that produces better-tasting ribs and chicken! Something about the way Hasty-Bake causes the outer crust to form on a rib and the way it crisps up the skin on chicken," he notes.

How will you feel after eating at Burn Co? Happy! They can't seem to make enough of this salad to satisfy customer demand. It is one of the first items to go on the "Sold Out" board at the front of the line. When you try it, you'll see why.

GRILLED POTATO SALAD

Serves 6 to 8

1½ pounds Yukon Gold B size
potatoes, skin on, diced extra-large

2 to 3 tablespoons olive oil

Salt and black pepper

1 medium bell pepper, any
color, diced extra-large

1 small red Spanish onion,
diced extra-large

1 small yellow Spanish onion,
diced extra-large

2 tablespoons rendered
bacon fat, melted

½ cup of your favorite spicy
mustard, or to taste (Burn Co.
uses chipotle mustard)

Toss the potato chunks with some of the olive oil, salt,
and pepper. Grill the potatoes in a grill topper (see Note)
until cooked through, stirring often. Transfer to another
pan to cool. Toss the bell pepper and onions with the
remaining olive oil, salt, and pepper and grill until soft.
Allow to cool, then combine in a large bowl with the
potatoes, bacon fat, mustard, and more salt and pepper
to taste. Chill for at least 1 hour before serving.

Note: A grill topper is a metal container with small holes
to place on top of your grill, making it possible to grill
small items. You may have to grill the potatoes and vegetables separately.

Potato Salad

Danny's Place

902 S. Canal St.
Carlsbad, NM 88220
505-885-8739
http://www.dannysbbq.com

anny's Place got its start as a Dairy Queen franchise—the only one to serve barbecue.

But when owners Danny and Carolyn Gaulden were pressured to stop serving barbecue and start serving standard DQ fare, they decided to remodel and open their own restaurant, Danny's Place. Danny's Place not only makes great smoked fresh ham (see page 100) but also serves great potato salad. Here is the recipe.

POTATO SALAD

Makes about 6 pounds, serving 12 hungry folks or about 16 average eaters

4 pounds russet potatoes

4 or 5 large eggs

1 medium-small onion, chopped

3 celery stalks, chopped

½ cup chopped pimientos or roasted red peppers

1 cup sweet pickle relish with juice

2 teaspoons salt

1 teaspoon black pepper

3 tablespoons yellow mustard

2 tablespoons apple cider vinegar

1 to 1½ cups Miracle Whip

Paprika, for garnish

Boil the potatoes until fork-tender. Cool and peel. Chop into pieces about fingernail size or smaller. Boil the eggs for 15 minutes, cool, peel, and chop into small pieces. Add the eggs, chopped onion, celery, pimientos, pickle relish, salt, pepper, mustard, vinegar, and 1 cup of the Miracle Whip to the potatoes and mix well. Add a little more Miracle Whip if the mixture seems too dry, but be careful; how much you need will vary depending on how starchy the potatoes are. Turn the potato salad into a serving dish and finish off with a dusting of paprika for a nice presentation. You can also add a couple of sliced boiled eggs on top if you want to get fancy. Refrigerate for 3 to 4 hours or overnight before serving.

Wilber's Barbecue

4172 U.S. Highway 70 East
Goldsboro, NC 27534
919-778-5218
http://wilbersbarbecue.com

Many people told us that Wilber's is a mandatory stop if you want the true flavor of eastern North Carolina whole hog. We tried it, and we're glad we did. These days many whole hogs in eastern North Carolina are cooked with gas, but at Wilber's you get it the traditional way, cooked in pits fueled with slow-smoking oak coals. After cooking all night, the meat is separated from the bones and chopped. Some dry seasonings are mixed in, but not enough to overpower the flavor of the hog. Wilber's vinegar-based barbecue sauce is on the table so you can add as much extra seasoning as you wish. Potato salad, slaw, and hushpuppies round out the meal. It's good enough that we wish Wilber Shirley would open a joint in Kansas City. He has been barbecuing pigs in North Carolina since 1962, so it's not likely he would entertain a move. We're just glad he's in Goldsboro, and we've joined the "Wilber's is a mandatory stop" chorus. We'll be back.

Mr. Shirley had left the premises shortly before we arrived, so we didn't get the pleasure of a visit with him. Had we done so, we would have asked for his potato salad recipe. We liked it, and we noticed that Wilber's is one of only a few barbecue joints in North Carolina that serve potato salad. Our version has a few extras that we like in a potato salad.

SOUTHERN-STYLE POTATO SALAD

Serves 6 to 8

2 to 3 pounds potatoes

4 hard-cooked eggs, peeled and chopped

4 celery stalks, chopped

½ cup sweet pickle relish

2 tablespoons canned diced pimiento

½ cup diced sweet onion

¼ cup diced green bell pepper

Sea salt and black pepper

1 cup real mayonnaise

2 tablespoons yellow mustard

Wash the potatoes and cover with water; bring to a boil and simmer for 30 to 40 minutes, until tender. Drain the potatoes and set them aside to cool. When the potatoes are cool, peel and dice them. Add the eggs, celery, relish, pimiento, onion, green pepper, and salt and pepper to taste. Stir until mixed. Stir the mayonnaise and mustard together until mixed and then add the mixture to the potatoes; mix well. Refrigerate for at least 1 hour before serving.

Barbecue Baked Beans

Boss Hawg's BBQ

2833 S.W. 29th St.
Topeka, KS 66614
785-273-7300
http://www.bosshawgsbbq.com

oss Hawg's BBQ is a family-owned Topeka-based barbecue joint that came about by way of barbecue competition. Hank and Elizabeth Lumpkin decided to take their championship barbecue to the commercial arena in 1986, and it's a winner. Boss Hawg's started out with carryout and catering only. They soon became successful and well known enough to open the present location in a shopping center off Southwest 29th Street. As far as we know, Boss Hawg's BBQ is the only barbecue that has an official annex that's a dining room in a U.S. Navy submarine, the USS Topeka.

Shortly before his untimely death in 2003 at age 38, Hank and Elizabeth opened the popular Pigskins Sports Bar adjacent to Boss Hawg's. They used money Hank had won on the TV show Jeopardy to pay for the bar. Fortunately for the barbecue consumer public, Elizabeth carries on the Boss Hawg's tradition. Hank would want it that way.

At Boss Hawg's, knotty pine walls and shelves are adorned with barbecue sauces, trophies, ribbons, and other awards from barbecue competitions, plus artfully framed barbecue memorabilia. The Boss Hawg's liquor license is framed with a picture of Carrie Nation, the famous nineteenth-century hatchet-wielding prohibitionist known for wreaking havoc in saloons. New owner Sarah Burtch is continuing the Boss Hawg's legacy established by Hank and Elizabeth. As Elizabeth used to say, "We care about you, our guests, in a way no chain or franchise ever could. We care about the quality of service and food you receive."

In our quest for America's best barbecue, asking each and every barbecuer for a recipe that has never been published was a chore in itself. It was even harder to ask for a specific recipe, which was usually not exactly what they wanted to give us. It was easy to get bean and coleslaw recipes, and we wanted some of those things,

but in most cases we had to decline those recipes and ask for others. In the case of Boss Hawg's, we really wanted the baked beans! Are these the best baked beans ever? Many people say they are, and we concur. Their baked beans are cooked in the pit for 2 to 3 hours, swimming in barbecue sauce with apples, raisins, onions, dark brown sugar, and bacon. Thanks to Boss Hawg's, here is the home version.

Boss Hawg's liquor license is displayed with a picture of Carrie Nation. It has a special irony since Carrie Nation was no stranger to Topeka. In January 1902 she was a guest speaker at a temperance convention there. She branded the hatchet as her saloon attack tool and had souvenir hatchet pins made. Sale of the pins helped further her cause and pay off a slander suit she lost. Carrie once said, "Oh, I tell you, ladies, you never know what joy it gives to start out to smash a rum shop."

BARBECUE BAKED BEANS

Serves 6 to 8

3 (16-ounce) cans pork and beans, rinsed and drained

2 cups dark brown sugar

1 cup cooked chopped bacon, barbecue pork (see page 59), or barbecue brisket (see page 42)

1 cup diced tart apple, such as Granny Smith

1 cup diced onion

1 cup barbecue sauce

¼ cup golden raisins

2 teaspoons liquid smoke

2 cloves garlic, pressed

½ teaspoon ground coriander

Combine all the ingredients in a 2-quart casserole dish and blend well. Bake in a 350°F oven until bubbly, 45 to 60 minutes.

Buffalo's Beans

Buffalo's BBQ

201 N. Hwy. 11
Sperry, OK 74073
918-288-6200
http://buffalosbbq.com

When you're sitting at the Buffalo's rugged sun-bleached picnic table that is chained to the Daylight Donuts sign at the side of Highway 11 in Sperry, Oklahoma, it's hard to believe that the bustling city of Tulsa is only 10 miles south. Whether you get it to go or enjoy it outdoors on location, Buffalo's BBQ is some of the best barbecue in Oklahoma, which of course means some of the best in America. Here's how Donny puts it: "The way I look at it, you take two pieces of bread or a bun. The bottom side is Texas. The top side is Kansas City. All the good stuff is in the middle."

Donny is another talented pitmaster whose success in competition barbecue inspired him to go into business. One of his many prestigious awards is Grand Champion at the Jack Daniel's World Championship Barbecue. He runs his low-overhead, one-man food trailer operation only a couple of miles from his home. When regular customers call ahead, Donny has their order boxed and brown bagged when they arrive to pick it up and pay for it. His antidote for formerly slow sales on Wednesdays is a prime rib special. Regular customers call in their order at least a day ahead to make sure there's a prime rib with their name on it before they're sold out. Although Donny's barbecue secrets are as hard to pull out of him as getting him to smile on cam-

era, he was kind enough to share his bean recipe with us. Donny told us he doesn't put meat in his beans due to differences in customer demand. Some want pork. Others want beef. Some prefer no meat in the beans. With this recipe you can go meatless or add your own.

BUFFALO'S BEANS

Serves 8

2 (16.5-ounce) cans baked beans, drained

1 tablespoon yellow mustard

¼ cup packed brown sugar

⅔ cup of your favorite barbecue sauce

2 teaspoons of your favorite rub

Preheat the oven to 300°F.

Combine all the ingredients in a baking pan and cover with foil. Bake for 2½ hours or until the beans reach 165°F.

Van's Coleslaw

Bob Syke's Bar-B-Q

1724 9th Ave.
Bessemer, AL 35020
205-426-1400
http://www.bobsykes.com

Van Sykes grew up in the barbecue business. His parents, Bob and Maxine Sykes, opened a barbecue joint in Birmingham, Alabama, in 1956, a year after Van was born. The combination of Maxine's business savvy and Bob's pit savvy made for a successful barbecue business launch from the get-go. A dozen years after the Birmingham opening Bob Syke's had moved to Bessemer and had spawned fourteen franchises in Alabama and Tennessee. Long hours and extreme stress took a toll on Bob Sykes in 1970. A stroke incapacitated him to the point that he could no longer work in the business. It was up to Maxine and her teenage son, Van, to keep the business going. They dropped the franchise businesses and focused on making the Bessemer restaurant the best it could be. To this day they have lived up to that legacy. Bob Sykes, who died in 1990, would surely be proud of his wife and son.

We have known Van by reputation over the past 25 years. When we tasted his barbecue sauce in 1984 at the first Diddy-Wa-Diddy National Barbecue Sauce Contest, we could tell he knew a thing or two about barbecue. Since then we've gotten to know him as fellow members of the Southern Foodways Alliance. At a symposium on barbecue we shared some bench-shaking belly laughs with Van while Calvin Trillin regaled us with straight-faced humor and insights related to the subject at hand.

Van upholds the high standards he learned from Bob: fresh, quality ingredients and no shortcuts. Van's barbecued pork, beef, and ribs are tender, smoky, and delicious. Try to save room for pie! According to Van, "Everybody loves a good slaw with their BBQ." Thanks to Van for the recipe he shared with us.

VAN'S COLESLAW

Serves 6 to 8

½ cup real mayonnaise (heavy-duty, not low-fat)

1½ tablespoons tarragon vinegar

1 tablespoon sugar

7 cups thinly sliced green cabbage

1 cup grated carrots

Salt and black pepper

Chopped fresh parsley, for garnish

Mix the mayonnaise, vinegar, and sugar in a large bowl. Add the cabbage and carrots and toss to coat. Season to taste with salt and pepper. Cover and refrigerate for up to 4 hours. Sprinkle with parsley and serve.

Coleslaw and Baked Beans

Woody's Bar-B-Que

5599 Hwy. 14 East
Waldenburg, AR 72475
870-579-2251
http://buywoodyssauce.com

Who said you couldn't set up your barbecue rig on a corner, make a living, and get famous too? Woody (William) and Cecelia Wood proved you could when they got into barbecue in 1985 to supplement Woody's crop-dusting income.

Truckers put Woody's on the map; they would pull their big rigs into the parking lot and chow down on his pig sandwich and ribs to go. "How about a bottle of your barbecue sauce?" they'd ask. "We don't bottle it" was the answer. "Well, if you ever do, I want a case to take back to Ohio!"

So Woody and Cecelia started making 5 gallons of barbecue sauce at a time and bottling it, but that made only about 2½ cases. That was OK for the first years; then they graduated to a 20-gallon pot and could make 10½ cases at a time.

Since then those sauces, along with Woody's barbecue and barbecue rubs, have won numerous awards at the National Barbecue Association (NBBQA) contest. Woody has taken home four or five first-place awards more than once and also won first place at the Dallas Gourmet Market. And business is still booming, with the truckers still spreading the word of great BBQ with their CBs blaring, "Good Q—come and get it!"

In fact the barbecue stand was doing so well and demand for his sauces was so high that Woody had several co-packers in the South make a sample of his sauce to make it more widely available. Not one of the five made it like Woody did, though. A close approximation was not what Woody and Cecelia had built their business and reputation on. So they did the only thing they could do: They built their own bottling plant. Now they sell several sauces, rubs, seasonings, and marinades—all award-winning.

Despite having their own plant, Woody's still does all of its barbecue business out of a Winnebago, with everything cooked on a large custom-built Klose barbecue pit. And it's open only three days a week—Wednesday, Thursday, and Friday—plus Saturdays during duck season.

It's worth heading to Woody's on one of those days for the outstanding pork sandwich. The slaw on it is a delicious sweet and sour, not too

COLESLAW

Serves 6 to 8

1 head green cabbage, shredded and chopped

½ cup sweet pickle relish

¼ cup Miracle Whip (not mayonnaise)

¼ cup sugar

Salt and black pepper

Combine all the ingredients in a large bowl and blend well. Adjust the seasonings to your taste.

WHY PICKLES WITH BARBECUE?

We have eaten at hundreds of barbecue joints across America. Seldom do we find one that doesn't serve pickles with the barbecue. Dill chips predominate, followed by dill spears or kosher deli spears. A few joints offer hot pickles or sweet pickles. Since the custom is near universal, we figured it would be easy to go online or in books about barbecue and find out when, where, and why it got started. Not so.

Our barbecue buddy and eminent historian of barbecue, Dr. Howard Taylor, may have nailed it. He told us that pickles were on deli sandwiches or on the side by the early 1800s and on hamburgers by the early 1900s. When Texas markets began selling barbecue in the late 1800s/early 1900s, eating barbecue with sliced white bread, onions, and pickles off butcher paper with no forks was quickly adopted as common practice. Pickles, onions, bread, and saltine crackers were already at hand and made a natural pairing. Around 1950, some Texas restaurants tried serving pickle relish on barbecued beef sandwiches, but luckily the idea died quickly.

BAKED BEANS

Serves 6 to 8

2 (16-ounce) cans pork and beans

¼ medium onion, coarsely chopped

1 tablespoon dark brown sugar

1 large green or red bell pepper, chopped

⅓ cup Woody's Original Mild Bar-B-Q sauce

2 teaspoons yellow mustard

Preheat the oven to 350°F. In a 1½-quart baking dish, combine all the ingredients, stirring to combine. Bake the mixture for 30 to 45 minutes, until hot and bubbling.

sweet and not too sour. Here is the recipe, more or less. It's all done to taste, so you be the judge of how sweet or sour you want it and add more or less of anything to taste. The baked beans are also quite good.

Coleslaw with Character

Character's Famous BBQ

7283 Adairsville Hwy. 140
Adairsville, GA 30103
678-481-6701

Our friend Vernee Green-Myers told us about Character's and helped us with this review, a blend of her words and ours. If Vernee says Character's is good, it's good!

Michael Character's Famous BBQ is located on a busy corner in the small town of Adairsville, Georgia, in a renovated old gas station. It's small, open certain days for lunch only until sold out. It's pretty much a one-man operation except for his friend, Tom, who helps him at barbecue competitions.

Michael spends Monday preparing for the week ahead. He cooks briskets and butts on Monday for Tuesday, but cooks ribs and chicken every day. He puts them on before 7 a.m. to have them ready at 11. After he puts on the chicken and ribs, he'll cook potato salad, make coleslaw, and bake a homemade pound cake, the only dessert on the menu. He makes his famous sauce fresh every day. As his friend Tom said, "There are no measuring cups in Character's. He makes it without a recipe every day, but it tastes exactly the same!" He sells out every day—on average, a case of butts and a case of baby back ribs.

Michael's has made appearances on national TV shows such as *Destination America* and *BBQ Pitmasters*. He also got bitten by the competition bug and has won a fair share of contests. Michael shared his coleslaw recipe with us, thanks to Vernee. Since he eyeballs everything, this was his best estimate of the amounts. You can squirt the mustard to your taste.

COLESLAW WITH CHARACTER

Serves 24

2 (32-ounce) bags coleslaw mix with carrots and purple cabbage

1 medium yellow onion, finely chopped in a food processor

2 tablespoons Morton Season-All

1 tablespoon salt

1 to 2 tablespoons lemon pepper

2 squirts yellow mustard (the length of the pan)

About ¼ cup mayonnaise

Combine all the ingredients in a large aluminum pan. Mix well, cover with foil, and refrigerate for 3 to 4 hours before serving so the juices mix together. Stir well before serving.

Eastern North Carolina Coleslaw

Stamey's

2206 High Point Rd.
Greensboro, NC
336-299-9888
http://www.stameys.com

 tamey's means "barbecue" to residents of Greensboro and the surrounding area. It has been so since 1930. The barbecue comes from a distinguished lineage that started in Lexington, where founder C. Warner Stamey learned the art and business of barbecue from Jess Swicegood and Sid Weaver. When Warner turned the business over to his sons, Keith and Charles, they had big shoes to fill and a stellar reputation to maintain. No problem. Under their leadership the business continued to thrive, as it does to this day with two longstanding locations in Greensboro. Since Keith's death in 2001, Charles and his son Charles Keith "Chip" Stamey have done an outstanding job of running Stamey's, including the Stamey tradition of hickory-smoked barbecue in custom-built pits.

If you've never tried a traditional Carolina pulled pork sandwich, it's time to treat yourself to one. After that, the only way you'll eat pulled pork is with a helping of great Piedmont-style coleslaw slapped on top. The sour notes in the slaw complement the sweetness of the pork. It is one of our all-time favorite flavor combos.

EASTERN NORTH CAROLINA COLESLAW

Serves 8 to 10

½ **cup sugar**

½ **cup ketchup**

½ **cup apple cider vinegar**

2 **teaspoons salt**

2 **teaspoons black pepper**

2 **teaspoons hot sauce,
preferably Texas Pete**

1 **medium head green cabbage,
coarsely grated**

In a large bowl, stir together the sugar, ketchup, vinegar, salt, pepper, and hot sauce until blended. Add the cabbage to the bowl and toss to coat. Cover and chill for at least 2 hours before serving.

Pink Coleslaw and Buttermilk Biscuits with Country Ham

A & M Grill

402 E. Center St.
Mebane, NC 27302
919-563-3721

The former A&M Grill opened just after World War II. It was modernized after several years, but kept its inviting, well-weathered feel. The tables were covered with checkered blue cloths and outfitted with rolls of paper towels for napkins. A bottle of the ubiquitous Texas Pete sauce was on each table.

When the founder's son, Charles McAdams, Jr., had to step aside for health reasons, the many fans of A&M Grill were relieved that the restaurant would not be shuttered. Thanks to Charles's wife, Donna McAdams, and daughters, Lisa Wright, Charlotte Regans, and Karen Lewis, Mebane's A&M Grill continued to serve its famous pork barbecue with pink slaw and hushpuppies. We had a good visit with Donna and Lisa before our order arrived the last time we were there and are grateful to have their recipe for slaw.

Ardie wished A&M had served a chopped pork and coleslaw omelet for breakfast, but it never made it to the menu before A&M closed in 2011. Paul came up with a good substitute, one of his southern country favorites that isn't exactly barbecue but was on A&M's menu: country ham on homemade biscuits. We're also including Paul's recipe for that.

PINK COLESLAW

Serves 6 to 8

½ cup real mayonnaise

¼ cup ketchup

1½ tablespoons white vinegar

1 tablespoon sugar

7 cups chopped green cabbage

Salt and black pepper

Mix the mayonnaise, ketchup, vinegar, and sugar in a large bowl; add the cabbage and toss to coat. Season to taste with salt and pepper. Refrigerate until ready to serve.

BUTTERMILK BISCUITS WITH COUNTRY HAM

Makes 12 biscuits

**3 cups all-purpose flour,
or more as needed**

1 tablespoon baking powder

1 teaspoon sea salt

¾ teaspoon baking soda

¾ cup Crisco or lard

¾ to 1 cup buttermilk

Lard or canola oil, for frying

**12 thin slices country ham,
or more if desired**

Preheat the oven to 450°F and put a rack in the middle. Sift the flour to make sure there are no lumps. Add the baking powder, salt, and baking soda. Slowly add the Crisco, working it into the dry ingredients with a large dinner fork or spoon or your hands.

Next add the buttermilk, working it into the mixture and adding only enough to moisten the dry ingredients. After everything is thoroughly mixed, plop it down on a floured counter or cutting board. Knead the dough until it is about the consistency of Play-Doh. If the dough is still sticky, sprinkle more flour on your counter or cutting board. As you knead your dough, it will pick up more of the flour.

When you have it the right consistency, you can shape your biscuits by hand or using a cookie or biscuit cutter. If using a cookie or biscuit cutter, roll the dough ½ inch thick on a lightly floured surface. Place the biscuits on a lightly greased baking sheet. Bake for 15 to 18 minutes, until golden brown.

While the biscuits are baking, heat a little lard or canola oil in a large skillet over medium-high heat. Fry the ham on one side until it just begins to brown, then turn and fry the other side. Remove the biscuits from the oven, split them, fill them with slices of country ham, and serve warm. If it's for lunch, add a side of Pink Coleslaw.

Mac 'n' Cheese

Smoque

3800 N. Pulaski Rd.
Chicago, IL 60641-3197
773-545-7427
http://www.smoquebbq.com

"YOU'D GIVE IT ALL UP TO RUN A BARBECUE JOINT?!" HIS WIFE EXCLAIMED. HE SAID YES.

Before we met Barry Sorkin, we had an axe to grind with him. Thanks to Barry and many other Chicago restaurant owners, Rudy "Tim" Mikeska shut down his barbecue joint in Taylor, Texas, in order to keep up with demand for his sausages in Chicago. After meeting Barry and eating Smoque's first-class barbecue, we buried the hatchet. Smoque does Rudy's sausage proud!

Smoque also turns out superbly tender, juicy beef brisket, baby backs, and spareribs that rival any of your favorite barbecue joints and pulled pork that could make our Alabama barbecue buddy "Sheepdog" stand on the table and howl!

Smoque is a small barbecue joint that is huge on flavor. The loyal customer base it attracted since opening day keeps coming back, along with throngs of others who have newly discovered what's happening on North Pulaski. Smoque turns out quality barbecue that's as good as the best joints we've tried. Take a bite of Smoque brisket or sausage or baby backs or spareribs or pulled pork or pulled chicken and we think you'll agree. Sauce it if you must, but Smoque meat doesn't need sauce. Their sweet-sour, western North Carolina–style sauce is good, but we prefer it on the fantastic fries instead of the meat.

Barry Sorkin applies himself 100 percent to whatever he does. The problem was that, although the pay was good at his previous job, he just wasn't into it. "You'd give it all up to run a barbecue joint?!" his wife exclaimed. He said yes. He partnered with four other "regular guys" who know barbecue, and Smoque was born.

Smoque goes beyond the same old, same old and raises the bar on barbecue excellence. The sides are even top-notch. The beans, fresh-cut fries, coleslaw, and corn bread are delicious, and their mac and cheese is absolutely some of the best we've ever eaten. We saved room for a peach crumble dessert that would rival any cobbler in any barbecue joint in the South. When you go to Chicago, get Smoqued!

MAC 'N' CHEESE

Serves 14 to 16

CHEESY BREAD CRUMB TOPPING

4 tablespoons butter

1½ cups bread crumbs

½ cup grated Parmesan cheese

MAC 'N' CHEESE

8 tablespoons (1 stick) butter

2 pounds elbow macaroni, cooked just short of al dente

1⅓ pounds sharp cheddar cheese, shredded, plus 2 cups shredded for spreading over the top

1 quart evaporated milk

4 large eggs

1 teaspoon dry mustard

½ teaspoon onion salt

½ teaspoon celery salt

½ teaspoon Louisiana hot sauce

To make the topping, melt the butter. Add the bread crumbs and Parmesan and mix until thoroughly combined. Set aside.

Preheat the broiler. To make the mac 'n' cheese, melt the butter in a large pot. Do not let it brown.

Add all the remaining ingredients except the 2 cups cheddar to the pot. Heat over medium heat, stirring almost constantly, until the cheese melts and the sauce thickens and reaches 160°F (this is important so the eggs don't scramble). Transfer to a large deep baking dish or half-size hotel pan.

Sprinkle the remaining 2 cups cheddar over the top.

Spread a thin (⅛-inch) layer of bread crumb topping over the top of the cheddar. You may have extra. Place the assembled dish under the broiler just until the bread crumbs turn golden brown. Serve immediately.

Cast-Iron Skillet Corn Bread

Skylight Inn

1501 S. Lee St.

Ayden, NC 28513

252-746-4113

 *ational Geographic* magazine once called the Skylight Inn the "Barbecue Capital of the World." The late Pete Jones, then owner, was so rightly proud of the distinction that he topped the roof of the joint with a metal dome meant to resemble the nation's capitol dome. The dome is still there, serving as a beacon and an icon.

We can't attest to how the barbecue at the Skylight Inn today compares to how it was when Pete ran the place, but you'll get no complaints from us. It was worth the trip. In fact it was so good we were seriously talking about moving to North Carolina. Well, not so seriously that we would actually leave Kansas City, also dubbed the barbecue capital of the world by other magazines and food writers. But we have no qualms about saying the folks who live close enough to frequent the Skylight Inn are fortunate indeed.

There's nothing fancy about the place, but there's ample seating and the comfortable feeling that you're in the right place, because the door keeps opening to admit more customers, and most look like this is business as usual for them. You'll hear the familiar chop-chop-chop of cleavers on a large butcher block lit with heat lamps. Something we liked that not every place

CAST-IRON SKILLET CORN BREAD

Makes 8 wedges

¼ **cup bacon drippings or butter**

2 **cups fine stone-ground white cornmeal**

1 **teaspoon salt**

½ **teaspoon baking soda**

½ **teaspoon baking powder**

1 **large egg**

1½ **cups buttermilk**

Preheat the oven to 450°F. Place the drippings in a 10-inch cast-iron skillet and pop the skillet into the oven to heat. In the meantime, combine the cornmeal, salt, baking soda, and baking powder in a large bowl. In a small bowl, beat together the egg and buttermilk. Add the buttermilk mixture to the cornmeal mixture and stir, using the absolute minimum number of strokes needed to moisten the dry ingredients.

Remove the hot skillet from the oven and swirl it around so the drippings coat the bottom and lower sides of the skillet. Then pour the remainder of the hot drippings or butter into the batter and stir a couple of times. Turn the batter into the hot skillet, place back in the oven, and bake until it is golden brown, 20 to 25 minutes. Remove from the oven, cut into 8 wedges, and serve warm.

does is the addition of pig cracklings to the chopped pork. They must put them in shortly before serving, as they were nice and crunchy in our sandwiches. This is basic North Carolina barbecue goodness: a chopped pork sandwich topped with coleslaw, with a side of skillet corn bread, Texas Pete hot sauce at the ready, and a glass of sweet tea.

Our barbecue buddy Carl Rothrock met us at Skylight. The staff was so busy serving customers none of us could get the recipe out of them, so Paul came up with this home version.

SAUCE MATTERS—

Many pitmasters have told us it's the sauce that matters. "Anyone can barbecue," they say, "but not everyone can make good sauce." On the other hand we've heard—especially in Texas—that "My barbecue is so good it doesn't need sauce." In some places it is house policy to prohibit sauce on the premises. Thus, the barbecue vs. sauce edict is reversed. "Anyone can make sauce, but not everyone can barbecue."

Questions also arise as to what makes a good sauce. Should the base be vinegar, tomato, mustard, mayonnaise, soy, fruit, peppers, or something else? Should sauce be spicy hot or mild? Are any specific herbs and spices essential? While we can agree on a few objective standards such as barbecue shouldn't taste like lighter fluid and it should be tender enough to chew easily, people part ways on the other questions. Barbecue aficionados debate all of these questions and many others. In the end there are no right or wrong answers when it comes to questions of individual taste.

OR DOES IT?

BBQ Corn Bread

Spencer's Smokehouse & Barbeque

9900 NE 23rd St.
Midwest City, OK 73141
405-769-8373
http://www.spencersbbqmenu.com

Mike Spencer has been mistaken for Tommy Lee Jones so many times that he smiles and takes it in stride. The resemblance is remarkable. Fortunately for barbecue aficionados, Mike's remarkable talents are at the barbecue pit and in the kitchen instead of on-screen.

Spencer's large dining area offers booth and table options. Old-fashioned farm and kitchen memorabilia are sprinkled throughout to lend homey ambience. We made a special trip to Spencer's on advice from our Oklahoma barbecue buddy, Darian "Kosmo" Khosravi, and we're glad we did. Besides top-quality standard barbecue meats, we especially liked the fried okra and Mike's seasonal favorite, barbecue corn bread. We didn't even have to arm-wrestle him for the recipe.

This has the makings of a complete meal in itself. It is worth the trip to Midwest City for Mike's original, fresh from the oven. When you can't make it to Spencer's, try this at home.

BBQ CORN BREAD

Serves 6 to 8

1 pound barbecued pulled pork

1 cup cornmeal

1 cup all-purpose flour

2½ teaspoons baking powder

½ teaspoon salt

1 cup sugar

¼ cup whole milk, or as needed

½ pound (2 sticks) butter, softened

4 large eggs

1 (14.75-ounce) can cream-style corn

1 to 2 fresh jalapeño peppers,
  seeded and minced, or to taste

1½ cups shredded cheddar cheese

TOPPING

4 tablespoons butter

3 tablespoons barbecue sauce

1 teaspoon garlic salt

½ teaspoon cayenne, or to taste

Preheat the oven to 350°F. Generously spray a 9 by 13-inch pan with nonstick cooking spray. Shred the pulled pork into fine pieces and set aside.

In a large bowl, stir together the cornmeal, flour, baking powder, and salt.

In a separate large bowl, stir together the sugar, milk, and softened butter. Stir in the eggs one at a time until well incorporated. Add the corn, peppers, cheese, and pulled pork and stir by hand (don't use an electric mixer) until blended.

Add the flour mixture to the corn mixture and stir by hand until well blended. Pour the batter into the prepared pan.

Bake for 45 to 50 minutes, until golden brown and a toothpick inserted into the center of the bread comes out clean.

To make the topping: Combine all the ingredients and melt in the microwave. Brush over the cooked corn bread and return to the oven for 5 to 7 minutes. Cool completely, then cut into squares and serve warm.

CINEMA 'CUE

Barbecue is a major or bit player in many famous and infamous movies. Some of our favorites:

- *Gone With the Wind* (1939). There's a barbecue at the beginning of the movie, and the word is uttered eleven times during the 3-hour-and-42-minute movie.
- *Giant* (1956). This blockbuster big-screen drama starring James Dean, Rock Hudson, and Elizabeth Taylor is based on Edna Ferber's best-selling novel. The barbacoa scene is truly memorable. No "mad cow" scares back then. "And do those brains taste sweet!"
- *Murphy's Romance* (1985). While Sally Field and James Garner romanced each other as Murphy Jones and Emma Moriarty, Kansas City's Rich Davis of KC Masterpiece Barbecue Sauce fame supervised the open-pit barbecue of a steer at Emma's ranch. Notice a bottle of KC Masterpiece on Murphy's kitchen table? This is an early example of the pre-*E.T.* product placement marketing so common in today's movies and TV shows.
- *Top Gun* (1986). Filmed on location in San Diego's Kansas City Barbeque restaurant. The joint, autographed bras, and other memorabilia burned down on June 26, 2008, due to a pit fire. Like a phoenix, a new joint has emerged from the ashes, just like old times.
- *Fried Green Tomatoes* (1991). Based on Fannie Flagg's best-selling novel *Fried Green Tomatoes at the Whistle Stop Café,* this movie is the Sweeney Todd of cinema 'cue thanks to some Alabama barbecue that you'll see on the screen.
- *Dancer, Texas – Pop. 81* (1998). A bottle of Bone Suckin' Sauce appears on the dining room table in a trailer home. We know it isn't a product placement marketing deal. We asked Sandi Ford at Ford Foods, home of Bone Suckin' Sauce, and she didn't know about the movie.

Walk the Line (2005). Is that Bozo's Hot Pit Bar-B-Q in Mason, Tennessee, where Joaquin Phoenix and Reese Witherspoon—as Johnny Cash and June Carter—are sitting? Yes!

She was happy to know her sauce is in the movie, however.

- *Primary Colors* (1998). Politicking and barbecue are naturals in this story about a former governor of Arkansas, played by John Travolta, in a race for the White House.
- *Secondhand Lions* (2003). The brawl scene takes place in the Cele Store, a Texas barbecue joint we want to try. Scenes from *A Perfect World* (1993) were also shot in the Cele Store.
- *The Cookout* (2004). Unexpected wildness and confusion occur when Storm P as Todd Anderson hosts a cookout to celebrate a $30 million contract with the New Jersey Nets. The DVD includes a special feature on how to have a good cookout, plus some good recipes from the cast.
- *Baptists at Our Barbecue* (2004). This comedy is about an attempt to bring peace to a divided community by throwing a barbecue with everyone invited.
- *Chef* (2014). Check out the scenes at Austin's Franklin Barbecue in this comedy about a chef who gets fired from a restaurant and ends up opening a food truck. Look for pitmaster Aaron Franklin in a cameo role.

Corn Bread Muffins

Branks BBQ & Catering

13701 24th St. East
Sumner, WA 98390
253-891-1789
http:www.branksbbq.com

Paul had the pleasure of visiting Branks BBQ at its original location, a nice small, homey barbecue joint in downtown Sumner, Washington. It became very successful, and there was no way to expand, so it moved to the industrial district. The decor is what you might call country with a lot of local history thrown in, things like bucksaws and other old logging items. The staff is young and friendly, the barbecue is cooked in the pit with wild cherry wood, and all the sides and desserts are made from scratch. Featured here is the recipe for Branks's great corn bread muffins. Paul is good for two or three every time he eats there.

CORN BREAD MUFFINS

Makes 12 muffins

1 cup yellow cornmeal

1 cup all-purpose flour

1/8 to 1/4 cup sugar

4 teaspoons baking powder

1/2 teaspoon sea salt

1 to 1 1/4 cups buttermilk

1 large egg, at room temperature

11 tablespoons butter,
    melted and cooled

Preheat the oven to 375°F and place a rack in the middle. Butter 12 regular (1/3-cup) muffin cups. In a medium bowl, combine the cornmeal, flour, sugar, baking powder, and salt, then sift the mixture into a large bowl. In the now empty medium bowl, mix the buttermilk and egg together with a wire whisk. Whisk in the melted butter. Pour the buttermilk mixture into the cornmeal mixture and stir just until incorporated. Do not overmix. Divide the mix equally among the prepared muffin cups. Bake for about 15 minutes, until a toothpick inserted in the center of a muffin comes out clean. The muffins will be a pale yellow. Cool on a rack for 10 minutes. Serve with real butter.

Roasted Garlic Chile Morita BBQ Sauce

The Ranch House

2571 Cristo's Road
Santa Fe, NM 87507
505-424-8900
http://www.theranchhousesantafe.com

We were saddened when Ardie's friend Elaine Anton decided to shutter her fantastic Santa Fe barbecue joint, R&B. Would anyone else fill the gap Elaine was leaving when the coals went cold in her Southern Yankee? Would anyone else turn out the flavorful, inventive dishes with a Santa Fe accent that R&B's was known for? To our delight, such a place was discovered for us by one of our favorite mystery writers, N. M. Kelby, author of *Whale Season* and *Murder at the Bad Girl's Bar and Grill*—and a BBQ goddess as well. While she was in Santa Fe as artist-in-residence at the Santa Fe Art Institute, Ardie asked her to see if Santa Fe had any good barbecue to offer beyond chain or franchise venues. To our delight, she discovered local chef Josh Baum. N. M. was kind enough to offer a report and a recipe for Roasted Garlic Chile Morita BBQ Sauce that Josh gave us. N. M. Kelby's background in journalism and food writing shines through in this piece. We're proud to share her review with you, and we thank her!

The things people do for love are truly amazing. Josh left behind the world of haute cuisine, working in France at Michelin three-star restaurants, to come to Santa Fe, and eventually he opened up a barbecue joint called Josh's Barbecue. And he did it for love, but not just love of barbecue—it was for the love of his wife.

Josh had always wanted to open his own restaurant, and when the opportunity arose he chose barbecue because the pace appealed to him. It was much more low key than working in the frantic world of fine dining. Josh's uncle owns Steve's Rib and Sports Grill in Oklahoma City, Oklahoma. "I used to watch my uncle at his place, and it was just great. He'd cook everything in the morning and then relax," Josh says. "I really wanted to spend more time with my wife." So, Josh's Barbecue was born. After five years, Josh decided to change the name and concept (though not his dedication to good barbecue) and opened a new place called the Ranch House, where he carried over most of the Josh's Barbecue menu.

Even though his work in France is far behind, the haute-cuisine sensibility is not. Josh won't offer a single item that is bought premade. Everything is made from scratch using the finest seasonal ingredients and hormone-free meats. The fare is mostly traditional, with ribs, pulled pork, brisket, and barbecued chicken. It's difficult to go wrong here. All are standouts in their own right. Josh smokes with a traditional Ole Hickory Pit using Texas oak, anywhere from 5 to 30 hours, depending on the meat, and the results are sublime.

Even the sides are worth driving for. The coleslaw has a nice hit of mustard, rice wine vinegar, and green chile. The Green Chile Corn

continued on page 160

ROASTED GARLIC CHILE MORITA BBQ SAUCE

Makes 4 cups

1 small yellow onion, chopped

2 tablespoons canola oil

4 morita chiles or chipotles in adobo, minced or diced

12 cloves roasted garlic

⅓ cup apple cider vinegar

2½ cups chicken stock

1 (14½-ounce) can diced tomatoes, drained

1½ cups ketchup

½ cup Thai sweet chili sauce

¼ cup molasses

½ cup packed brown sugar

2 tablespoons fresh orange juice

2 tablespoons fresh lemon juice

Salt and black pepper

Sauté the onion in the canola oil in a medium saucepan over medium heat until soft, 5 to 7 minutes. Add the chiles and roasted garlic and toast lightly for 3 to 4 minutes. Add the vinegar and cook until the mixture is reduced by half, 15 to 20 minutes.

ROASTED GARLIC

2 heads garlic

1 tablespoon extra-virgin olive oil

Sea salt and freshly ground black pepper

Preheat the oven to 325°F. Line a small baking dish with aluminum foil. Cut the top quarter from each head of garlic and place the garlic cut side up on the prepared dish. Drizzle with oil and season lightly with salt and pepper. Turn the garlic cut side down and roast until the cloves are soft and golden brown, about 1 hour. Remove from the oven and let sit until cool enough to handle. Squeeze the garlic from the skins and discard the skins. This makes more than you'll need for Josh's recipe, but you can store it in an airtight container in the refrigerator for up to a week and use it in a variety of dishes.

To make a garlic paste: When cool enough to handle easily, put the roasted garlic into a small bowl, mash with a fork, and add oil from the pan until a paste forms. The paste makes great garlic bread!

Add the stock, canned tomatoes, ketchup, chili sauce, molasses, brown sugar, orange juice, and lemon juice. Bring to a boil; then lower the heat and simmer for 30 minutes. Remove the pan from the heat and set it aside to cool. Once the mixture has cooled, puree it in a blender and pass it through a fine-mesh strainer. Season with salt and pepper to taste and serve. Goes great on poultry!

continued from page 158
Bread is cakelike and more sweet than hot. In fact, most things are just hot enough; they won't make you sweat.

Josh puts a regional spin on traditional barbecue offerings. "I really want to cook barbecue for the locals," Josh says. So, not only does he serve a toothsome brisket, smoked for 18 hours and as moist and tender as I've ever had, but he offers a local variation, Green Chile Brisket, in which he resmokes the basic brisket with Hatch chiles for a grand total of 30 hours. The result is as complex as any French sauce. The chiles and brisket become an amazingly complex combination of smoke, sweetness, and heat. Good eats. One of the big must-haves here is the chips and homemade queso with the green chile brisket. If you don't like chips, you can have them pour it over a spud.

Nearly all Josh's meats are served dry (some do have a brush of glaze), so Josh offers several sauces every day. This is where his chef's training truly shows. The "traditional" sauce is anything but. Loaded with flavor, some heat, and only a slight hint of smoke, its base is Thai sweet chili sauce. The hot version is just that—the same great sauce turned up a notch.

The sauces are fresh tasting, and each flavor is married to the other in the French style—which is to say that there is no one dominant taste or overwhelming heat—they are just dang fine sauces and a perfect complement to the moist, smoky meat.

Like any good culinary school graduate, Josh believes in specials. When I was there, the special was baby backs with a red chile glaze. Right as he finishes cooking the ribs, he brushes them with the sweet, hot paste and then serves a bowl of it on the side. Totally addictive. I found myself pouring the glaze all over my baked potato.

JET Sauce

JET Bar-B-Q

1100 E. 3rd St. N.
Wichita, KS 67214
316-262-7299
http://www.jetbbq.com

For someone who didn't aspire to be a firefighter when he grew up, John Edwin Thien, Wichita's JETMAN barbecue pitmaster, matured into a fire tamer who works magic with fire, smoke, and meat. In 1997, after 16 years at his original location on Central, he and his wife, Suzy, jumped at the opportunity to move JET Bar-B-Q into the former Firehouse Number 8. "I thought it would be cool to be located in a firehouse and *start* a fire every day,'" John told us. JETMAN had been serving up some of America's best barbecue for almost two decades, but when his meat fires flared up in that old firehouse, his barbecue reached the pinnacle of perfection.

Thanks to JETMAN, Firehouse Number 8 is now equipped with two vintage Oyler barbecue pits, a prep room, kitchen, serving station, and engine company dining area. In good weather he opens the tall doors on each end of the firehouse for drive-thru barbecue.

Although the sliding poles are gone and the holes are covered, there is no mistaking that you're in a firehouse. Helmets, clothing, memorabilia, and gear adorn the walls and floor around the perimeter.

Ardie has been a fan of JET Bar-B-Q since he ate his first rib at the original joint some three decades ago. When he introduced Chef Paul to JET ribs, JET got a new convert. Ardie swears he heard Chef Paul exclaim, "Holy smoke, this is good!" upon first bite.

Chef Paul remarked to JETMAN, "I've passed by at least four times on business trips, and you haven't been open." "Just remember W-T-F," JETMAN replied. "Wednesday, Thursday, Friday. That's when we're open—with the exception of Black Friday, when we're always closed."

JET's tender, moist, smoky ribs kissed with JET's signature tomato-base sauce with a clove accent can verge on being addictive. Wise and considerate pitmaster that he is, JETMAN serves his ribs dry so you can add as much or as little sauce as you wish. They are delicious without sauce, but we like JET sauce so much that we add a little. We also love JET brisket, sausage, pulled pork, and turkey.

How does he do it? Here's what the JETMAN told us: "Good 'cue comes from paying attention to your product and your temperature gauges. When you have temperature and humidity changes, as we have in Kansas, there is no

continued on page 162

JET BARBECUE SAUCE

Makes about 9½ cups

SAUCE BASE (ABOUT 8 CUPS)

1½ tablespoons whole celery seeds

1½ tablespoons onion salt

1½ tablespoons dry mustard

1 cup hot water

1¼ cups cranapple juice

1½ tablespoons ground cloves

1 cup packed light brown sugar

¾ cup of your favorite dry rub

3 tablespoons liquid smoke

1¼ cups blackstrap molasses

40 ounces tomato paste

SAUCE

3½ cups Sauce Base

3 cups Cattlemen's BBQ Sauce or your favorite

3 cups tomato puree

To make the sauce base: In a large bowl, combine the celery seeds, onion salt, and dry mustard with the hot water and mix well. Add the remaining ingredients and blend well. What you don't use in the sauce can be frozen for later use.

For the sauce, combine the base, Cattlemen's, and tomato puree and blend well. Refrigerate and use within 2 weeks or freeze for later use.

continued from page 161

set time or temperature. Knowing your equipment and your wood is vital to consistency. You should never stop trying to improve no matter what you do. Experimentation is the adrenaline of the soul."

On one of our visits, the day before Thanksgiving, a steady stream of customers frequented the pickup counter to get a preordered JETMAN-smoked Thanksgiving turkey. More than half walked out with a JET sandwich or JET ribs, brisket, pulled pork, sausage, or "The Jester," a beef and hot link sandwich. JET beans and potato salad sides are popular takeout choices. As a special Thanksgiving "thank you for your business," JETMAN offered a complimentary shot of Wild Turkey to his smoked turkey customers. That's a tradition worth keeping!

There is real barbecue, and there is fake barbecue. There is good barbecue, and there is bad barbecue. JET barbecue is real good barbecue!

Goode Company BBQ Beef Rub

Goode Company Barbeque

5015 Kirby
Houston, TX 77098
800-627-3502 or 713-643-5263
http://www.goodecompany.com

Jim Goode, pitmaster at Goode Company Barbeque in Houston, Texas, started the company in 1977. Today there are four Goode Company restaurants, plus a mail-order business called the Barbeque Hall of Flame. Cooking tools, barbecue products, books, pies, and other great products can be ordered from the Hall of Flame online or with a phone call.

To our good friend and barbecue buddy the late Brian Heinecke, a stop at the original Goode Company to dine and to visit with Jim was a favorite highlight of any trip to Texas. We can't think of Goode Company without remembering Brian.

The walls of Goode Company are full of cowboy memorabilia, photos, and taxidermy. Customers line up and order cafeteria style and then find a place to dine at one of the many long picnic tables. It's one of those many barbecue places where the enjoyment of the barbecue brings people from all walks of life together, like a community gathering.

Jim's rub is great for beef, including ribs, roasts, and brisket, but it also enriches pork and lamb. Thanks to Jim, here's the recipe.

GOODE COMPANY BBQ BEEF RUB

Makes ¾ cup

2½ tablespoons dark brown sugar

2 tablespoons paprika

2 teaspoons dry mustard

2 teaspoons onion powder

2 teaspoons garlic powder

1½ teaspoons dried basil

1 teaspoon ground bay leaves

¾ teaspoon ground coriander

¾ teaspoon ground savory

¾ teaspoon dried thyme

¾ teaspoon freshly ground black pepper

¾ teaspoon white pepper

⅛ teaspoon ground cumin

Salt

To make the rub, combine all the ingredients, including salt as desired, in a small bowl. Store the mixture in an airtight container for up to 6 months. There's no need to refrigerate it.

To use the rub, massage it into the meat thoroughly the night before you plan to grill. Wrap the meat well in plastic wrap and place in the refrigerator until grilling time so that the flavors will be absorbed into the meat.

Championship Rib Rub & All-Purpose Seasoning

Johnny's Barbecue

5959 Broadmoor
Mission, KS 66202
913-432-0777
http://johnnysbbq.net

Johnny White is a longtime friend. We eat often at Johnny's, and we wrote parts of this book there. That said, Johnny's is here because Johnny's belongs here.

This former pizza place is now one of the most popular barbecue joints in Kansas City. A mix of southwestern art and barbecue artifacts lends eye candy to the scene, but what we like most about the decor are the barbecue sauces on display from across America and elsewhere. At Johnny's request, Ardie got him started with sauces from his *Great BBQ Sauce Book* collection. Since then, with customers bringing in sauces from all over the country, Johnny has the world's largest collection of barbecue sauces, bar none.

Hats off to the entire Johnny's team, including Johnny's son Eric, who runs Johnny's in Olathe; Brian White, Johnny's brother; Mike "Bubba" Brouhard, Johnny's brother-in-law; Terri Brouhard, Johnny's sister; Shannon Hammer, Johnny's niece; and Jason Ossana and Jan Monty, who try to keep a lid on our rowdiness. That's a special challenge on First Wednesday each month when the barbecue faithful convene for lunch, networking, and BS.

Johnny learned the barbecue business years ago when he worked at Rosedale Barbecue with the late Anthony Rieke. Although the Rosedale influence is noticeable, Johnny has developed his own original style, and it's a winner. His award-winning all-purpose rub will up your barbecue game.

CHAMPIONSHIP RIB RUB
& ALL-PURPOSE SEASONING

Makes about 6 tablespoons

2 tablespoons kosher salt

1 tablespoon coarse black pepper

1 tablespoon paprika

1 teaspoon sugar

1 teaspoon whole celery seeds

1 teaspoon cayenne

1 teaspoon dried oregano

1 teaspoon garlic salt

1 teaspoon chili powder

½ teaspoon ground cumin

Combine all the ingredients in a tightly sealed clear plastic food storage bag, shaking until blended. If not using the rub immediately, you can store it in a cool, dark place for up to 6 months.

Apply the rub to ribs and refrigerate, covered, for 4 to 6 hours for the best results before cooking as desired.

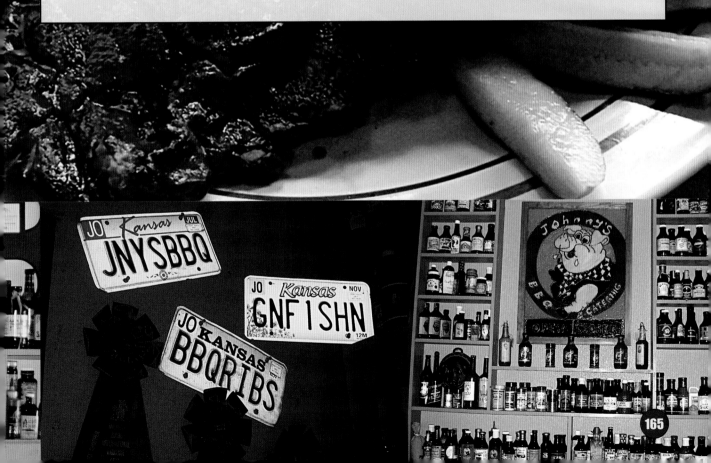

Fried Okra

Perry's Original Roadside BBQ

See Web site for location.
941-724-1702
http://www.perryssauce.com

We're not bona fide snowbirds who head south to Florida annually when winter arrives. We did venture south last winter, however, in search of sun, surf, seafood, and barbecue. We heard there was a man named Perry in Sarasota who cooks outstanding barbecue. Eager to find out, we checked the schedule posted on his Web site and found Perry on a Sunday afternoon on Siesta Key in front of Entersection Pub on the patio. There he was, at a folding table under a portable tent, wrapping a large order of brisket, ribs, and chicken in aluminum foil for a New York City customer ready to fly home. When it was our turn to order, everything was sold out except a portion of brisket. We took it, Perry sliced it, and it was truly great—moist, tender, and flavorful. Other customers have raved about Perry's chicken and ribs, and we'll be back for that, but on the merits of his brisket alone we can tell Perry knows his way around the barbecue pit.

Washington Perry has been barbecuing for almost 40 years. He learned the basics from his uncle and mother during his growing-up years in Dawson, Georgia.

"I learned how to barbecue the old-fashioned way—out back with a 55-gallon drum and a whole hog," he told us. Perry's longtime dream was to cook and serve the best barbecue possi-

ble. His many enthusiastic fans agree that he has achieved that dream. Perry is glad his barbecue is received so well, but he doesn't rest on his laurels. Like all of the best barbecue pitmasters we know, Perry hasn't stopped learning. "There are always new ideas coming up," he said. "My uncle told me, 'I don't care what you do in life—cooking or whatever—your chief occupation is to always be a student.'"

Perry also emphasized that his mother, Alice Perry, "was everything to my success." During the Perry family's early years in Sarasota, Alice opened a café called Alice's Soul Food. All of the items on Perry's catering menu today are from Alice's original recipes. "She was the one to teach us how to do all that," said Perry.

Perry's Original Roadside BBQ is so named "because that's where it all started—selling barbecue on the roadside," he said. He has a kitchen for preparing catered meals and will cook whole hog for special occasions, but when he's on the road at scheduled locations in Sarasota, the customers want spareribs, brisket, and chicken. "There's not much call for whole hog," he said.

Perry uses his own original recipes for rub and sauce. His rub is a mix of granulated garlic, seasoned salt, black pepper, Old Bay Seasoning, and ground cinnamon. "The cinnamon gives the meat an apple flavor, like it's been cooked with apple wood," Perry said. Perry's Original Roadside BBQ Sauce is made with tomato ketchup, mustard, vinegar, molasses, peppers, sugar, spices, "and LOTS OF LOVE!" His smoke

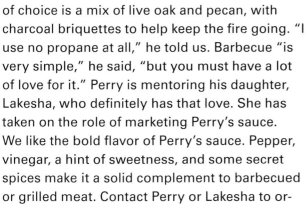

of choice is a mix of live oak and pecan, with charcoal briquettes to help keep the fire going. "I use no propane at all," he told us. Barbecue "is very simple," he said, "but you must have a lot of love for it." Perry is mentoring his daughter, Lakesha, who definitely has that love. She has taken on the role of marketing Perry's sauce. We like the bold flavor of Perry's sauce. Pepper, vinegar, a hint of sweetness, and some secret spices make it a solid complement to barbecued or grilled meat. Contact Perry or Lakesha to order a bottle or a case. We recommend a case, because after you try it you'll want to share it with friends and keep a supply in the cupboard so you won't run out. "We have a lot of fun," Perry told us. Commitment to excellence, lifelong learning, lots of love, and a lot of fun is Perry's winning formula for life and barbecue. We think he's on to something!

Reading Perry's catering menu could inspire a trip to Sarasota to book an Original Roadside catering event. Besides barbecued pulled pork, beef brisket, ribs, and chicken, your choice of sides is black-eyed peas, their famous mac and cheese, collard greens, Brunswick stew, coleslaw, potato salad, fried green tomatoes, fried okra, or corn bread. We didn't get Alice's original recipe for fried okra, but this is a good one.

FRIED OKRA

Serves 6 to 8

Vegetable oil, for deep-frying

1½ pounds whole fresh okra

1 cup self-rising cornmeal

½ cup all-purpose flour

1 teaspoon salt

½ teaspoon black pepper

Preheat a deep-fryer with vegetable oil to 375°F. If you don't have a deep-fryer, you can use a skillet over medium-high heat. Just be sure to use enough oil to cover the okra.

Wash the okra under cold running water and drain well. Prepare the okra for cooking by trimming the tip and stem ends. Cut the okra into ½-inch slices. Set the cut okra aside while you prepare the cornmeal coating.

Combine the cornmeal, flour, salt, and black pepper in a brown paper bag or a resealable plastic bag. Shake the mixture well.

Drop the okra into the bag and shake well to coat it uniformly. Drop the okra into the deep-fryer without crowding and fry until the okra turns golden brown and floats to the top, 6 to 8 minutes. If you're using a skillet, once the okra begins to brown on one side, turn it over and brown on the other side for 3 to 4 minutes total. Once the okra is done, remove it from the oil and drain it on paper towels. Serve warm.

Pecan Pie

BBQ Co
Pull Pork
Cream Corr
Jalapeños
Grated Chees

DESSERT

Fresh Baked
Cobbler 2⁶⁰
With Ice Cream
3²⁵

Homemade!
Bread Pudding
served with
Butter Rum
sauce

$2.00

chocolate
Cake

Apple
Dum

ownies
nd Cak
ana Nu
Bread
$1.95
ERT. ALL BROWNIES HAVE NU

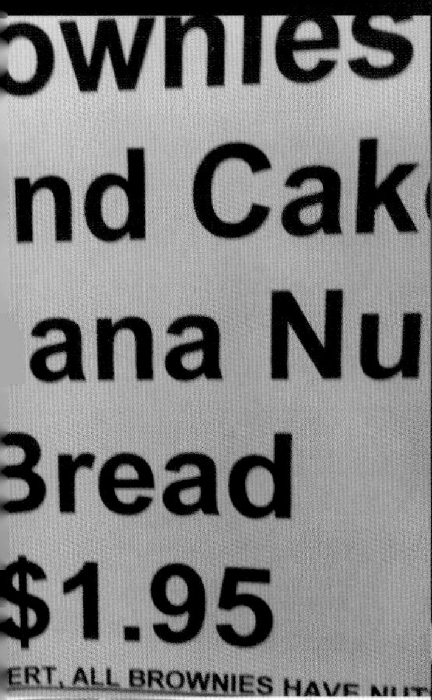

Desserts

It isn't easy to save room for dessert when you're eating great barbecue. That's why many joints don't serve dessert. Some do, however, and the ones we give you here are worth your restraint in the earlier courses of the meal. From banana cream pie to fried peach pie, apple dumplings, homemade vanilla ice cream, and more, they look good, taste good, and will bring you back for more. Desserts needn't complement the menu. They are in a category all their own.

Individual Apple Pies

Boneyard Grill

113 W. Harrison
Guthrie, OK 73044
405-293-9615
http://boneyardgrillguthrie.com/
index.htm

The City of Guthrie, Oklahoma, marks a couple of major milestones in the month of April—one territorial, the other culinary. The Great Land Rush for 2 million acres of land in Oklahoma Territory started at noon on April 22, 1899. Some 50,000 individuals took part in the rush, seeking up to 160 acres apiece that could become theirs through homesteading and improving the property. President Benjamin Harrison was authorized by the U.S. Congress to make the land available to settlers. On that day in April, Guthrie blossomed from uninhabited prairie to a city of 10,000 in only 6 hours.

The great culinary milestone in Guthrie happened on April 6, 2007, when Ralph Mann and Wayne Machtolff opened the original Boneyard Grill on South Division Street. The Boneyard

name was inspired by rib bones from a rib-eating and beer-drinking session with friends of Ralph and Wayne. Today they are going strong in a new, larger restaurant downtown in a spacious, historic brick building on West Harrison.

We liked the Boneyard Grill so much on our first visit that we decided to take a risk and feature them in the first edition of this book. Boneyard's winning combination of ambience, friendly service, quality food, and reasonable prices has proved a success. Boneyard clearly benefits from Ralph and Wayne's prior experience as chefs in other restaurants.

Grilled steaks, pulled pork, ribs, chicken, and honey-pecan crusted catfish are only part of their extensive menu. You have to visit several times to graze through it all. We especially like the ribs, which we clean to the bone. But we always save room for apple pie.

Here's the official Boneyard Grill Apple Pie— the original recipe from Ralph's grandmother, Oma Sczksczeika. Although Boneyard calls these individual apple pies, they can feed 3 or 4 in Ardie's opinion, but then he's not a big dessert person.

INDIVIDUAL APPLE PIES

Makes 2 pies

PASTRY

3 cups all-purpose flour

¼ cup granulated sugar

1½ teaspoons fine sea salt

10 ounces (2½ sticks) unsalted butter, very cold, cubed

⅓ cup all-vegetable shortening, very cold or frozen, cut into small pieces

6 to 7 tablespoons ice water

FILLING

7 cups peeled, cored, and diced apples

2 tablespoons unsalted butter

½ cup packed light brown sugar

½ cup granulated sugar

1½ teaspoons ground cinnamon

¼ teaspoon ground nutmeg

¼ teaspoon ground cloves

⅓ to ½ cup heavy whipping cream

Natural, demerara, or sanding sugar, for sprinkling

Vanilla ice cream, for serving

In a food processor fitted with a metal blade, pulse together the flour, sugar, and salt until well-combined. Add the butter and shortening and pulse a few times, until the butter and shortening pieces are evenly dispersed, with the largest pieces about the size of peas. Be careful not to overmix. Add the ice water, a tablespoon or two at a time, and pulse to combine, until the dough is evenly moistened. Pinch a bit of dough together between two fingers to test. The dough should stick together. If it seems dry, add a few more teaspoons of water and pulse again.

Transfer the pastry to a well-floured work surface and divide in half. Gather each half into a ball, then flatten into a round disk and wrap tightly in plastic wrap. Refrigerate for 1 hour. (If refrigerated longer, you'll need to let the pastry soften slightly before rolling.)

Heat a skillet over medium-heat. Add the apples, butter, sugars, and spices to the pan and stir to combine. Cook until the butter is melted and the apples are just soft but not mushy, 2 to 3 minutes. Remove from the heat and transfer the apple filling to a mixing bowl to cool to room temperature.

Preheat the oven to 375°F. With a floured rolling pin, roll one pastry disk into two rounds 1 inch larger than two upside-down, 5½-inch glass pie plates. Transfer the rounds into the pie plates, pressing firmly against bottom and side. Divide the filling between the shells.

Roll the other pastry disk into two 7-inch rounds. Top each pie with a round, cut slits to vent, and trim, press, and crimp the edges. Brush the top of each pie with whipping cream and sprinkle sugar over the top. Cover the edges with a 2- to 3-inch-wide strip of foil to prevent excessive browning.

Bake for 20 to 30 minutes, until the pies are golden and cooked through. Let cool for 10 minutes on a rack. Serve warm with a scoop of vanilla ice cream.

Apple Crisp

Hole in the Wall Barbecue

3200 W. 11th Ave.
Eugene, OR 97401
541-683-7378
http://www.holeinthewallbbq.com

Hole in the Wall Barbecue is a perfect example of how the craving and desire for good barbecue can move mountains. In 1992, Richard and Linda Becker returned from Arizona to Oregon, where they grew up. "To satisfy our barbecue cravings, we decided to open our own restaurant," they told us. And their lives were changed forever.

Hole in the Wall Barbecue first opened August 2, 1993, for lunch only on weekdays, from 11 a.m. to 2 p.m., and on Fridays and Saturdays until 8 p.m. The menu was limited, with three sandwiches, chili, barbecue beans, potato salad, and coleslaw—all made from scratch. With their ever-growing barbecue and catering business they "bit the bullet" and expanded their hours to 8 p.m. Tuesday through Saturday. They also added St. Louis–style ribs, barbecue chicken, hot links, french fries, and sweet tea, as well as other seasonal items.

Hole in the Wall's reputation has spread far and wide. Paul has enjoyed eating their award-winning barbecue since 1994, when they were only 8 months old. Their outstanding brisket sandwich and barbecue ribs are his favorites, and their award-winning chili is also worth the trip. One of their signature desserts is apple crisp, and as everything else at Hole in the Wall, it's made from scratch.

APPLE CRISP

Serves 8 to 10

FILLING

¾ cup granulated sugar

2 teaspoons ground cinnamon

3 pounds apples, peeled, cored, and sliced

TOPPING

⅓ cup light brown sugar

⅓ cup all-purpose flour

½ teaspoon baking powder

¼ teaspoon baking soda

6 tablespoons butter, frozen

½ cup quick oats

Preheat the oven to 350°F. Combine the granulated sugar and cinnamon in a large bowl and blend well. Add the apples and toss until the apples are well coated.

Mix the brown sugar, flour, baking powder, and baking soda and blend well. Using a metal scraper blade or pastry knife, cut the butter into the flour mixture until it reaches the consistency of peas. Add the quick oats and mix well.

Spray a 9-inch square baking pan with nonstick spray. Add the apple mixture and spread the oat topping evenly over the top. Bake, uncovered, for 20 minutes, rotate the pan, and bake for another 20 minutes, until the topping is golden brown and the apple filling is bubbling.

Apple Dumplings

Rooster's Bar-B-Q

2001 Capps Rd.
Harrison, AR 72601
870-741-5888
http://www.roostersbar-b-q.com/
index.html

One of Rooster's signature desserts is apple dumplings, which are great served topped with cream or ice cream. Here is our version of their trade-secret dumpling.

APPLE DUMPLINGS

Makes 1 dozen

2 to 2½ cups all-purpose flour

2 teaspoons baking powder

1 teaspoon sea salt

¾ cup shortening

½ cup whole milk

4 to 6 Granny Smith or other cooking
   apples, peeled, cored, and sliced

About ½ cup sugar, for
   sprinkling on the apples

Ground cinnamon

Ground nutmeg

8 tablespoons (1 stick) butter,
   cut into small pieces

SYRUP

2 cups sugar

¼ teaspoon ground cinnamon

¼ teaspoon ground nutmeg

2 cups hot water

4 tablespoons butter or
   margarine, melted

Heavy cream or ice cream,
   for serving (optional)

Preheat the oven to 375°F. Lightly grease a 9 by 13-inch baking dish or a 12-cup muffin tin.

Combine the flour, baking powder, and salt in a bowl. Cut in the shortening until the mixture resembles coarse meal. Gradually add the milk, stirring to make a soft dough. Roll the dough into a ⅓-inch-thick rectangle on a lightly floured surface; cut it into twelve 5-inch squares.

Place 3 or 4 slices of apple on each square. Sprinkle each dumpling with 2 teaspoons sugar and a sprinkling of cinnamon and nutmeg to taste; dot with butter. Moisten the edges of each dumpling with water; bring the corners to the center, pinching the edges to seal. Place the dumplings 1 inch apart in the prepared baking dish.

To make the syrup, combine the sugar, cinnamon, nutmeg, hot water, and butter; stir to dissolve the sugar. Pour the syrup over the dumplings and bake for 35 to 45 minutes, until golden brown. Serve hot with cream or ice cream.

Crullers

SMOKE Restaurant

901 Fort Worth Ave.
Dallas, TX 75208
214-393-4141
http://smokerestaurant.com

Our friend Dr. Howard Taylor told us about SMOKE when we were looking for places that serve real barbecue for breakfast. SMOKE serves barbecue for breakfast and more.

When you first step inside, you may think you're underdressed. Is this retro-1940s, white stucco, renovated Belmont Hotel dining room with white tablecloths really a barbecue joint? What put us at ease was the SMOKE-branded butcher paper positioned atop the white tablecloths. The small plates with a pink silhouette of a pig, steer, chicken, or lamb at each setting also put us at ease. And like all real barbecue joints, SMOKE attracts customers of all ages. We're of an older demographic than the young exuberant folks gathered at the bar, but no matter. It's an upscale, friendly barbecue joint.

Although we have yet to enjoy a SMOKE breakfast, we give high marks to what pitmaster/chef/co-owner Tim Byres serves for lunch and dinner. Chef Tim's commitment to the "Bloom Where You Are Planted" national campaign is evident in the food and beverage menus. Texas meat, vegetables, and brews are featured, along with some prized items from other states. Some of SMOKE's vegetables and herbs are grown in a garden behind the hotel. The menu varies seasonally and according to what Chef Tim has dreamed up as an original creation. We hope that some, such as the Pimento Croquettes with Grilled Romaine and the Foie Gras & Chicken Liver Pâté, stay the course. Oysters vary from raw to roasted. Thus far they are from the sea, not the prairie. When you're in a seafood mood, SMOKE will not disappoint. We go for the barbecue, and it's all good. If you arrive early enough to get the Big Rib, don't miss it. Served with hominy casserole and fresh herb chimichurri, it's a Texas classic with a gourmet accent. Chef Tim lends a cowboy campfire twist to another Texas classic with his coffee-cured or -rubbed brisket. The pork spareribs, pulled pork, strip steaks, and pork chops will meet the high standard you expect at SMOKE. And at SMOKE you should always save room for dessert.

Here is Chef Paul's rendition of the churros we enjoyed at SMOKE. Chef Tim's original recipe and a pantry full of other inventive recipes and smoke basics are available in his excellent book, *SMOKE: New Firewood Cooking*.

CRULLERS

Makes about 12

½ cup milk

½ cup water

8 tablespoons (1 stick) unsalted butter

¾ cup sugar

¼ teaspoon kosher salt

1 cup all-purpose flour

3 large eggs

Oil, for deep-frying

1 cup sugar mixed with 1 to 2
   tablespoons ground cinnamon

1½ cups caramel sauce (store-
   bought or homemade)

Sweetened whipped cream,
   for serving (see Note)

Orange marmalade, for garnishing

Bring the milk, water, butter, sugar, and salt to a full sim-mer in a medium saucepan over medium-high heat. Re-duce the heat to low and stir in the flour with a wooden spoon, stirring vigorously until the dough "cleans" the sides of the pot (no longer sticks). Scrape this mixture into a large bowl and use electric beaters or a stand mixer fit-ted with the paddle attachment to beat on medium speed for about 2 minutes to cool it a little. Using the lowest speed on the mixer, add one egg at a time, blending until fully incorporated.

Heat the oil in a deep-fryer to 350°F (or use a deep pot and measure the oil temperature with a deep-frying thermometer).

Fill a piping bag fitted with a large star tip with the batter (you may have to work in batches). Pipe small pieces, 2 to 3 inches long, on lightly greased parchment paper and gently slide them into the oil, trying not to splash, while removing the paper. You can also flip the piped crullers onto a slotted spoon and lower them into the oil.

Fry the crullers for about 2½ minutes, turn, then cook for about 2½ minutes more. Lift the crullers out with a slot-ted spoon and place them on a paper-towel-lined plate to cool. Dust with cinnamon sugar and serve immediately with caramel sauce and whipped cream, garnished with a dab of marmalade.

Note: To make fresh whipped cream, place 1 cup heavy whipping cream in a chilled small glass bowl. Using chilled beaters, beat until it begins to thicken. Add 3 tablespoons confectioners' sugar and ½ teaspoon vanilla extract and beat until soft peaks form.

Peach Cobbler

Allen & Son

6203 Millhouse Rd.
Chapel Hill, NC 27516
919-942-7576

After a long-awaited visit to the Ginger Young Art Gallery, where they added a couple of treasures to their outsider art collection, Ardie and his wife, Gretchen, told Ginger that their next stop was Allen & Son for lunch. Ginger said, "Oh, yes! That's one of our favorite places." She assured them they were in for a delicious lunch and asked them to give proprietor Keith Allen her hello.

Before eating lunch, Ardie and Gretchen wanted to visit with Keith. "He's out back" was the answer. Out back is a working woodpile of huge hickory logs in various states of preparation to become charcoal for cooking some of the best barbecued pork shoulders in the world. A long rectangular building houses the pits on one end and a kitchen/prep room on the other. There was also the unmistakable chopping sound Ardie and Gretchen had become accustomed to already, only two days into their North Carolina barbecue tour.

The man doing the chopping was Keith Allen, the son in Allen & Son. Tall, rugged, handsome, and strong as an ox, Mr. Allen gave Ardie and Gretchen a friendly reception. This is a pitmaster with a passion for serving top-quality barbecue.

How he does it isn't easy. "People come here and want to learn how I do it," he said. "But they don't last long." After a few days of getting up at the crack of dawn and doing barbecue the Keith Allen way, they burn out and leave. Doing barbecue eastern North Carolina style as Keith Allen does it demands strength, know-how, long hours, time management, and serious dedication to excellence in barbecue. Keith has all of that. Here is some of what he gets done in a day:

Keeps a steady supply of hardwood on hand

Keeps a steady supply of pork shoulders and other kitchen supplies for made-from-scratch sauce, sides, and desserts

Keeps a steady supply of hot coals at the ready for shoveling under the shoulders every half hour

Saws and chops wood into pieces small enough to fit into his charcoal pit

Converts wood into charcoal

Schedules and plans catering jobs

Chops cooked shoulders for serving

During the 30-minute periods between coal shoveling, he'll be doing a variety of tasks such as making cobblers, making homemade ice cream, preparing sauce or sides—all that and more. Yet, if you catch him at the right

PEACH COBBLER

Serves 6

8 tablespoons (1 stick) butter

2 cups sugar

1 teaspoon ground cinnamon

1 cup all-purpose flour

½ teaspoon salt

1 tablespoon baking powder

1 cup milk

3 generous cups peeled and sliced peaches, with their juices

Preheat the oven to 350°F. Place the butter in a 9 by 13-inch baking dish and place the dish in the preheating oven. In a small bowl, combine ½ cup of the sugar with the cinnamon and mix well. Set aside. In a medium bowl, sift together the flour, the remaining 1½ cups sugar, the salt, and the baking powder. Blend in the milk, stirring just until the mixture forms a batter. When the butter in the baking dish has melted, remove the dish from the oven and pour the batter into it. Spoon the peaches and their juice on top of the batter and sprinkle with the reserved sugar and cinnamon mixture. Bake for 35 to 45 minutes, until the peaches are bubbling. As the cobbler bakes, the batter will rise up around the peaches. Remove from the oven and allow to cool for about 20 minutes before serving.

time, he is willing to visit with strangers and answer questions.

Allen & Son has a friendly homestyle feel to it. Nothing fancy. A mix of tables and chairs perhaps recruited from yard sales, flea markets, friends, and neighbors. The cinder-block walls are a green color reminiscent of Starnes in Paducah, Kentucky. Pig stuff and a few photos adorn the walls. Brunswick stew, chopped pork, coleslaw, fries, hushpuppies, and iced tea, with peach cobbler topped with homemade vanilla ice cream, made one of the best barbecue feasts Ardie and Gretchen had enjoyed over the years. Just a touch of the homemade vinegar-based sauce with melted butter, pepper, and other spices is a delicious complement to the sweet, smoky pork. The fries aren't stiff like fast-food fries, but they are delicious. Keith told us the basics of how he makes the cobblers, and we're sharing our own similar version here. Our hats are off to Keith Allen. He does North Carolina proud.

Fried Pies

A&R Bar-B-Que

1802 Elvis Presley Blvd.
Memphis, TN 38106
901-774-7444
http://www.aandrbbq.com

There are two other A&R locations in Memphis, but our favorite has always been on Elvis Presley Boulevard. The first four times we ate there, we were so full from the heavenly chopped barbecue pork sandwiches topped with coleslaw that there was no room for dessert. Lately we've saved room for the homemade crescent-shaped fried pies, and they're so good we now make it a regular practice to save room for fried pie. Sometimes we get it for carryout for later enjoyment, but we don't leave A&R without one unless they're sold out. Like the restaurant, there's nothing fancy about these pies, but the flaky fried piecrust enveloping a filling of your choice—peach, apple, sweet potato—is a treat not to be missed.

To our knowledge, no one has explained why fried pies settled in Tennessee and Arkansas barbecue houses. True, you'll find them in non-barbecue houses elsewhere, including mass-produced versions at fast-food places, but the true southern fried pie is best enjoyed in Tennessee and Arkansas. Some of the finest we've had are at A&R in Memphis.

FRIED PEACH PIES

Makes 10 to 12

2¼ cups all-purpose flour

1 teaspoon salt

½ cup shortening or lard

½ cup milk

1 (21-ounce) can peach pie filling

1 cup vegetable oil or
   shortening, for frying

To make the crust: In a large bowl, mix together the flour and salt. Cut in the shortening until the mixture is crumbly. Mix in the milk and stir until the dough forms a ball. Roll out the dough and cut it into ten to twelve 6-inch circles. Set aside.

Put the oil or shortening in a small, deep skillet over medium heat (350°F if using a thermometer). Spoon equal amounts of filling into each pastry circle and fold in half. Seal the pastry with a fork dipped in cold water.

Fry the pies one at a time in the hot oil, browning them on both sides, 7 to 10 minutes. Drain the pies on paper towels.

Note: Use fresh oil or shortening for frying. Otherwise, flavors from previously fried fish, onion rings, or fries will be absorbed in your piecrust.

Root Beer Cake

Joe's Real B-B-Q

301 N. Gilbert Rd.
Gilbert, AZ 85234
480-503-3805
http://www.joesrealbbq.com

he barbecue at Joe's Real B-B-Q is pure Texas and has attracted a large following. We recommend starting with the sampler plate of ribs, chicken, beef, and pork, with a side of cheesy potatoes and pit beans. Root beer aficionados won't be disappointed with Joe's real root beer on tap or with this recipe they generously shared with us.

JOE'S REAL B-B-Q ROOT BEER CAKE

Serves 12

CAKE

10 ounces (2½ sticks) butter

1¼ cups root beer (Joe's or your favorite)

2½ tablespoons cocoa powder

2¼ cups (4 ounces) miniature marshmallows

2½ cups granulated sugar

2½ cups all-purpose flour

1½ teaspoons baking powder

1½ teaspoons baking soda

2½ to 3 large eggs

½ cup plus 2 tablespoons buttermilk

1 tablespoon vanilla extract

FROSTING

3 tablespoons butter

⅓ cup root beer (Joe's or your favorite)

2¼ teaspoons cocoa powder

4 cups (12.8 ounces) sifted powdered sugar

⅓ cup chopped pecans

Preheat the oven to 300°F and put a rack in the middle. Grease a 9 by 13-inch baking dish.

To make the cake, bring the butter, root beer, cocoa powder, and marshmallows to a boil in a large saucepan over medium heat. Cook, stirring, just until the marshmallows melt. Remove the pan from the heat and set it aside.

In the bowl of a stand mixer, combine the sugar, flour, baking powder, and baking soda. Pour in the hot butter mixture and mix for 5 minutes on medium speed, until well combined. Add the eggs, buttermilk, and vanilla and mix for 5 more minutes, until smooth. Pour the batter into the prepared pan and bake for about 1 hour or until a skewer or toothpick inserted in the middle of the cake comes out clean.

During the last few minutes the cake is baking, make the frosting. Combine the butter, root beer, and cocoa powder in a medium saucepan and bring it to a boil over medium heat. Add the powdered sugar and mix until smooth. Stir in the pecans. Pour the hot frosting over the hot cake and spread it evenly with a spatula. Let the cake cool for at least an hour before slicing and serving it.

Lexington Banana Pudding

Speedy's Barbecue, Inc.

1317 Winston Rd.
Lexington, NC 27295
336-248-2410 or 336-248-2092
http://speedysbbqinc.com

Lexington is the pork barbecue capital of America to many—but don't include Memphians among them. All barbecue aficionados, however, agree that Lexington has earned a prominent spot on America's best barbecue map. Wayne Monk, the dean of Lexington barbecue, deserves a great deal of credit for Lexington's famous 'cue. Thanks to that fame, although Wayne's barbecue is still the hallmark, he has some outstanding competition, and Speedy's is among them. Speedy's, in our judgment, is a necessary stopping place for swine dining if you're anywhere within 100 miles or more of Lexington.

You can tell by the look of the building and by the logo—a pig on skates with a tray of barbecue—that Speedy's has a history as a drive-in. Today it's a dine-in or carryout joint. Wood-paneled walls, booths and tables, miscellaneous movie posters on the walls—it is by no means fancy. The ambience, service, and food, however, are laudable. This family business, owned and operated by brothers Roy and Boyd Dunn, puts the emphasis on what they call "the 3-Qs: Quality, Quantity & Quick Service."

Our chopped pork sandwich with coleslaw, hushpuppies, and fries was outstanding. We got regular chopped, unlike the diners next to us, who made sure the server understood they wanted theirs chopped "extra fine." That's how they got it, and judging from their body language, the Boyd brothers had once again lived up to their 3-Qs motto.

The banana pudding is homemade, and it is one of the best we had in North Carolina. That being said, we regret that we couldn't get the exact recipe. Paul came up with one that is sure to please and reminds us of what we had at Speedy's, plus meringue.

SPEEDY'S BARBECUE, INC

BEST BARBECUE IN LEXINGTON

(336) 248-2410   (336) 248-2092

BARBECUE

Barbecue Sandwiches		Barbecue Plates	
Chopped	3.15	Chopped	
Sliced	3.30	Sliced	
Coarse Chopped	3.45	Coarse Chopped	

(Skin 75¢ extra on BBQ Sandwiches)

(Served with slaw, french fries, SA rolls or hushpuppies)

"Quality plus Quantity spells SPEEDY'S BBQ"

BAKED BEANS
POTATO SALAD
BANANA PUDDING

LEXINGTON BANANA PUDDING

Serves 8

½ cup plus 6 tablespoons sugar

Pinch of salt

3 tablespoons all-purpose flour

4 large eggs, 3 separated, the whites set aside at room temperature

2 cups whole milk

40 to 50 vanilla wafers

3 to 4 ripe bananas, sliced

½ teaspoon cream of tartar

Preheat the oven to 375°F.

Blend ½ cup of the sugar with the salt and flour. Add the whole egg and the 3 yolks and mix. Stir in the milk. Cook in the top of a double boiler over boiling water, stirring with a wire whisk until thickened. Remove from the heat and cool.

In a 1½-quart baking dish, arrange a layer of whole vanilla wafers, a layer of sliced bananas, and a layer of custard. Continue, making 3 layers of each.

To make the meringue, put the egg whites and cream of tartar into a stainless-steel or copper bowl. Using a wire whisk, whip to medium-soft peaks. Beat in the 6 tablespoons sugar and continue to beat until the egg whites are glossy and hold a firm peak. Spread the meringue over the banana mixture, being sure to seal it to the edges of the baking dish.

Transfer the baking dish to the oven and bake until the meringue is browned, 10 to 12 minutes. Chill and serve cold.

BARBEFEUDS: JUSTICE AND THE PITS

We like to think that barbecue brings more people together than it pulls apart, but that's not always the case. Barbecue is no stranger to civil and criminal courts—more the former than the latter, thank goodness. Here are a couple of notable civil cases we've heard about:

Bozo the Clown sued Bozo's Hot Pit Bar-B-Q over the name. The court battle lasted for several years, with Thomas Jefferson Williams, nickname "Bozo," of Bozo's Hot Pit Bar-B-Q emerging as the winner. He had the nickname and named his barbecue joint after it in 1923, before Bozo the Clown, aka Larry Harmon, came along in 1949. The two Bozos were in court again in 1982 in a dispute over whether Bozo's barbecue could trademark its name nationally. The courts said yes.

Smokaroma vs. the United States of America. This company in Boley, Oklahoma, manufactures a barbecue cooker that is part pressure cooker/part smoker. It doesn't comply with the official U.S. government definition of barbecue, and the feds won't budge.

Bananas Foster

Danna's Bar-B-Que & Burger Shop
963 State Hwy. 165
Branson, MO 65737
417-272-1945

We hesitated when we saw the big bold yellow sign at Danna's that says, "Best Burgers in Branson." Could we trust the barbecue in this place? Short answer: Yes! Don't worry about the "burger" in Danna's name or the burgers on the menus of other Branson barbecue joints. In a town that attracts so many tourists, if you don't have America's favorite fast food, you'll lose customers. Burgers were on the menu at every barbecue joint we checked in Branson. Fried burgers, not smoked or charcoal grilled.

Danna's interior decor is what we call Ozark funky. Old-fashioned signs, pig art, old arcade machines, assorted wooden tables and chairs, high ceilings, and the buzz of happy customers give the place a welcome feel.

Saturday is Ardie's traditional day for a lunchtime fried burger. It goes back to his childhood, when his mother fried burgers every Saturday for the family lunch. He ordered a Danna burger as a side dish to ribs, pulled pork, chicken, beans, fries, and slaw. The former Split-T charcoal-grilled burger with onion and mayo in Oklahoma City is still Ardie's all-time favorite, but Danna's served him one of the best fried burgers he's ever eaten, except the ones his mother served, of course.

Danna's spareribs and pulled pork are winners on appearance, tenderness, and taste—easy to chew, not too heavy on the smoke. The chicken was our favorite—smoky, tender, juicy, and flavorful. If you have to turn down the fries, beans, and slaw to save room for dessert, do it. Although the apple dumpling and Kentucky bourbon pecan pie are memorable, treat yourself to bananas Foster first.

One might ask why a dessert as elegant as bananas Foster at a barbecue joint. That's easy to answer. Any recipe using bananas is a great complement to barbecue. Banana pudding is traditionally served at almost every barbecue joint in the Carolinas, including Speedy's (see page 181). Then there's the fantastic banana cream pie at Big Bob Gibson in Decatur, Alabama (see page 184).

This isn't Danna's secret recipe, but we think you'll like it, and it makes an impressive tableside presentation.

BANANAS FOSTER

Serves 4

4 tablespoons butter

1 cup light brown sugar

½ teaspoon ground cinnamon

¼ cup banana liqueur

4 bananas, peeled, cut in half lengthwise, and halved

¼ cup Myers dark rum

4 scoops vanilla ice cream, homemade (see page 189) or store-bought

Combine the butter, brown sugar, and cinnamon in a flambé pan or skillet. Place the pan over low heat either on an alcohol burner or on top of the stove and cook, stirring, until the sugar dissolves.

Stir in the banana liqueur and then place the bananas in the pan. When the banana sections soften and begin to brown, after 3 to 4 minutes, carefully add the rum. Continue to cook the sauce until the rum is hot; then tip the pan slightly to ignite the rum.

When the flames subside, lift the bananas out of the pan and place 4 pieces over each portion of ice cream. Generously spoon the warm sauce over the top of the ice cream and serve immediately.

Banana Cream Pie

Big Bob Gibson Bar-B-Q

2520 Danville Rd., Southwest
Decatur, AL 35603
256-350-0404
http://www.bigbobgibson.com

e've known and admired Don McLemore and Chris Lilly and their families for years. Don, grandson of the late Big Bob Gibson, and Chris, Don's son-in-law, are well known on the barbecue competition circuit as well as in the barbecue restaurant industry. Chris has produced and starred in a series of barbecue instructional videos, as well as co-hosting in a cable TV series. Don, Chris, their spouses, and extended family make you feel like family when you enter their contest cooking area or their restaurants.

continued on page 186

BANANA CREAM PIE

Serves 8

PIECRUST

1¼ cups all-purpose flour

1 teaspoon sea salt

1 tablespoon sugar

3 tablespoons vegetable shortening or lard, chilled

4 tablespoons unsalted butter, cut into ¼-inch pieces

4 to 5 tablespoons ice water

CREAM FILLING

½ cup sugar

¼ cup cornstarch

¼ teaspoon sea salt

5 large egg yolks, lightly beaten (reserve 4 whites for the meringue)

2 cups whole milk

½ cup evaporated milk

1 to 2 teaspoons vanilla extract

2 tablespoons unsalted butter

2 medium firm-ripe bananas, sliced into ¼- to ½-inch-thick rounds

MERINGUE TOPPING

1 tablespoon cornstarch

⅓ cup water

¼ teaspoon cream of tartar

½ cup superfine sugar

4 egg whites, at room temperature

½ teaspoon vanilla extract

To make the crust, process the flour, salt, and sugar in a food processor until combined. Add the shortening and process until the mixture has the texture of coarse sand, 10 to 12 seconds. Scatter the butter pieces into the flour and process until the mixture is pale yellow and has the texture of coarse crumbs, with butter pieces no larger than a small pea, ten to twelve 1-second pulses. Turn the mixture into a medium bowl.

Sprinkle ¼ cup of the ice water over the mixture. Using a rubber spatula, fold the mixture a few times. Press down on the dough with the spatula to see if the dough sticks together. Add 1 more tablespoon of ice water if needed and then fold and test again. When the dough holds together, flatten the dough into a 4-inch disk. Wrap in wax paper or plastic wrap and refrigerate for at least 1 hour or overnight.

Remove the dough from the refrigerator and let it come to room temperature. Roll the dough on a lightly floured surface or between sheets of plastic wrap or parchment paper to a 12-inch circle. Roll the dough over the top of your rolling pin and transfer it to a 9-inch pie plate. Work the dough down the sides to the middle of the plate, gently pressing it into the bottom of the pan. Trim the edges to extend about ½ inch beyond the edge of the pan. Fold that excess ½ inch of dough under itself; pinch the dough to flute it or use the tines of a fork to flatten the dough against the rim of the pie plate. Refrigerate for about an hour to firm up the dough.

Preheat the oven to 375°F and place a rack in the center. Remove the pie plate from the refrigerator. Place a doubled 12-inch square of aluminum foil over the dough and press down.

Fill the foil with 2 cups dried beans or ceramic or metal pie weights. Bake for 25 to 30 minutes, or until the crust is a light golden color under the foil. Carefully remove the weights and foil and continue baking until the dough is light brown, 7 to 8 minutes. Remove from the oven and cool on a wire rack.

To make the filling, whisk the sugar, cornstarch, and salt together in a medium saucepan. Add the egg yolks, then immediately but gradually whisk in the milk and evaporated milk. Cook over medium heat, stirring constantly, until the mixture thickens and begins to simmer, 8 to 10 minutes. Cook for another minute, stirring constantly. Remove the pan from the heat and whisk in the vanilla and butter.

Pour the filling into a heatproof bowl and press a sheet of plastic wrap against the top of the filling to prevent a skin from forming; cool for 20 to 30 minutes. Pour half of the filling into the cooled baked piecrust. Top with the banana slices and then the remaining filling. Place another piece of plastic wrap directly on the filling. Refrigerate for at least 3 hours, until completely chilled.

Preheat the oven to 350°F.

To make the meringue, mix the cornstarch with the water in a small saucepan; bring to a boil, whisking as it comes to a boil. Continue whisking until the mixture becomes translucent, then remove from the heat. In a small bowl, mix the cream of tartar and sugar together. Place the egg whites and vanilla in a medium stainless-steel or copper bowl and beat them until frothy. Beat in the sugar mixture, 1 tablespoon at a time, until all of the sugar mixture is incorporated and the whole mixture forms soft peaks. Beat in the cornstarch mixture 1 tablespoon at a time and continue beating until it's incorporated and stiff peaks form.

Remove the pie from the refrigerator and remove the plastic wrap. Top with the meringue, forming peaks. Place the pie in the oven and bake for 12 to 14 minutes, until the meringue is set and the meringue begins to turn golden brown. Cool before serving.

on the Food Network site, but we recommend the real sauce from the restaurant. You can get it by calling or ordering online.

Big Bob Gibson's has a reputation for great barbecue and great pies. Whenever we go to a barbecue contest and we know that Big Bob Gibson is entered, after all the pleasantries have been exchanged and the right opportunity presents itself, we ask Carolyn and Don McLemore, "Did you bring pies?" And most of the time Carolyn will say with a smile, "Why, yes we did, and we will be serving some about seven o'clock. Please stop by."

continued from page 184

Big Bob Gibson's Alabama white barbecue sauce has been famous since 1925. In recent years Don and Chris have added some award-winning tomato-based sauces to the Big Bob Gibson lineup. Their impressive wins at Memphis in May, the American Royal, and other major contests give them bragging rights that are second to none—but their humility and southern hospitality trump any bravado.

You can get the recipe for Big Bob Gibson's grilled chicken breast with white sauce from its Web site, and the white sauce recipe is posted

Big Bob Gibson presents a real dilemma when you go to one of the restaurants. Do you save room for dessert and order less barbecue or order the usual amount of barbecue and hope to have room for a slice of the fabulous pie? Believe us, this is a real problem. Rather than repeat the chicken and sauce recipes, we wanted to treat you with a famous Big Bob Gibson signature pie, but that's a trade secret to be kept within the family. When you can't enjoy pie at a Big Bob Gibson restaurant or cooking contest, we know you'll like this one.

BIG BOB GIBSON'S BAR-B-Q
1721 Bee-Line 31 So. East — Ph. EL 3-9935

186

Mud Pigs

Southern Girls BBQ Roadshow

The mission of Vernee Green-Myers and Kellie Henry—the Southern Girls BBQ Roadshow—is to travel throughout the southern United States on assignment for the *National Barbecue News* and report on all things barbecue—contests, restaurants, backyard barbecues, pitmasters, and fantastic recipes. When we told them about mud pigs, they searched far and wide for some on their beat, to no avail. Undaunted, they decided to make their own mud pigs. Theirs were so good that friends and relatives started coming out of the woodwork as if the Girls had won the lottery! We begged them to share their recipe with us. We've been asked,

"ARE MUD PIGS BETTER THAN SEX?"

We think what Cheryl Litman (see page 58) used to say about barbecue is the best reply:

"IT DEPENDS ON WHO MADE THE MUD PIGS AND WHO YOU'RE HAVING SEX WITH."

MUD PIGS

Makes 13 to 15 pieces

1 pound thick-sliced bacon (preferably Hormel Black Label thick-sliced or thick-sliced cherry wood smoked)

1 (11-ounce) bag Nestlé Peanut Butter & Milk Chocolate Morsels

1 (12-ounce) bag Ghirardelli Chocolate Dark Melting Wafers

1 tablespoon coconut oil (refined, so no fragrance)

Cook the bacon until crisp, then drain on paper towels and set aside to cool completely.

Bring water to a boil in the bottom of a double boiler. Melt the peanut butter and chocolate chips in the top. Immediately turn the heat to low and stir to maintain a smooth consistency.

Dip or brush the melted chips onto each slice of bacon, leaving 1 inch uncovered to use as a handle to hold the bacon while eating. (The Girls use a silicone sauce brush after dipping to help fill the cracks and crannies of the bacon.) Place on wax paper to set. (If you use two double boilers and want to speed things up, you can place the dipped bacon in the freezer for about 1 minute to set faster.)

Melt the dark chocolate and coconut oil in a clean double boiler. Dip or brush the chocolate onto the bacon about halfway up the peanut butter and chocolate mixture so both colors show. Place on wax paper to set before serving.

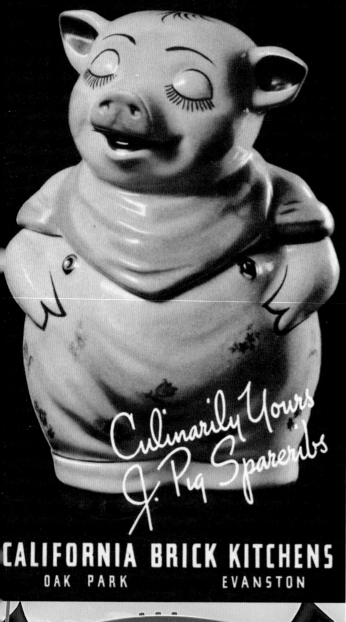

Ice Cream

Stamey's

2206 High Point Rd.
Greensboro, NC
336-299-9888
http://www.stameys.com

We've heard so much good talk about Stamey's Barbecue that we had to try it. And why not try it with friends in Greensboro who are barbecue experts and have eaten at Stamey's for years? David Bailey, senior editor of *O. Henry* magazine and one of the most refreshing, entertaining, and informative barbecue bloggers of all, said, "Let's meet at the Stamey's across from the Coliseum." We met him there, with his wife, Anne, for a memorable feast of chopped pork, slaw, beans, fries, Brunswick stew, iced tea, and peach cobbler topped with homemade ice cream.

It's no wonder the pit crew at Stamey's has mastered the art of hickory-smoked pork shoulder barbecue. The Stamey legacy goes back to when founder C. Warner Stamey lived in Lexington and learned barbecue from local experts Sid Weaver and Jess Swicegood when he was in high school. By 1930 Warner was out of high school, had returned to his hometown of Shelby, and started selling barbecue there. Greensboro became his chosen city in 1953, and Stamey's has been a community fixture ever since, now with two locations.

David Bailey has a genuine gift with words. We asked him for a quote about Stamey's.

ICE CREAM

Makes about 6 cups

4 large eggs

2 cups sugar

1 (14-ounce) can sweetened
    condensed milk

1 (10½-ounce) can evaporated milk

¼ teaspoon salt

2 tablespoons vanilla extract

Milk, 2% or whole, if desired

Beat the eggs well in a large bowl. Add the sugar, condensed milk, evaporated milk, salt, and vanilla, beating well. Pour the mixture into an ice-cream freezer. You can add a little milk if desired until the mixture is 2 to 4 inches from the top of the freezer can. If you add the milk, mix thoroughly. Follow your ice-cream freezer manufacturer's instructions for freezing the ice cream.

Note: If the freezer stops or hangs up, add about ½ cup or so of water to the ice-cream mixture to aid in thawing, enough so it begins to turn freely.

Variation: You can mix about 4 cups of sweetened fresh fruit (your choice) into the mixture just before you transfer it to the ice-cream freezer.

Here's what he gave us: "I've been eating Stamey's since my daddy first took me to the big city of Greensboro and my mama gave me a spit bath after I'd made a mess of myself and my Sunday-go-to-meeting clothes. It's every bit as good today as it was way back then—consistent, clean, classic, with a sauce that demonstrates that a little bit of ketchup's not a bad thing. If you don't think they use hickory, just sniff the air, look at the woodpile out back, and get your taste buds checked by your doctor."

We couldn't get an original Stamey's recipe, but this recipe has served us well, and you'll know why when you try it.

Pop's Salt Lick Sundae

The Salt Lick Bar-B-Q

18001 FM 1826
Driftwood, TX 78619
512-858-4959
http://www.saltlickbbq.com

Driving along the rural road between Dripping Springs and Austin, Texas, most people would not expect to happen upon a world-class barbecue joint standing by itself in a cattle pasture sprinkled with post oak and large Texas-size shade trees. But there it is, made of limestone and timber, fitting perfectly into the landscape. Out back the gravel parking lot covering several acres of former pasture hints at how popular this joint is. The picnic shelter waiting area outside the restaurant entrance also tells you that this joint is no stranger to crowds.

The Salt Lick Bar-B-Q is a destination. Few customers just happen upon it. The huge parking lot fills up with busloads of tourists and carloads of locals from nearby Dripping Springs and Austin 7 days a week. You may have to wait, but you'll get a table.

Imagine a bunch of wood-beamed picnic shelters stuck together, but with walls and screens instead of open air. Add a round stone holding pit inside the entrance, loaded with barbecue meats that look so good you want to grab a bite right now. Add a reception desk with cash register, shelves of sauce, shirts, and gimme hats for sale, busy servers taking orders and delivering orders, picnic tables filled with people enjoying the bar-

becue and filling the air with laughter, animated gestures, and gustatory exclamations, and you've found the Salt Lick. It is living proof that barbecue attracts people the way salt licks—blocks of solid salt placed in pastures and woods—attract deer, cattle, and other furry critters.

In hunting season a salt lick can prove dangerous for deer. People attracted to the Salt Lick Bar-B-Q get a much better deal. They feast on tender, lean, juicy mesquite-smoked barbecued beef brisket, pork ribs, chicken, sausage, and/or turkey, with sides of potato salad, coleslaw, beans, bread, pickles, and onions. You get full, satisfied, with reasonable hopes to live another day, and your wallet doesn't take a beating. Be sure to bring cash. The Salt Lick doesn't take credit cards. Excellent Texas barbecue at reasonable prices. Fast, friendly service. Ambience galore.

Hold it! We should have warned you up front to save room for dessert. The homemade pecan pie and the peach cobbler à la mode are not to be missed. If you're adventuresome, however, try a dessert that is not on the menu that you can make for yourself at your table. Mind you, this is not an official Salt Lick menu item. It is the invention of Ken Wilson, jewelry maker and postcard collector/dealer, in Dripping Springs. Ken's grandchildren call him "Pops." Ardie and his wife, Gretchen, have enjoyed several delightful feasts at the Salt Lick with Ken, his wife, Debbie Little-Wilson, artist/print maker with a special interest in women's suffrage and cowgirl themes, and Mary Fischer, ceramics artist who is famous for her ceramic houses. Each time, Ken finishes his meal with a scoop of Blue Bunny ice cream, topped with some

117
2/28/06
Ken saucing his ice cream @ The Salt Lick. He said it's delicious!
Ice Cream

The Salt Lick
BBQ

original Salt Lick Bar-B-Q Sauce. We call it Pops's Salt Lick Sundae. Debbie has tried it and likes it. Gretchen, Mary, and Ardie haven't yet, but maybe on another visit! Since up to now Ardie's favorite unusual barbecue sauce combo has been McClard's barbecue sauce on fresh cantaloupe, Salt Lick sauce on ice cream oughta be no problem. Make sure you use Salt Lick sauce. You can get it at the restaurant, online, and at gourmet stores and supermarkets.

POP'S SALT LICK SUNDAE

Serves 1

2 scoops vanilla ice cream

¼ cup Salt Lick Original Bar-B-Q sauce—no substitutions

Put the ice cream in a sundae vessel or bowl, top with barbecue sauce, and enjoy.

Bread Pudding with Whiskey Sauce

The County Line Bar-B-Q

6500 Bee Cave Rd.
Austin, TX 78746
512-327-1742
http://www.countyline.com

We've never been disappointed at any of the County Line locations, although we're partial to the original. The view of metropolitan Austin, the roadhouse history, and the rustic woodsy Texas Cowboy Country Club ambience feel right to us.

Before you sate your appetite on those gargantuan barbecued beef ribs the County Line is famous for, stop yourself. You have to save room for dessert—especially the bread pudding with whiskey sauce. Portions are big enough for two or more, so go easy or plan to take some home.

Legend has it that this former roadhouse is haunted by the ghost of a young woman who lost her life there years ago. We think we saw her about 5 minutes after we cleaned the last remnants of our whiskey sauce from the plate!

The County Line has their "Mom's Bread Pudding Recipe" online. Here's our version, which is similar and slightly easier to make. Our whiskey sauce is adapted from the County Line's recipe.

BREAD PUDDING WITH WHISKEY SAUCE

Serves 6 to 8

2 cups cream, half-and-half, or whole milk

4 tablespoons unsalted butter

¾ cup granulated sugar

3 large eggs

1 tablespoon ground cinnamon

½ teaspoon ground nutmeg

1 teaspoon vanilla extract

3 cups bread torn into small pieces (French bread works best)

½ cup raisins or berries (optional)

TENNESSEE WHISKEY SAUCE

1 pound (4 sticks) Grade A butter

2¼ cups packed light brown sugar, no clumps

1 cup heavy whipping cream

¼ cup Jack Daniel's Tennessee Whiskey (your choice of Black Label, Green Label, Single Barrel, or Gentleman Jack) (no substitutes)

Preheat your oven to 350°F and place a rack in the center. In a medium saucepan over medium heat, heat the cream just until a film forms over the top. Add the butter to the cream, stirring until the butter is melted. Cool to lukewarm.

In a mixing bowl, combine the granulated sugar, eggs, cinnamon, nutmeg, and vanilla. Beat with an electric mixer at medium speed for 1 minute. Slowly add the cream mixture to the sugar mixture.

Place the bread in a lightly greased 1½-quart casserole dish. Sprinkle with raisins or berries if desired. Pour the batter on top of bread. Bake for 45 to 50 minutes, until set.

While the bread pudding is baking, make the whiskey sauce. Melt the butter in a clean, heavy stainless-steel pan over medium heat. Be careful not to burn the butter. Slowly add the brown sugar, stirring constantly with a wooden spoon until the sugar is dissolved and the mixture is smooth and hot but not simmering. Simmering or boiling will make the sauce too thick, so avoid too much heat. Slowly add the heavy whipping cream, stirring as you add it. Blend well and remove from the heat. Add the Jack Daniel's whiskey and whip it into the sauce, mixing well. Pour a generous portion atop the finished bread pudding and lick the pan clean!

OUR FAVORITE BARBECUE RESTAURANTS

ARDIE'S TOP 10

1. Franklin Barbecue—Austin, TX

2. Arthur Bryant's Barbecue—Kansas City, MO

3. Snow's BBQ—Lexington, TX

4. Louie Mueller Barbecue—Taylor, TX

5. Oklahoma Joe's Bar-B-Que—Broken Arrow, OK

6. Johnny Harris Restaurant & Barbecue Sauce Company—Savannah, GA

7. Arapahoe Café & Pub/Bonnie Q BBQ—Dillon, CO

8. Allen & Son—Chapel Hill, NC

9. Smoque—Chicago, IL

10. Back Door Barbecue—Oklahoma City, OK

PAUL'S TOP 10

1. The Dixie Pig—Blytheville, AR

2. Coopers Bar-B-Q & Grill—Junction, TX

3. Lillie's Q—Chicago, IL

4. Franklin Barbecue—Austin, TX

5. Oklahoma Joe's Bar-B-Que—Broken Arrow, OK

6. Arthur Bryant's Barbecue—Kansas City, MO

7. Snow's BBQ—Lexington, TX

8. Joe's Kansas City Bar-B-Que—Kansas City, KS

9. Louie Mueller Barbecue—Taylor, TX

10. Smoque—Chicago, IL

LEGACY RECIPES

Red's Barbecued 'Coon

Ira Ray "Red" Gill
Razorback Cookers Catering
Blytheville, AR

Ira Ray "Red" Gill was born in the very small town of Dell, Arkansas, in 1928. He used to say that the only way the population ever went up was when someone was born and the only way it went down was when someone died. Ray died on June 3, 2003, in Blytheville, Arkansas, at age seventy-five.

Ray was one of the most colorful characters we have ever met on the barbecue trail, and it had nothing to do with his red hair. He was short in stature and a teller of tall tales, a rodeo clown, a brahma bull rider, a jack of all trades, and one hell of a good barbecuer. Besides being a legend on the barbecue circuit, he was asked to cater President Clinton's first inaugural party.

Ray was a World War II and Korean War veteran, serving in both the U.S. Army and the U.S. Air Force. After his military career, Ray settled in Blytheville, Arkansas, with his wife, Eva Lannum Gill. He loved barbecue and had been doing it all his life, so naturally he established a barbecue catering business, Razorback Cookers Catering. By age thirty-seven Ray had been honored by the Jaycees as one of the Outstanding Young Men of America.

In 1986, at the age of fifty-eight, Ray formed the River City Spice Company. Inspired by great-grandfather William Thomas Gill, Ray adapted some secret family recipes into a line of barbecue seasonings and sauces (which you can order at http://www.rivercityspice.com). River City Barbecue Products was born, branded as Razorback Bar-B-Q. Razorback products and the Razorback cooking team established a winning reputation in the worldwide barbecue contest network.

Ireland, Scotland, Wales, and twenty-six states in the United States have awarded Red and his son, Ray Alan, and the Razorback Cookers championships, including World's Best Barbecue Sauce, World's Best Baby Back Ribs, Best Ribs in the World, Virginia Invitational World Barbecue contest, Best in the West . . . the list goes on. The Memphis in May World Championship Barbecue Cooking Contest committee awarded Ray a plaque that reads: "To Red Gill and his Razorback Cookers, A great showman and the World's Best Barbecue and Pork promoter."

Ray will be remembered for his clever way with words. Here are some of his great sayings:

"SERVE NO SWINE BEFORE ITS TIME; SERVE NO BEEF AT ANY TIME."

"GOOD FOOD AIN'T CHEAP. CHEAP FOOD AIN'T GOOD!"

195

> "YOU GOTTA START WITH GOOD MEAT AND YOU GOTTA HAVE SLOW COOKING. YOU GOTTA COOK IT LOW AND COOK IT SLOW."
> —Ray "Red" Gill, DP, UHOH (Doctor of Porkology, University of High on the Hog)

Everything now is run by a new legend in the making, Ray and Eva's son, Ray Alan, along with his wife, Glenda, and the help and direction of Eva Gill.

Before his death, Ray posted several recipes on his Web pages for posterity. The barbecued raccoon recipe stands out as the most unusual. We can easily imagine Ray embellishing the recipe with stories and cooking tips. May he rest in peace.

RED'S BARBECUED 'COON

Serves 10 to 12

1 (8- to 10-pound) raccoon, dressed

2 medium onions, chopped

3 to 5 dried red peppers

Salt and black pepper

Razorback Brand Barbeque Sauce, hot or mild

Wash the raccoon and cut it into 10 to 12 serving-size pieces. Cover with cold water in a Dutch oven. Bring to a boil for 15 minutes. Pour off the water and add fresh water along with the onions, dried peppers, and salt and black pepper to taste. Boil for 1 to 2 hours, until tender. Remove and dry on paper towels. Dip the meat in barbecue sauce and place on a hot grill for 45 minutes, basting frequently. Remove from the grill and place in a shallow pan. Pour the sauce over the meat and bake at 350°F for 1 hour.

Grilled Rattlesnake

Jim Quessenberry
Arkansas Trav'ler

Jim Quessenberry was one of those larger-than-life characters in the barbecue network who will never be forgotten. He was a big man with big dreams and a big appetite for excellent barbecue and fun. Jim was a great storyteller and practical joker.

Anytime you visited Jim in his cooking area at a contest, he'd treat you like family. He would offer you a drink, invite you to sit down and rest your feet, and then ask, "Did you hear about what kind of mess old so-and-so got himself into?" That, or a similar question, was the platform for a tall tale or a joke. Anyone was fair game for Jim's practical jokes; ladies had to be especially on guard. We remember the year Jim brought a big bullfrog to the Memphis in May World Championship Barbecue Cooking Contest. He rigged up an inconspicuous trapdoor at the back of his porta-potty. Since access to a private facility has always been a premium at the contest, Jim was quick to oblige when friends were in need. The Year of the Bullfrog was one of his finest moments. After giving a female guest sufficient time to be seated inside, Jim would quietly slip the bullfrog through the trap door. Soon there would be a scream and the door would burst open. We'll leave it at that, except to note that one time the joke didn't work. A lady who could be described as a "country girl" not given to fear of critters didn't—to Jim's surprise—come bursting out the door, nor did she scream. "The funniest darn thing happened in there," she told Jim. "I looked down and saw a big bullfrog sitting next to me. Poor thing took a hop to his demise when I stood up." Jim decided against rescuing the unfortunate critter.

We're baffled as to why Jim never took the grand championship at Memphis in May with his whole hog. He barbecued some of the best hogs we've ever tasted, right up there with what Ed Mitchell turns out. As far as we know, Jim and Ed never met, but they would have been instant buddies and an unbeatable whole-hog cooking team. Jim did, however, win the Irish International Barbecue Cooking Contest in Lisdoonvarna in 1985 and 1987, plus many other contests in the United States.

Jim wasn't the first or last Arkansan to call himself the Arkansas Trav'ler. It was a term he used mostly for branding his team and his products—Sauce Beautiful and Spice Beautiful. To the many barbecuers who knew him and loved him, he was "Ques" (pronounced "Kwez"). Fortunately, Jim's hot and mild Sauce Beautiful and his Spice Beautiful did not pass away with him like a dream. That would have been sad poetic justice, since Jim swore with a straight face that the recipes came to him in a dream. Wherever the source, they were tasty and beautiful, and Jim was wise enough to pass along the recipes to his sons, Lee and Michael. You can visit the product site and order at www.bbqberry.com.

We never asked Jim exactly how he cooked his Hogs Beautiful. Unless he taught his sons, or his faithful sidekick, Arthur, the recipes and techniques went with Jim to the Great Barbecue in the Sky. We do remember, however, what he told us about how to cook rattlesnake.

ARKANSAS TRAV'LER RATTLESNAKE BEAUTIFUL

Serves 8 to 12 as an appetizer

RATTLER RUB

1½ tablespoons sea salt

1½ tablespoons black pepper

2 teaspoons granulated garlic

2 teaspoons paprika

RATTLESNAKE

1 rattlesnake, about 12 ounces, skinned

2 tablespoons canola oil

¼ cup Rattler Rub or Spice Beautiful

Combine the sea salt, black pepper, granulated garlic, and paprika and mix well.

Using a very thin, sharp fillet knife, start at the middle of the snake's backbone and work around the bone to the belly. Take your time. This is very delicate and expensive meat. Cut into bite-sized fillets.

Coat the fillets with canola oil and lightly sprinkle with the Rattler Rub or Spice Beautiful. Use a grill topper to avoid dropping the meat through the grill grate. Grill over medium heat for about 1 minute per side, until done. Overcooked rattlesnake will be rubbery.

Volcanic Goat Cheese

Gordon's on the Green

This recipe is so good we had to keep it as volcanic comfort food for Gordy's and Gordon's former customers and as a fantastic discovery for all who didn't get the opportunity to dine there. Gordon's used Demitri's Bloody Mary Seasoning, but you can use any brand.

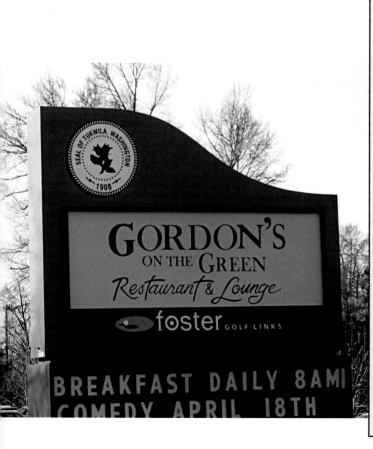

VOLCANIC GOAT CHEESE

Serves 4

3 Roma tomatoes, cut in half and seeded

1 tablespoon balsamic vinegar

2 teaspoons Montreal steak seasoning, finely ground

2½ cups tomato juice

½ cup Bloody Mary mix

1 cup barbecue sauce

1 tablespoon granulated garlic

1 tablespoon granulated onion

1 to 2 tablespoons chipotle chiles in adobo sauce

¾ pound goat cheese

Fresh chives, for garnish

Low-calorie garlic crostini, for serving

Preheat your smoker to 250°F. Place the tomatoes on a sheet pan and sprinkle with the balsamic vinegar and seasoning. Smoke for 40 to 60 minutes, until soft to the touch. Cool down and save the juices.

Remove the tomato skins and process the tomatoes, the reserved juices, tomato juice, Bloody Mary mix, barbecue sauce, garlic, onion, and chiles in a food processor.

Warm 2½ ounces of the sauce in each of 4 rarebit dishes or ramekins and place three 1-ounce slices of goat cheese in the sauce. Place under the hot broiler just to warm the top of the cheese. Garnish with chives cut about 1 inch long. Serve with the crostini.

Jalapeño Hushpuppies

Rudy Mikeska's Bar-B-Q

Say "Mikeska" to a native Texan, and the reply will be "barbecue." The Mikeska barbecue legacy began in the late nineteenth century, when a penniless family from Czechoslovakia moved to Texas to build a better life. First there was farming, and then there was barbecue—barbecue on a massive scale through several restaurants run by Mikeska family members and through huge catering events in Texas, the rest of the United States, and abroad.

We were saddened when Rudy Mikeska told us that Rudy Mikeska's in Taylor is closed. Rudy and his crew are so busy making and selling their famous sausages all over the country that they didn't have time and staff to keep the Taylor store open. The good news is that there are plenty more Mikeska family barbecue joints in Texas to satisfy your hunger for authentic Texas barbecue.

Jalapeño Hushpuppies were a popular item on the original Rudy Mikeska's Bar-B-Q catering menu. We give you our version here.

JALAPEÑO HUSHPUPPIES

Serves 6 to 8

2 cups yellow cornmeal

1 cup all-purpose flour

¾ teaspoon seasoned salt

½ teaspoon cayenne

1 teaspoon baking powder

1 teaspoon baking soda

½ cup chopped scallions

1 or 2 jalapeño peppers

2 large eggs

1 cup buttermilk

2 tablespoons bacon grease

Canola oil or lard, for deep-frying

In a large bowl, mix the cornmeal, flour, seasoned salt, cayenne, baking powder, and baking soda until combined. Add the scallions and jalapeño peppers and stir to combine. Add the eggs, buttermilk, and bacon grease. Stir it all up until the flavors are thoroughly blended.

Heat the oil in a deep-fryer to 350°F (or use a deep pot and measure the oil temperature with a deep-frying thermometer). When it's hot, use a tablespoon to drop your hushpuppies in. Allow them to brown on all sides. They will begin floating when done, after 5 to 7 minutes. Be careful not to overcook them. Drain on paper towels.

REFLECTIONS OF AN OMAHA PITMASTER

Our longtime friend Mason Steinberg, proprietor of the former Mason's Old Mill Bar-B-Que in Omaha (see page 206), wrote the following piece of personal barbecue history for us to share with you. It's a keeper!

"This Bar-B-Que Should Satisfy All," New Orleans–born restaurant critic for the *Omaha World-Herald* Jim Delmont said in his three reviews of Old Mill Bar-B-Que in five years.

I opened Old Mill in 1990 because I couldn't get my style of barbecue in Omaha anymore. I like green-hickory-smoked brisket, pork butt, and spareribs, like I got in the early fifties at Omaha's premier barbecue joint, The Silver Pit. I will never forget the first time I walked in the Silver Pit and walked up to the pit boss, Jasper Jones. He asked me what I wanted, and after looking at the menu board I ordered a rib sandwich. Four spareribs, two slices of barbecue bread, and sauce on the side. To drink, Whistle Orange out of the 10-cent Coke machine next to the screen-door entrance.

From that moment on, I was addicted and never wanted to go through treatment. My many years traveling all over the world eating barbecue helped feed my addiction.

In 1989, while reminiscing about our high school years, the discussion got around to my favorite food . . . you guessed it: barbecue. Talk then focused around late-night trips to the black community in North Omaha for barbecue.

Most that night agreed that the old-style barbecue we had as big-shot high school athletes was no longer available.

Having had too many Jack Daniel's and water, I opened my mouth and said I could open a barbecue restaurant within six months and it would taste just like the old days. Barbecue bread and all!

It happened in October 1990 and gave me some of the best years of my life—my customers, friends I met, knowledge I gained about barbecue, traveling, and all the time feeding my addiction. Who could ask for anything more?

I featured triple-deck thin-sliced brisket sandwiches, pulled pork, spareribs, whole smoked chickens cut into two-bone, four-bone, or whole birds, and naturally everything came with barbecue bread and mild, medium, or big-boy hot sauce on the side.

After a couple of years I added brisket burnt ends, smoked catfish, and smoked feather bones. Feather bones (riblets, for the unenlightened) were a Sunday all-you-can-eat special from noon until we sold out. Record: eighty-four pieces and three pitchers of beer.

An all-time favorite is the homemade smoked beans—rich, dark, spicy, on the sweet side, smoky, with large cubes of smoked brisket in a thick sauce, cooked with our special blend of bean seasoning, all smoked in our hickory pit.

Barbecued Pork Shoulder

Gary Wells

**Founder and Former President,
Kansas City Barbeque Society**

The people of barbecue are not just friends; they are family. One well-known barbecuer said it this way: "You can always say that your barbecue is better than his barbecue. What you don't say is anything derogatory, for instance, saying his barbecue tastes like mud or is as tasty as a piece of wood. It's just a common courtesy. You don't tear down your barbecue family."

Gary Wells belongs in the legacy section of this cookbook. Although he owned a restaurant and hotel once, Gary never owned or managed a barbecue restaurant. Gary's involvement in the sport of barbecue, however, has resulted in an explosion of new pitmasters and barbecue restaurateurs.

Gary and his wife, Carolyn, started the Kansas City Barbeque Society (KCBS), the world's largest and foremost barbecue organization. The KCBS can be viewed as a Barbecue Restaurant Farm System. Out of the barbecue contest system and training programs Gary and Carolyn started, many successful barbecue teachers, pitmasters, and restaurateurs have emerged.

When Gary cooked barbecue in competition, he especially liked to cook pork shoulder. Here is one of his treasured recipes.

GARY WELLS'S BARBECUED PORK SHOULDER

Serves 8 to 10

¼ cup onion salt

2 tablespoons celery salt

2 tablespoons seasoned salt

½ cup packed light brown sugar

¼ cup paprika

2 tablespoons black pepper

1 tablespoon cayenne

1 (18- to 20-pound) whole pork shoulder, trimmed, with skin on

2 (24-ounce) bottles Wicker's Original Marinade

Preheat your smoker to 250°F. Combine the onion salt, celery salt, seasoned salt, brown sugar, paprika, pepper, and cayenne and blend well. Rub all of the exposed meat with the rub, but don't season the skin.

Place the shoulder in the smoker skin side up. Turn and baste the meat side with the Wicker's every 3 hours. Cook until the internal temperature is 185°F for slicing or 195° to 205°F for pulling or chopping (see page 59). Serve with your favorite barbecue sauce on the side.

4 Legs Up
Smoked Prime Rib

http://www.4legsupbbq.com/index.html

**A**fter a successful run with their barbecue restaurant and catering business in Great Bend, Kansas, Kelly and Roni Wertz decided to shutter the restaurant and devote time to teaching barbecue classes all over the country. They also plan to roll out a full line of barbecue rubs and sauces, and they still compete in major contests. We like their smoked prime rib so much that we had to keep it here for you.

SMOKED PRIME RIB

Serves 10 to 12

HORSERADISH SAUCE

½ cup prepared horseradish

1 cup mayonnaise

1 cup sour cream

2 tablespoons Worcestershire sauce

1 tablespoon lime juice

1 tablespoon black pepper

2 tablespoons Bad Byron's Butt Rub or
  your favorite barbecue seasoning

SEASONING

¼ cup ground cumin

¼ cup sea salt

2 tablespoons chili powder

2 tablespoons sugar

2 tablespoons garlic powder

2 tablespoons onion powder

2 tablespoons black pepper

1 tablespoon paprika

1 tablespoon dried oregano

2 teaspoons cayenne

1 whole lip-on certified Angus beef
  rib roast (12 to 15 pounds)

Combine all the horseradish sauce ingredients in a nonreactive bowl. Cover and refrigerate.

Combine all the seasoning ingredients in an airtight container and blend well.

Place the roast bottom side up in a large roasting pan. Season the bottom of the roast heavily with about a third of the seasoning and rub it in. Flip the roast fat side up.

With a sharp knife, score through the fat cap just into the top layer of red meat; do not score too deeply. Score every inch or so at a 45-degree angle from the upper left corner to the lower right corner of the roast, going all the way to the lip (the hard fat on the narrow end of the roast).

Season heavily with the rest of the seasoning, rubbing and pressing the seasoning into the scores. Allow the roast to rest overnight in the fridge—a good 12 hours.

Preheat your smoker to 250°F using the wood of your choice. Roast the meat for 4 to 6 hours, until the internal temperature is no greater than 130°F. The roast will be rare in the center.

Remove the roast from the smoker and wrap in several layers of plastic wrap. Allow to rest for at least 1 hour before carving; then place the roast on a cutting board in a sheet pan. Cut the plastic wrap and allow the juice to drain into the sheet pan. The juice can be served straight with the prime rib or reduced by half in a saucepan on the stove with a tablespoon or so of butter added at the last minute to smooth the sauce. Do not use premade or canned beef "au jus." Slice the meat and serve with the juice and the horseradish sauce.

Bistecca alla Fiorentina

Giancarlo Gianelli
Barbecue Baron of Tuscany

The call came when Ardie and his dining companions had finished one of the most memorable meals of their lives: a fantastic multicourse dinner of Tuscan gourmet delights prepared by Chef Giancarlo Gianelli. They were visiting with and praising Giancarlo in the outdoor courtyard of his small restaurant, the Locanda dell 'Oste Poeta, at Tocchi, Monticiano, Siena. "Giancarlo, I just shot a wild boar in my cornfield," his friend, Vittorio, said over the phone. "Will you please come help me butcher it?" Giancarlo asked, somewhat hesitantly, so as not to offend the diners, if they would like to come along. Having just dined on grilled wild boar chops marinated in balsamic vinegar and herbs—plus seven other superb Tuscan dishes, with complementary local table wines— they were ready for adventure.

It was a very dark night as they navigated a narrow dirt road in the Tuscan hills to Vittorio's farm. The darkness was broken occasionally with flickering gravesite candlelights in cemeteries, honoring the dead. Giancarlo hopped out and opened a gate, crafted of sticks and branches from nearby trees, and they proceeded into Vittorio's farm. In the doorway of the barn was a huge dead male wild boar, still warm, resting in a big stainless-steel wheelbarrow below chains on a pulley to hoist him up by the hind legs for butchering. Opera music filled the air. Tools and paintings adorned the walls. It was like walking into a Fellini movie with the set designed by Salvador Dalí—but it was real.

Giancarlo went to work on the boar—hoisting it upside down by the back legs, slicing through the belly and spilling the contents into the wheelbarrow. Vittorio tossed some of the organs outside to his exuberant, barking hunting dogs. Soon the boar was stripped of its hide and removed to a cooler for further processing later. It was done. Everyone cheered and toasted with a round of Chianti. This is only one of many memories that friends of Giancarlo were left with in the wake of his untimely death from a respiratory illness at age fifty-seven. His dear wife, Adriana, preceded him in death by two years—two years of grief and deep sorrow for Giancarlo.

When Ardie first met Giancarlo in 1995, he and Adriana ran a restaurant in leased space in the small village of Stigliano. Robust and bearded, he was grilling a spatchcock chicken, covered with a brick, on his Tuscan grill with oak charcoal. Ardie's rudimentary Italian and Giancarlo's rudimentary English didn't make for a smooth conversation, but with gestures and words their rapport was instant—especially when a mutual passion for barbecue and Jack Daniel's became apparent. Ardie dubbed Giancarlo the "Barbecue Baron of Tuscany," and asked that he please have wild boar on his menu the next time Ardie came to Italy, despite the Tuscan custom of only serving wild boar—except in the form of cured sausage—in the winter months.

Two years later Ardie returned to Tuscany, bringing some barbecue and Jack Daniel's memorabilia and encouraging Giancarlo to compete in the Jack Daniel's World Championship Invitational Barbecue. Lo and behold, he eventually found a sponsor and made the trip. He, Adriana, and their friends Susan Pennington from Montestigliano and Ellen and Peter Brown from Minneapolis, formed team Allegri Cinghiali. Thanks to Cliff and Donny Weddington of Oink, Cackle & Moo, team Allegri Cinghiali had a pit and some excellent mentoring. Billy Bones also stopped by to welcome them and share a few tips for success. To Giancarlo's regret, the grand championship eluded him, but he and Adriana were thrilled to take home the First Place trophy for "Home Cooking from the Homeland." Giancarlo was truly a Renaissance man—chef, poet, artist, expert on Etruscan dietary habits, teacher, father, husband, friend, and founder of a movement dedicated to contemporary interpretations of Tuscan cuisine, the "Blue Kerchiefs."

What follows is a recipe adapted from Giancarlo's self-published book, *The Taste of Memories*. Giancarlo was a native of Florence, where he learned the Florentine manner of cooking. His many Florentine dishes were second to none, including this classic Florentine steak.

BISTECCA ALLA FIORENTINA (STEAK IN THE FLORENTINE MANNER)

3 T-bone or porterhouse steaks, cut to a thickness of 3 fingers each

Salt and freshly ground black pepper

Extra-virgin olive oil

Remove the steaks from the refrigerator at least 3 hours before they are to be cooked so that the middle of the finished steaks will not be cold. Giancarlo would suggest that at the same time you open a bottle of good Chianti that has been aged for at least 3 years. Place a large amount of charcoal under the grill, set the grate above it (preferably at least the width of four fingers above the coals), and preheat it until it is glowing but with no flame.

Place the steaks on the grill. Let them cook on one side, without adding salt and under no circumstances prodding them with a fork. When they have formed a crust (after 7 to 8 minutes), turn them over with a spatula, sprinkle the cooked side with salt, and grill them on the other side for 7 to 8 minutes. Turn over again and salt the other side. At the end they should still be rare in the middle and well cooked on the outside. Before serving, season each steak with a little freshly ground black pepper and a couple of drops of extra-virgin olive oil. This and only this is the real fiorentina—a T-bone cut of sirloin steak, no lemon, never well-done, and only grilled over charcoal.

Note: One day the man who taught Giancarlo to cook suggested packing the steaks in some dry hay and putting them in the refrigerator for 5 or 6 hours so that the meat absorbs the most intense of the flavors on which the animal feeds. Giancarlo sometimes did that, and he would also burn the same hay next to them as they cooked. He thought it might be a rather sacrilegious thing to do, but a little bit of blasphemy every now and then is certainly not going to get us sent to hell.

3 for the Money
Barbecued Ribs

Mason Steinberg
Old Mill Bar-B-Que, Omaha, NE

ason Steinberg was the creator and facilitator of Old Mill Bar-B-Que, which is closed now but may be reopened in the Omaha area soon by his son Jason.

We would venture to say that Old Mill Bar-B-Que was one of the best barbecue restaurants in the Midwest, with good food, ambience, and great barbecue. Mason, being a very frugal person and good businessman, would buy natural-fall ribs (full slab, untrimmed), 3 and down spare ribs, which means the slabs weighed 3 pounds or less. Mason cut the slabs into St. Louis–style ribs, which means he squared up the slabs and cut the breastbone and the gristle from the top of the slab. These are called rib tips. When you do this, you also take the skirt (a flap that is attached to the diaphragm) off the inside of the slab. It's all clear as mud, right?

3 FOR THE MONEY BARBECUED RIBS

Ribs serve 4 to 6; rib tips serve 2; skirts serve 1

2 slabs St. Louis spareribs

2 rib tips

2 skirts

1 cup barbecue rub of your choice

Remove the membrane from the back of the ribs and trim any excess fat. Season the ribs all over with your favorite barbecue rub. Cook the ribs and rib tips using the indirect method at 230° to 270°F for 5 to 6 hours, until the ribs tear easily. Rib tips take 4 to 5 hours. Grill the skirts at 400° to 500°F using the direct or indirect method, which will take 1 to 3 hours.

Mason barbecued ribs every day for his business, and he saved the rib tips to run a Saturday night special. For Sunday afternoon, he ran a barbecued skirt special. That's why we dedicate this 3 for the Money Barbecued Ribs recipe to Mason.

206

MASON'S BARBECUED FEATHER BONES

Serves 6 to 8

1 tablespoon garlic powder

1 tablespoon onion powder

1 tablespoon salt

1 teaspoon ground allspice

1 teaspoon chili powder

1 teaspoon black pepper

½ teaspoon ground nutmeg

½ teaspoon cayenne

¼ teaspoon ground cinnamon

2 pounds feather bones (1½ by 3½-inch bones cut from a hog's backbone)

In an airtight container, combine the garlic powder, onion powder, salt, allspice, chili powder, black pepper, nutmeg, cayenne, and cinnamon. Mix well, seal, and store in a cool, dry place until ready to use, up to 6 months.

Preheat your offset smoker to 225° to 250°F. You can also use your grill for smoking (see page 217). Season the feather bones fairly heavily with the spice rub. Then let the meat sit at room temperature for about 1 hour. Place the meat bone side down on a screen or baking sheet in your smoker and smoke for about 30 minutes. Turn the meat so that you'll have marks on both sides; then smoke for another 30 minutes. The internal temperature of the meat should be about 160°F when it is finished. Make sure there is plenty of smoke in the smoker throughout the cooking time and do not sauce the featherbones while cooking, as the heat and smoke should give them a nice mahogany color with a wonderful flavor. If you do serve sauce, do so as a light dipping sauce with plenty of barbecue bread (see page 75) for mopping up the juices and maybe some sauce.

Note: You can cook the feather bones the day before you plan to serve them. Cook until they reach an internal temperature of 140°F on an instant-read thermometer, let them cool, and refrigerate overnight. Let sit at room temperature for 1 hour before placing them in your smoker at 225° to 250°F for about 30 minutes, until the internal temperature reaches 160°F.

Barbecued Baby Back Ribs

John Willingham
www.willinghams.com

The late John Willingham is a barbecue legend, icon, and entrepreneur. His barbecue contest awards could fill an entire room in a barbecue hall of fame. Not one to rest on his laurels, John was fully engaged each day in the pursuit of barbecue excellence. John was proud of his loving wife, Marge, as well as their three daughters and seven grandchildren. John's popular cookbook, *John Willingham's World Champion Bar-B-Q*, spells out some of his many secrets to barbecue success.

John's search for the best way to cook barbecue prompted his invention of the famous patented W'ham Turbo Cooker. He also developed an award-winning line of W'ham seasonings, both dry and wet. John was one of the first barbecuers to use Worcestershire powder and powdered vinegar. His rubs and sauces are available online and in select stores.

John's world championship cooking team, the River City Rooters, continues his legacy at various contests and events. John owned three barbecue restaurants in his long tenure as "the man of Memphis barbecue." He is dearly missed in the barbecue community and beyond.

John was known for his great championship ribs. Here's a recipe he gave to Paul, saying, "It's simple. Just use my W'ham seasonings and you can't go wrong."

W'HAM-STYLE SEASONING

Makes about 2¾ cups

½ **cup sugar**

½ **cup onion salt**

½ **cup garlic salt**

2 **tablespoons chili powder**

2 **tablespoons Worcestershire powder**

1 **tablespoon lemon pepper**

1 **tablespoon black pepper**

1 **tablespoon vinegar powder**

1 **teaspoon cayenne**

1 **teaspoon rubbed sage**

1 **teaspoon dried basil**

½ **teaspoon ground rosemary**

Combine all the ingredients and blend well. Store in sealed jar in a cool, dark place until ready to use, up to 6 months.

BARBECUED BABY BACK RIBS

Serves 4 to 6

2 slabs baby back ribs

½ cup W'ham seasoning of your choice (or use the recipe opposite)

Apple juice, for basting

Set up your smoker to cook indirectly at 250° to 275°F. This temperature is a little higher than usual, but John believes that ribs should be cooked hotter than most barbecue. To prepare the ribs, trim them of excess fat. Do not remove the membrane from the back of the ribs before you cook them. John, like many other Memphis pitmasters we've met, says that leaving the membrane on keeps the meat juices in. Paul and John have a friendly disagreement on this technique. Sprinkle the ribs all over with the W'ham seasoning. Place the ribs in the smoker. If you hang the ribs like John and Paul do, you don't have to turn them. Just baste them with apple juice after 1½ hours. If you cook the ribs on a grate or in a rib rack, turn them after 1½ hours and baste with apple juice. Cook the ribs for 3 to 4 hours, until you can take two ribs side by side and easily tear them apart. When the ribs are finished cooking, remove the membrane and serve.

THE BEANS OF BARBECUE

We're told that barbecue was commercialized in the early 1900s of necessity. Recent immigrant butchers, the story goes, discovered that the barbecue method of cooking transformed tough, hard-to-sell cuts of meat such as beef brisket and pork spareribs into tender, juicy, smoky irresistible meat feasts. Tough scraps could also be ground into meat for sausage, burgers, and chili.

It figures that beans are one of the most popular side dishes with barbecue. Dried beans are cheap and tough. When soaked in water, drained, and simmered in fresh water until tender, with a variety of seasonings added, they rock! As with barbecue, you'll find bean side dishes in a variety of presentations in barbecue joints across the country. Pit-baked or oven-baked beans in barbecue sauce with meat scraps and other ingredients such as onion and peppers are very common. In central Texas we found mostly pinto beans with jalapeños, sometimes as a free, help-yourself side dish. Fresh or canned green beans are served in some joints, too.

Cheesy Taters

Hickory Creek Bar-B-Que

Through no fault of his own, and to our lament, pitmaster/proprietor Ric Gere sold his equipment and closed the doors at the late great Hickory Creek Bar-B-Que in Baldwin City, Kansas. No more contest-quality hickory-smoked ribs, pulled pork, brisket, sausage, and turkey at 711 High Street. We couldn't part with Ric's Hickory Creek Cheesy Taters recipe. It will complement any style of barbecue you put on the table.

CHEESY TATERS

Serves 12

½ **cup minced onion**

2 **cups shredded cheddar cheese**

1 **(16-ounce) container sour cream**

8 **tablespoons (1 stick) butter, melted**

1 **(10.75-ounce) can cream of chicken soup**

1 **(32-ounce) package frozen shredded hash browns, thawed**

Salt and pepper to taste

Preheat your smoker to 230° to 250°F. Combine all the ingredients in a large bowl and mix well. Spray a 9 by 13-inch baking pan with nonstick spray, fill the pan with the mixture, cover, and smoke for about 3 hours, until the top forms a golden crust.

210

BBQ Mutton

Otis Boyd

Boyd 'n' Son Bar-B-Q, Kansas City, MO

tis Boyd was a pitmaster's pit-master and a Kansas City barbe-cue icon. He has gone on to his heavenly reward, and it is only appropriate that where his barbecue restaurant stood at 5510 Prospect Avenue is now a church. Thank you, Otis, for your wonderful barbecue and for being a true gentleman.

Over the course of a 6-hour visit several years ago, Mr. Boyd shared his recipe for barbecued mutton. His was one of the few places in town that sold mutton. It was smoked to tender perfection and sauced with Mr. Boyd's tomato-based barbecue sauce for a perfect complement.

BBQ MUTTON

Serves 6 to 8

3 slabs mutton breast (ribs)

2 quarts buttermilk

BARBECUE RUB

½ cup sea salt

½ cup packed dark brown sugar

1 tablespoon ground allspice

1 tablespoon finely ground black pepper

2 teaspoons ground coriander

2 teaspoons ground juniper berries

1 teaspoon ground rosemary

1 teaspoon ground thyme

½ teaspoon ground nutmeg

MUSTARD SLATHER

2 large cloves garlic, peeled

½ teaspoon sea salt

½ cup Dijon mustard

1 tablespoon soy sauce

1½ teaspoons ground rosemary, thyme, or oregano

2 tablespoons fresh lemon juice

¼ cup olive or peanut oil

Heat your grill or smoker to 230° to 250°F. Trim any excess fat from the ribs and place the ribs in a large plastic bag. Pour the buttermilk over the ribs, press the air from the bag, seal the bag, and place it in the refrigerator to marinate for 8 hours or overnight.

Combine the rub ingredients in a small bowl and blend well. To make the mustard slather, mash the garlic with the salt in a small bowl. Whisk in the mustard, soy sauce, herb, lemon juice, and then the oil, to make a mayonnaise-like cream.

Remove the ribs from the marinade, shake off any excess marinade, and blot with paper towels. With a pastry brush, lightly brush the mustard slather on the bone side of the ribs; then season that side with the rub. Repeat with the meat side. Place the ribs in your cooker and cook for about 6 hours, until the ribs pull apart easily.

Seafood-Stuffed Lobster

DennyMike Sherman
http://www.dennymikes.com

ennis Michael Sherman, aka "DennyMike," caught the barbecue bug from longtime friend and native Texan, the late Charlie Arriaga. After years of grazing on barbecue in Kansas City, Memphis, and throughout the South, he kept coming back to the one that brought him: Texas style. He ended a successful run as pitmaster/owner of DennyMike's Smokehouse BBQ and Deli in Old Orchard Beach, Maine, to devote full time, with his wife, Patty, to manufacturing and marketing DennyMike's Sauces & Seasonings throughout America and beyond.

Although Maine is better known for lobster rolls than barbecue, the scene is changing. New England now sports some championship barbecue teams and respectable barbecue restaurants. Hats off to DennyMike and the New England Barbecue Society for making this happen!

Seafood-Stuffed Lobster features Maine lobster barbecued to perfection. Thanks to DennyMike and our barbecue buddies, Steve and Hope Rowley, for this legacy recipe.

SEAFOOD-STUFFED LOBSTER

Serves 6 to 12

6 (1- to 2-pound) lobsters

SMOKED SEAFOOD

¾ pound bay scallops, with juices

¾ pound Maine shrimp, peeled, deveined, and washed

1½ pounds Alaskan king crabmeat, with juices

3 tablespoons DennyMike's Fintastic seasoning or seafood seasoning of your choice

6 tablespoons butter, melted

SMOKED STUFFING

6 tablespoons butter

6 tablespoons minced celery

6 tablespoons minced yellow onion

1½ tablespoons minced shallot

3 tablespoons snipped parsley

1½ tablespoons minced jalapeños

3 tablespoons dry sherry

1½ tablespoons Dijon mustard

Juice of 1 lemon

3 sleeves Ritz crackers, crumbled

3 cups Italian bread, cut into ¼-inch cubes

2 tablespoons DennyMike's Fintastic seasoning or seafood seasoning of your choice

3 large eggs

1 lemon, cut into sixths

1 to 2 tablespoons paprika, or to taste

½ cup finely grated Parmesan cheese

Fill a steamer pot large enough for all of the lobster claws with water and bring it to a boil. Kill the lobsters (instructions follow), remove their claws, and toss the claws into the steamer to cook until they turn red. Do not overcook. Use tongs to transfer the claws to a plate to cool slightly, then crack the claws and remove the claw meat in one piece.

Split open the lobsters and remove the bad stuff, saving half of the tomalley (liver) to add to the stuffing. Discard the extra half of the tomalley or save it for another purpose. (Or be like Paul and eat it!) Reserve the lobster shells for stuffing.

Set up your smoker to cook at 180°F, preferably with apple wood.

To make the smoked seafood, combine the scallops, shrimp, crab, and seafood juices with the Fintastic seasoning and butter in a large baking dish or foil pan. Set aside.

To make the stuffing, place the butter, celery, onion, and shallot in a saucepan and sauté until translucent. Add the parsley, jalapeños, sherry, mustard, and lemon juice. In a large bowl, combine the cracker crumbs, bread cubes, sautéed mixture, Fintastic, eggs, and reserved tomalley. Mix well. Transfer the stuffing to a large baking dish or foil pan.

Place the seafood and stuffing pans in the smoker and cook for about 1 hour, stirring twice. The scallops will take on a nice brown color from the smoke.

Remove the seafood and stuffing from the smoker and increase the heat of the smoker to 350°F. Combine the smoked seafood with the smoked stuffing and mix well. Place the lobster shells in a large baking dish or foil pan and layer with about ½ inch of the stuffing and seafood mixture. Layer the claw meat on top of that and generously top with the remaining seafood and stuffing mixture. Sprinkle the lemon juice, paprika, and grated Parmesan cheese over the top.

Put the pan on a baking sheet and place it in the smoker to cook until the internal temperature reaches 180°F on an instant-read thermometer, 1½ to 2½ hours.

Note: The most humane way to kill a lobster is first to render it unconscious by placing it in the freezer for 1½ to 2 hours. When the lobster is cold and no longer moving, place it on a heavy board, take a strong sharp knife, and drive it through the center of the cross on the back of its head.

Onion Strings

RUB (Righteous Urban Barbecue)
New York City

To our regret, RUB (Righteous Urban Barbecue), near the famous Chelsea Hotel in New York City, is now closed. Paul developed the menu and recipes and trained the kitchen staff. His name and caricature were all over the joint. RUB was an oasis of real barbecue in a city with a mix of real and fake barbecue. We and thousands of New Yorkers miss it. These lightly battered, deep-fried, spicy, crispy onion strings will jump-start your appetite. Pair these strings with your favorite craft beer and raise a righteous toast to RUB!

ONION STRINGS

Serves 6 to 8

1 large yellow onion

1 quart whole milk

Lard or canola oil, for deep-frying

8 cups (2 pounds) all-purpose flour

1 tablespoon salt

**1 tablespoon finely ground
   black pepper**

Barbecue rub

Slice the onion crosswise as thin as you can, about 1/16 inch thick. If you have a mechanical meat slicer, set it on 2 or 3, depending on your machine. Separate the onion slices, place in a bowl or other container, pour the milk over the strings, and toss gently to cover. If the milk does not cover the onions, add water. Cover the onion mixture and refrigerate for at least 3 hours or overnight.

Put the lard or oil in your deep-fryer and preheat to 350°F (or in a deep pot and measure the oil temperature with a deep-frying thermometer). Combine the flour, salt, and pepper in a large bowl and blend well. Remove a handful of onions from the milk marinade, shaking off any excess. Place the onions in the flour mixture, scatter some of the flour on top of the strings, and toss to coat thoroughly. Shake off any excess flour. Deep-fry the strings until golden brown, 3 to 5 minutes, separating the strings with metal tongs. Drain on paper towels and sprinkle with your favorite rub to taste. Repeat with the rest of the onion strings and serve hot.

BARBECUE BASICS

WHAT IS BARBECUE?

There is no easy answer. Barbecue is a method of cooking. Barbecued meat is also barbecue. A gathering of people to eat barbecue is a barbecue, too.

The barbecue method of cooking involves cooking meat at low temperatures (225° to 275°F) for several hours—from 4 to 24, or more. The result is meat that is tender and smoky, with about 25 percent of the original bulk lost through rendering of fat and juices. When barbecue is called "smoking," the reference is to "hot smoking" in a barbecue pit, as opposed to "cold smoking," which involves cooking brined meats at a low temperature, usually for several days. Traditionally that is done in a smokehouse. Both methods impart smoke flavor in the meat.

The word *barbecue* is sometimes used interchangeably with *grilling.* Grilling is a method of cooking foods directly or indirectly over hot coals or flames for short periods of time, from a few seconds to more than an hour. Thus, grilling is hot and fast; barbecue is slow and low.

Purists insist that grilling is not barbecue. While technically that is true, we have no argument with backyard cooks who invite friends and family to a "barbecue" featuring grilled hot dogs, sausages, steaks, or burgers.

DIRECT VS. INDIRECT GRILLING

Direct grilling is a method of quickly cooking food by placing it on a grill rack directly over the heat source. Direct grilling works best with smaller portions of food and foods that require short cooking times, such as burgers and/or foods with a low fat content, such as well-trimmed steaks and chops. It is faster than indirect cooking because more intense heat is provided and allows for browning on the outside of foods. Food is often cooked uncovered on a charcoal grill but covered on a gas grill.

Indirect grilling is a method of grilling slowly, to one side of the heat source, over a drip pan in a covered grill. Hot air circulates around the food, much like in a convection oven, and it cooks more slowly because less heat is provided. Indirect grilling is ideal for larger cuts of meat that require longer cooking times.

BARBECUING EQUIPMENT

Barbecue joints use a variety of cooking equipment, from custom-made to commercially manufactured. Fifty-five-gallon drums made into cookers; cinder-block pits—above or below ground—with grates and steel plates for lids; brick pits with carousel grates; "aquarium" pits with glass walls; stainless-steel pits fueled with gas, wood, electricity, or wood pellets; and large steel custom-made pits are what we've seen most often at barbecue joints.

FOIL DRIP PAN FOR INDIRECT GRILLING

A drip pan is a helpful accessory for indirect grilling. Make a foil drip pan by tearing off a sheet of heavy-duty foil about 2½ times as large as the food you will be cooking. Fold the foil in half; then fold up the edges to make 2-inch-high sides. Crease the corners to seal.

Home barbecue equipment can range from low-tech and inexpensive to high-tech and very expensive. If you don't already have a grill, we recommend starting with the low-tech and inexpensive icon of backyard cooking, the kettle grill. In either case, begin with studying the owner's manual for basic guidance and tips.

GRILLS: GAS OR CHARCOAL?

Both gas grills and charcoal grills have their proponents. When we barbecue, we prefer charcoal and wood, but not everyone feels that way. Paul has done two blind taste tests using gas vs. charcoal, and gas won both times.

The recipes in this book are from barbecue restaurants and professionals, where they almost always use charcoal, but you can use what you have and what you're comfortable with. The results may not be exactly the same, but you'll still end up with some great barbecue.

Here's a quick summary of gas and charcoal grill features.

GAS GRILLS

Gas grills come in all shapes and sizes. They use propane tanks or a natural gas hookup. They are essentially a metal box lined with tube-shaped liquid propane burners on the bottom. The burners are topped by a heating surface of metal bars, lava rocks, which are natural rock resulting from volcanic lava, or ceramic briquettes, which are radiant materials compacted into a brick shape. Ceramic briquettes don't burn completely as charcoal does. Lava rocks and metal plates are more similar alternatives to charcoal. Lava rocks can be used many times but eventually need to be replaced.

BENEFITS OF GAS GRILLS

Gas grills are quick to preheat—10 to 15 minutes. Multiple burners allow you to control the heat better than a charcoal grill. Gas grills are also less messy—no charcoal or fire starters—and they burn longer than charcoal. One 20-pound tank lasts for 12 to 14 hours. It's easier to maintain higher temperatures on a gas grill than on a charcoal grill, but if you're cooking for long periods of time, you'll use a lot of gas.

WHAT TO LOOK FOR

When selecting a gas grill, look for one made from materials such as cast aluminum, stainless steel, or porcelain-coated steel. Stainless-steel or porcelain-enamel-coated grill racks are easy to clean. Push-button ignition allows easy, safe lighting.

You'll want a minimum of three burners that work independently for greater grilling flexibility and heat control. A gas gauge to monitor fuel levels is especially helpful for barbecuing, when you're cooking for long periods of time. Also look for a built-in thermometer to monitor grill temperature.

Other options you'll find are removable secondary grill racks, side burners for cooking other foods while you're grilling, extra outside shelving for storage, extra outside work space for food prep, and rotisserie fittings.

An offset smoker is nice to have if you do a lot of smoking, but if you only occasionally smoke food, you can use your grill. You can purchase an accessory metal smoker box, a small perforated metal container placed on a gas grill's lava rocks or ceramic briquettes to hold wood chips and provide smoke. It can also be used on the grill rack of a charcoal grill. If you don't want to purchase a smoker box, you can put soaked wood chips in heavy-duty foil, seal and poke holes in the top, and place on the hot briquettes, rocks, or coals.

MAINTENANCE
Simple maintenance adds years to the life of a gas grill. Check the gas fitting for leaks each time you connect and disconnect by using a mixture of soap and water. Bubbles indicate a leak. You'll also want to periodically check the tubes connecting the propane tank to the grill to ensure there are no cracks or holes. Regularly empty the grease catch pan to prevent flare-ups and fires. Store the tank outdoors, not in an enclosed space, and detached from the grill.

After every use, turn your grill on high for 10 to 15 minutes with the lid closed. Turn off the grill and let it cool slightly. Loosen the residue from the grill rack with a brass-bristle brush. This not only prevents sticking but also helps to prevent flare-ups. When the grill is completely cool, wipe the inside and outside surfaces of the grill with a soft cloth and warm, soapy water. Rinse with clean water and wipe dry.

CHARCOAL GRILLS
Charcoal grills have either a round or square box construction. A kettle grill is a popular round one with a heavy cover that can be used for either direct or indirect grilling. A charcoal grate holds coals on the bottom, and a grill rack above the coals holds the food. Vents on the bottom and in the lid help control temperature (on most models).

BENEFITS OF CHARCOAL GRILLS
Charcoal grills are more affordable than gas grills, and they can reach higher temperatures.

WHAT TO LOOK FOR
Vents on both the top and bottom allow greater temperature control. Use stainless-steel or nickel-plated cooking and charcoal grates

BARBECUE TERMINOLOGY

Stick burner—Barbecue contestants' jargon for cooks who use hardwood as their primary fuel instead of charcoal, charcoal briquettes, or wood pellets.

Pellethead—Barbecue contestants' jargon for cooks who use pellet-burning barbecue pits.

WSM—Acronym for Weber Smokey Mountain Cooker Smoker. Due to its shape, it is also called the Weber Bullet. It is built for the slow and low barbecue method of cooking. Hot briquettes are placed in the bottom; a water pan and two racks for meat fill the remainder of the bullet. More information on the WSM is on the Weber Web pages.

(sometimes referred to as *grill grates* or *grids*). The grill should have a heavy-gauge bowl, a tight-fitting lid, a porcelain-coated finish, sturdy legs and construction, and heatproof handles. Look for preassembled or welded parts, which are more stable and less likely to rust.

Some charcoal grills include a built-in thermometer, which helps you maintain the right temperature for the foods you're cooking. A hinged grill rack will give you easier access to replenish coals, which is especially helpful when you're barbecuing. An ash catcher underneath the grill makes cleaning more convenient, and you can buy fire retardant mats to place under your grill to protect the ground beneath it.

MAINTENANCE
Charcoal grills are pretty easy to maintain. Keep the grill rack clean, and after the grill cools, remove the ashes to ensure proper air flow the next time you grill. When the grill is completely cool, wipe the inside and outside surfaces of the grill with a soft cloth and warm, soapy water. Rinse with clean water and wipe dry. To help protect the body from the weather and minimize white spots and oxidation, use a paper towel to apply a light coating of vegetable oil to the outside of the grill while it's cool. You can also buy a water-resistant cover to protect your grill when not in use.

HANDY UTENSILS AND EQUIPMENT
Long-handled tongs, basting brushes, spatulas, and heavy-duty oven mitts are useful for tending foods while cooking. It's also a good idea to keep an ABC fire extinguisher handy, just in case.

CLEANING YOUR GRILL GRATES
It's easiest to clean your grill grates when they're warm. After each use, scrub the grates with wire brushes and scrubbers so that they're clean and ready to go next time you grill. Use brass-wire brushes on stainless-steel grates and stainless-steel brushes on cast-iron grates. You can also use crumpled pieces of foil to remove buildup. Another way to clean them is to turn up your gas grill to high or build a hot fire in a charcoal grill and cover the entire grate with heavy-duty foil, weigh it down with bricks or rocks, cover the grill, and let it burn for about 10 minutes. Remove the foil with tongs and dispose of it. Hit the grate with a long-handled brush, and the charred bits will turn to powder that will fall off into the fire.

COOKING WITH CHARCOAL
You can buy two different kinds of charcoal. Charcoal briquettes made of compacted ground charcoal, coal dust, and starch are most common. They come in standard and easy-lighting. Easy-lighting briquettes are pretreated with a lighting solution for a quick start and need to burn for only 10 minutes before they are ready for grilling. They can be a real time-saver, but we don't recommend them because they can lend a petrochemical flavor to whatever you are grilling or barbecuing. You can also use lump charcoal, the carbon residue of wood that has been charred, usually in the form of lumps.

Try one of the following setups for direct or indirect grilling.

For direct grilling: Use long-handled tongs to spread the coals evenly in a single layer. Extend them about 1 inch beyond the area of the food.

For indirect grilling: You need a disposable drip pan large enough to cover the surface below the food. Use a purchased disposable foil pan or make your own (see page 216). Place the drip pan in the center of the firebox. Use long-handled tongs to arrange the coals around the pan.

LIGHTING A CHARCOAL GRILL

Charcoal grills are easy to start if you know the tricks of the trade. Remove the top grill grate and set it aside. Leave the lower charcoal grate in the grill, as you'll need to put the charcoal on top of that, not directly on the bottom of the bowl.

There are several ways to light the charcoal. The best and easiest way for home grilling is to use a chimney starter. You can stuff the bottom of the chimney starter with paper, turn the chimney over, put it on the fire grate, fill it with briquettes (around 92 in a standard chimney), and set the paper on fire. The fire will then move to the coals. Once the coals are ash gray (20 to 30 minutes), use a fireproof glove or mitt to grasp the chimney handle and dump the hot coals on one end of the fire grate.

The way Paul likes to light his fires is to use a small propane torch, available at most major hardware stores; it's also known as a *weed burner.* Mound the coals in the center of the grill, follow the torch manufacturer's instructions for lighting the torch, and hold it on the coals until they ignite. Once the coals have preheated, use long-handled tongs to distribute the coals how you want them. Or you can use an electric starter to light coals. To do this, place the starter in the coals and heat for the manufacturer's suggested time. Unplug the starter, remove it from the coals, and place it on a heatproof surface away from children and pets to avoid accidental burns. Distribute the coals when you're ready to cook.

Using lighter fluid is a very popular way to light your fire, and that's the only reason we mention it. It's the very last way we would light a barbecue fire because it usually leaves a petro-chemical taste on all cooked products. To light the coals using fluid, arrange them in a mound in the center of the firebox. Add lighter fluid according to the manufacturer's directions. Let stand for about 1 minute and then ignite with a match. Never add more lighter fluid after the fire has started. Once the coals are ready, use long-handled tongs to distribute them for cooking. You can also light your charcoal fire or chimney with gelled alcohol starter, such as Sterno, or just crumpled newspaper. If using a chemical fire starter, make sure all chemical residue has burned off before putting the meat in the kettle.

Once the coals are lit, allow them to heat for 20 to 30 minutes (10 minutes for easy-lighting) or until they turn ash gray in daylight or glowing red at night. When the coals are ready, use an oven mitt to close any two of the three vent holes in the bottom of the kettle. This lets oxygen in, which fuels the flame. Rub vegetable oil on the grill grate (or spray it with nonstick cooking spray) and put it in the kettle. Place the meat opposite the hot coals. If using wood chips, drain the water from them and dump them atop the hot coals. Put the lid securely on the kettle with lid vents open.

You can monitor temperature with a thermometer in the lid vent hole, and you can maintain your desired temperature by controlling oxygen intake to coals by adjusting bottom vent holes. More air means faster, hotter cooking. Less air allows for slower cooking. If you're direct grilling with an uncovered grill, charcoal briquettes will burn for 40 to 45 minutes, as a general rule. If you leave the lid on, most kettle grills will hold a steady temperature of 225° to 275°F for at least 6 hours. Avoid lifting the lid to check the meat, as this will prolong the cooking time. Turn items only once (halfway through cooking time). When you must lift the grill cover, lift it to the side rather than straight up—suction may otherwise draw ash onto the food.

To keep the grill going for several hours, you'll probably need to add more charcoal. It's best to maintain a constant temperature while barbecuing, and you can do that by adding hot coals instead of fresh briquettes when you need to refuel. Just before you put the grill grate over your first batch of coals, remove two and place them in the bottom of a chimney starter. Then fill the chimney starter with fresh briquettes and set it aside on a heatproof surface, such as concrete or bricks (not asphalt), so that it can preheat while you put your meat on the grill. By the time you need to add more coals to your fire, the coals in the chimney should be preheated and ready to go.

Cooking times will vary depending on the type and weight of meat. Don't leave your grill unattended while it's lit. When the meat is done, remove it from the grill and let it rest for 5 to 15 minutes before slicing, chopping, or pulling.

COOKING WITH GAS

You will want to refer to your owner's manual for specific directions for direct and indirect cooking on a gas grill.

In general, for indirect cooking on a two-burner gas grill, after preheating with both burners, you will turn off one burner and place the food over the unlit side, away from the heat source. For three-burner gas grills, you will turn off the mid-

dle burner after preheating and place the food in the center of the grill. Drip pans are required for foods that have juices, such as roasts and ribs. The food is placed on a rack in a roasting pan, and the roasting pan is set on the grill rack. The lid of the gas grill is then closed for grilling.

LIGHTING A GAS GRILL

As with a charcoal grill, it's a good idea to lightly coat your clean grill grates with a little bit of vegetable oil or nonstick cooking spray. Be sure to follow your owner's manual when lighting a gas grill. Before starting your gas grill, open the lid and turn all the burner control knobs to off. Turn the gas on at the source. From this point you should refer to your owner's manual for specific lighting instructions. After lighting your grill, close the lid and preheat the grill on high for 10 to 15 minutes. Again, you will want to refer to your owner's manual for the recommended preheating time and instructions for adjusting the heat while you're cooking. Avoid lifting the lid while you're grilling, as that will prolong the cooking time. When the meat is done, remove it from the grill and let it rest for 5 to 15 minutes before slicing, chopping, or pulling.

Tip: You can help keep your meat moist while cooking by spritzing it with apple juice, which won't change the flavor of the finished meat.

AVOIDING FLARE-UPS

Sometimes meat juices drip into the coals, briquettes, or rocks, causing flare-ups that can burn your meat. Flare-ups can, in fact, wreck a great meal in seconds.

To avoid flare-ups when barbecuing, place the meat opposite the hot coals, briquettes, or rocks. This creates a cool zone so that you can

WOODS

Natural wood chips and chunks can be added to a fire to impart a smoky flavor to food as it cooks. Alder, apple, cherry, hickory, maple, mesquite, oak, and pecan are commonly used. The chips are soaked in water, drained well, and added to a fire just before putting food on the grill. In kettle grills or gas grills, water-soaked wood chips or dry smoke pellets work best. Large cookers with a firebox on the side take well to wood logs or chunks.

We encourage the use of the hardwoods available locally. In the Pacific Northwest, that would be alder. In the Midwest and South, hickory, pecan, and oak. In the Southwest, mesquite. In the Northeast, maple. Also check for availability in your area of fruit woods such as apple, peach, cherry, and pear. If you're partial to a certain wood that isn't local—say, you're a Texan living in Maine—no problem. Barbecue woods of any variety can be shipped worldwide from a variety of suppliers. Call your local barbecue supply store or search online.

move meat back and forth from flames to cool zone as necessary. Trimming excess fat from the meat also helps prevent flare-ups. You can also try lowering the heat by raising the grill rack and spreading the coals so there is more space between them. Or you can remove some of the coals or cover the grill.

For excessive flare-ups in a charcoal grill, you may need to remove the meat from the grill and mist the flames with a water-spray bottle. Once the flames die down, you can return the food to the grill and resume grilling. Do not mist flare-ups on a gas grill. Simply close the lid and wait for the flare-up to die down. Some lava rock systems can collect grease that may result in flare-ups, so be especially watchful when using them and change them once a season if you use your grill a lot. When you open your propane tank valve, it might help to turn it only one turn so that you can turn it off in a hurry in the event of a flare-up.

TESTING GRILL TEMPERATURE

Most grills have thermometers, and if yours didn't come with one, you can purchase one. If you plan to do a lot of barbecuing, it's a good investment. If you don't have a grill thermometer, you need to be able to judge how hot the heat is coming from your grill, because not all foods are cooked at the same temperature. Hold your hand, palm side down, where your food will cook and at the same height as the food that will be grilled. Count by saying "one thousand-one, one thousand-two" for each second you can hold your hand there.

**1 second (or less) =
Very Hot Fire—600°F or higher**

2 seconds = Hot Fire—550°–599°F

3 seconds = Medium-Hot Fire—500°–549°F

4 seconds = Medium Fire—400°–499°F

5 seconds = Low-Medium Fire—301°–399°F

**6 seconds (or more) =
Low Fire—300°F or less**

These are rough estimates and can vary depending on where you place your hand. For example, there may be more heat in one location than another.

TESTING FOR DONENESS

A meat thermometer guarantees perfectly cooked meat every time. Insert the meat thermometer into the center of the thickest part of the uncooked meat. The thermometer should not touch any fat, bone, or the grill. The chart on page 225 gives suggested doneness temperatures for a variety of meats. When the meat reaches the desired doneness, remove it from the grill. Let it stand for about 15 minutes before slicing. This will make the meat easier to slice.

If you don't have a meat thermometer, the following are general cues for meat doneness:

Rare doneness: The center should be bright red, raw, and room temperature. This is generally not considered to be safe, as the meat does not get hot enough to kill any germs or bacteria that may be in it.

Medium-rare doneness: The center of the meat should have a bright red color and be slightly springy when pressed. This is not recommended for veal, pork, or ground meats.

Medium doneness: For this doneness, the center of the meat should have a slightly pink to red color. The meat will be slightly firm and springy when pressed.

Medium-well doneness: The center of the meat should have very little pink color and be firm and springy when pressed.

Well doneness: The center of the meat should have no pink color and be firm when pressed.

BASIC DIRECTIONS FOR BARBECUED MEAT

Some of the recipes in this book call for barbecue in a salad, baked potato, or other dishes. Here's some basic guidance for readers who don't have a favorite barbecue joint nearby or who want to cook barbecue at home. Follow the step-by-step procedures below, varying cooking times as follows:

Pork Shoulder: 8 or more hours until tender.

Beef Brisket: 12 or more hours until tender.

Whole Chicken: 1½ to 2 or more hours until done.

Sausages: 45 minutes to 1 hour until done.

Prepare meats as follows:

If you like to season meat before cooking, use your favorite rub or this all-purpose rub:

ALL-PURPOSE RUB

2 parts ground black pepper

1 part kosher salt

1 part granulated garlic

Stir the ingredients together. Sprinkle the rub on the meat lightly, the evening before or prior to putting meat in the grill.

PORK SHOULDER

Sold as the leg portion (arm shoulder) or upper, blade shoulder (Boston butt). The latter is popular with barbecuers.

To prepare pork shoulder, little if any trimming is needed. Sprinkle the meat with rub. Cook fat side up at 225° to 250°F for 2 hours per pound until tender. Cooks take pride in cooking a butt so tender that the shoulder blade can be pulled out with ease.

BEEF BRISKET

For best results, get a whole (7- to 10-pound) brisket in Cryovac. Do minimal trimming of fat. Sprinkle all surfaces lightly with rub. Cook fat side up at 250° to 275°F for 10 to 12 hours or more, until tender. Remove from the grill and let sit for 30 minutes before slicing against the grain.

WHOLE CHICKEN

Decide whether you want to barbecue the chicken whole intact or flat, spatchcock. The latter will take less time. For spatchcock preparation, refer to the B's Barbecue recipe on page 113. For whole chicken, lightly sprinkle it with rub and place it upright in the grill, opposite the hot coals. Cover the grill and cook at 125° to 150°F for 1½ to 2 hours, until done.

SAUSAGE

Cooking times will vary by type of meat in the sausage, size, and whether the sausage is raw or smoked. If it's smoked, it's enough to simply heat it in a microwave, conventional oven, or skillet.

If it's not already smoked, you'll need to cook it longer, and a grill or pit is a great way to do it. To prevent sausages from burning on the grill, precook or poach the sausages in water before barbecuing. To do this, put them in barely simmering water and poach for 20 to 30 minutes. Be careful not to cook them too fast or the skins will burst. Grill the precooked sausage for 5 to 10 minutes over medium-hot heat (see page 221).

This will heat the sausages through, giving them color and a smoky flavor.

Remember these golden rules when cooking sausages:

- **Cook sausages slowly to ensure that the skin doesn't burst.**

- **Never prick a good-quality sausage, as the casing helps to retain moisture.**

- **Cut the links between the sausages cleanly with a sharp knife. When cooked, a sausage should be cooked right through but still juicy and succulent and not charred.**

For more information on grilling sausages, you can also refer to the Meyer's Elgin Smokehouse recipe on page 92 or the Black's Barbecue cooking procedure on page 42.

THE BASICS OF MEAT FOR BARBECUE
PORK RIB BASICS

Baby backs: Loin back ribs. The term is often applied to any size slab of loin back ribs, but a true baby back rib slab is 1¾ pounds or less.

Spareribs: The intact rib section removed from the belly; may include costal cartilages with or without the brisket bone (breast bone) removed and diaphragm trimmed. A slab of spareribs should have at least eleven ribs.

St. Louis–style ribs: Spareribs prepared by removing the brisket bone parallel to the rib side, exposing cartilage on the brisket bone side. Skirt meat is usually removed. If left on, the outside edge of the skirt should be trimmed.

Skinned: The membrane on the back, or bone side, of the rib slab has been removed.

Long end: The first six ribs from the breastbone end.

Short end: The meatier ribs from number 7 to the end of the slab.

Wet: Ribs served with barbecue sauce on them.

Dry: Ribs served with a dry rub on them.

Shiners: Bones that show through the meat.

PORK BUTT BASICS

Pork butt/shoulder/ham: A pork butt is the top half of a swine's front legs; the bottom half is known as the *picnic.* The two pieces together are known as the *pork shoulder*; both picnic and shoulder have the feet removed. The hams are the back legs of the pig with the feet removed.

Bark: Bark is the crust on the outside of the piece of meat that you are barbecuing, which develops with the long barbecuing process.

Bone in/bone out: Pork shoulders can be purchased boneless or with the bone blade in. It is a matter of pride and accomplishment when a cook's shoulder is so tender that the bone can easily be pulled out when the meat is done.

Brown and white: The outside of a barbecued shoulder is dark, or brown, from cooking. Past the bark the meat is light, or white. You can order brown only, white only, or a mix of brown and white.

Sliced, pulled, or chopped: Refers to pork or any barbecued meat. Sliced meat is cut across the grain of the meat for a tender cut. Pulled meat has been cooked to 195° to 205°F and shredded with the grain of the meat. You can use two heavy-duty dinner forks to do this, or you can use your hands, wearing heavy-duty rubber gloves. Some cooks like to use heavy-duty plastic "claws" to pull pork. Chopped meat is cooked to 185°F and chopped across the grain into small pieces.

Carolina style: Barbecued pork shoulder is the meat of choice in western North Carolina, compared to the preference for whole hog in eastern North Carolina. Some places serve pulled pork. Others serve chopped pork. Texture ranges from coarsely chopped to finely chopped. The latter is done by special request.

BRISKET BASICS

Anatomy: A cut of beef taken from the breast section under the first five ribs. Brisket is usually sold without the bone and is divided into two sections. The flat cut has minimal fat and is usually more expensive than the more flavorful point cut, which has more fat. Brisket requires long, slow cooking and is best when barbecued.

Flat/point: The flat cut or first cut is the lean part of the brisket. The point, or deckle, is the fat end and is the tastiest part of the brisket.

Food Doneness and Temperature

FOOD	DONENESS	INTERNAL TEMPERATURE
BARBECUED PORK	Sliceable and Chopped	180°F (82.2°C)
SHOULDERS, PICNICS	Sliceable, Pullable, and Chopped	185°F (85°C)
BOSTON BUTTS	Pullable	195°–205°F (91°–96°C)
BARBECUED BEEF BRISKET	Sliceable	185°F (85°C)
BEEF STEAKS	Rare	135°F (57°C)
	Medium-Rare	140°F (60°C)
	Medium	145°F (63°C)
	Medium-Well	160°F (71°C)
	Well Done	170°F (77°C)
BEEF ROAST	Rare	130°F (54°C)
	Medium-Rare	140°F (60°C)
	Medium	145°F (63°C)
	Medium-Well	160°F (71°C)
	Well Done	170°F (77°C)
CHICKEN		
Whole or Pieces	Done	170°F (77°C)
Breast	Done	165°F (74°C)
CORNISH HEN	Done	170°F (77°C)
DUCK	Done	170°F (77°C)
GROUND MEAT	Medium	165°F (74°C)
BEEF, PORK, LAMB	Well Done	170°F (77°C)
HAM		
Fully Cooked	Well Done	140°F (60°C)
Not Fully Cooked	Well Done	160°F (71°C)

FOOD	DONENESS	INTERNAL TEMPERATURE
LAMB CHOPS AND RACK	Rare	120°F (49°C)
	Medium-Rare	125°F (52°C)
	Medium	130°F (54°C)
	Medium-Well	140°F (60°C)
LAMB ROAST	Rare	115°F (46°C)
	Medium-Rare	125°F (52°C)
	Medium	130°F (54°C)
	Medium-Well	140°F (60°C)
PHEASANT	Well Done	165°F (74°C)
PORK CHOPS	Medium-Rare	130°F (54°C)
	Medium	140°F (60°C)
	Medium-Well	150°F (66°C)
PORK TENDERLOIN	Medium-Rare	135°F (57°C)
	Medium	140°F (60°C)
	Medium-Well	150°F (66°C)
SAUSAGE	Well Done	170°F (77°C)
TURKEY		
Whole	Done (Check Thigh)	175°F (79°C)
Breast	Done	165°F (74°C)
Dark Meat	Done	175°F (79°C)
VEAL CHOPS & ROAST	Medium-Rare	125°F (52°C)
	Medium	140°F (60°C)
	Medium-Well	150°F (66°C)
VENISON	Medium	160°F (71°C)

JOINTS WE LIKE TO VISIT

ere's where we get to go over the hundred mark with a tip of our hats to some other great places.

ANGUS PIT STOP

608 S. Service Rd.
Calera, OK 74730
580-434-7867

You'll find Angus Pit Stop off Highway 69, only 10 miles beyond the Red River when you've crossed over from northern Texas to southern Oklahoma. You may think you haven't left Texas at the Angus Pit Stop, however. Like the joints in central Texas and elsewhere, you choose your mesquite-charcoal-smoked meats from a holding pit, and then they're sliced and weighed. Meats include brisket, pork chops, sausage, chicken, spareribs, tri-tip, and ham. Grote, "The Boss," has been slow-smoking barbecue since the late 1970s, and you can tell by the tender smokiness that he has learned a thing or two about barbecue over the years. Make room for a tasty hot cobbler or other dessert prepared by Diane, a certified gourmet cook.

BAD BRAD'S BAR-B-Q

3317 E. 6th Ave.
Stillwater, OK 74074
405-377-4141
http://www.badbrads.com

You can't beat the cowboy roadhouse ambience of this place, loaded with western memorabilia. If you're anywhere near Stillwater, head on out Highway 51 for some Bad Ribs and Rocky Mountain Oysters. Brad is also Bad in nearby Pawhuska.

BBQ PETE'S

6621 S. 211th St., Ste. 106
Kent, WA 98032
425-251-0778
http://bbqpetes.com

We're glad BBQ Pete's is back, thanks to Pete's son, Ryan. It was a sad day for us when Pete retired in 1995. Now the BBQ Pete's reincarnation is serving the same great-quality barbecue pork, beef, ribs, chicken, links, and sides that we enjoyed from the 1970s.

THE CATS RESTAURANT AND TAVERN

17533 Santa Cruz Hwy.
Los Gatos, CA 95033
408-354-4020
http://thecatsrestaurantandtavern.com

If you are a history buff and like good barbecue,

this has it all. The history goes back to the days of the stagecoach, but it was also a brothel and several restaurants and is on the National Register of Historic Places. One of their specialties is barbecued tri-tip, and they have some of the best BBQ ribs you will ever eat.

CHARLIE VERGOS' RENDEZVOUS

52 S. Second St.
Memphis, TN 38103
901-523-2746
http://www.hogsfly.com
The late Charlie Vergos is a Memphis icon. Charlie's son Nick and his siblings run the restaurant now. We know Charlie's legacy is in good hands.

COUCH'S CORNER BAR-B-Q

5323 E. Nettleton Ave.
Jonesboro, AR 72401
870-932-0710
http://www.couchsbbq.com
When our travels take us anywhere near Jonesboro, we make sure we stop at Couch's for a chopped pork sandwich. Someday we'll try the Couch Potato, if for no other reason than we like the name.

CORKY'S

5259 Poplar Ave.
Memphis, TN 38119
901-685-9744
http://www.corkysbbq.com
Our favorite Corky's is the original on Poplar Avenue. It is one of the most popular barbecue joints in town, and you'll know why when you dine there. We especially like the wet ribs with beans and fries.

COZY CORNER

745 N. Parkway
Memphis, TN 38105
901-527-9158
http://www.cozycornerbbq.com
We love the Cornish hen, baloney, and rib tips. Although we still really miss the presence of the late Ray Robinson, we know he'd be proud that his wife, Desiree, continues the Cozy Corner legacy.

EARL QUICK'S BAR-B-Q

1007 Merriam Ln.
Kansas City, KS 66103
913-236-7228
http://www.quicksbbqandcatering.com
You can tell that Ron Quick, pitmaster/ proprietor, learned his barbecue lessons well from his dad, Earl Quick, and the late Anthony Rieke of Rosedale Barbeque fame. One hundred percent hickory-smoked barbecue, slab specials on Wednesdays, friendly service. What could be better?

PAPPY'S DINER & BBQ

207 S. May Ave.
Oklahoma City, OK 73108
Diner: 405-235-0915
BBQ: 405-290-7551

Thank Tom Muir, owner, for maintaining a friendly corner on Oklahoma City's north side, near the state fairgrounds. Julia Roberts found it, and so can you. Get your breakfast at Pappy's Diner while you wait to chow down on ribs and brisket next door at Pappy's BBQ. By the time pitmaster Bob Moore is ready to pull the barbecue from Pappy's Cookshack smoker, manager Karen Hamilton and cashier/greeter Brenda Campbell will unlock the door and welcome you to a little piece of barbecue heaven on the red dirt urban prairie. Come back at dinnertime to feast on Oklahoma's traditional favorite onion burgers with fries at the diner, born of the Great Depression Dust Bowl era, when gobs of onion were fried with beef patties as a way to stretch the quantity with two delicious foods that were born to line dance together. Eat at Pappy's corner all day long!

PAYNE'S BAR-B-Q

1762 Lamar Ave.
Memphis, TN 38114
901-272-1523

Now we see why so many readers urged us to eat at Payne's. Payne's ribs, chopped pork sandwich, beans, and a fried pie = Barbecue Heaven!

Q39

1000 West 39th St.
Kansas City, MO 64111
816-255-3753

In Kansas City, where everyone is picky about barbecue, you have to be good or naïve to open a new barbecue restaurant. Rob and Kelly Magee, Q39 co-owners, are beyond good! Rob's chef training at the Culinary Institute of America, plus years of experience as a chef in high-end restaurants and his impressive wins in competition barbecue are all evident in this full-service restaurant with traditional competition-quality barbecue, burnt end burgers, white bean cassoulet, and dozens more creative sandwiches and sides. They also offer a more extensive wine and craft beer menu than any other barbecue joint in the city. Hint: Don't let Rob hear you call it a "joint."

RJ'S BOB-BE-QUE SHACK

5835 Lamar Ave.
Mission, KS 66202
913-262-7300
http://www.rjsbbq.com

RJ's has an excellent all-around menu and a friendly atmosphere. Certified Executive Chef Bob Palmgren is French trained. After successful gigs in some of Kansas City's finest restaurants, he caught barbecue fever, and his many fans are glad he did. Paul likes to meet there for the country breakfasts on weekends. Ardie is a fan of the pork butt burgers.

ROSEDALE BARBEQUE

600 Southwest Blvd.
Kansas City, KS 66103
913-262-0343
http://www.rbjb.com/rbjb/restaurants/
rosedale.htm

The oldest continuously operated barbecue joint in Kansas City still offers the most barbecue for your money. Beer is no longer served in buckets as it was in the 1930s, but you can get a quart bottle of beer to enjoy with your feast.

SMOKIN' GUNS

1218 Swift Ave.
North Kansas City, MO 64116
816-221-2535
http://www.smokingunsbbq.com

Phil and Linda Hopkins know their way around the barbecue pit, and they have the awards and satisfied customers to prove it. Most notable among their many awards is the 1999 Grand Championship at the Jack Daniel's World Championship Invitational Barbecue. "The Jack," as it is called in the barbecue network, is the most prestigious barbecue contest in the world. We can't go near North Kansas City without grazing at Smokin' Guns. On your first visit, share a combo platter with baby backs, brisket, pulled pork, and chicken, with beans and onion rings on the side. You won't have room for dessert, but take home some peach crisp to enjoy later.

TIN ROOSTER AT TURNING STONE RESORT CASINO

5218 Patrick Rd.
Verona, NY 13478
1-800-771-7711
http://turningstone.com/dining/
tin-rooster

If you like Old South food, the Tin Rooster is a destination to check out. Since opening in 2013, they have put out some great barbecue. Try the appetizer or small plate selection with Deviled Eggs with Green Onion, Pickled Jalapeños, Fried Pickles, and Fried Green Tomatoes and Brisket Chili. You will enjoy your adventure!

WHEN PIGS FLY BAR-B-QUE

7011 W. Central Ave., Ste. 116
Wichita, KS 67212
316-295-2150
http://whenpigsflywichita.com

We can't get near When Pigs Fly without stopping for ribs. Every customer gets friendly service and big bad barbecue here, even Red Sox fans. We're not saying that Pitmaster Brian Choy, "biggest and baddest in the land of BBQ," will give you a free rib if you're wearing a Red Sox cap, T-shirt, hoodie, or jersey, but maybe that pig will fly!

JOINTS WE'D LIKE TO VISIT

hen we look back on our barbecue travels, we think of that Johnny Cash song "I've Been Everywhere." We add more barbecue joints to our "been there" list each year, but there is so much barbecue, so little time. Here are a few joints that are still on our Wish List.

BIG BRICKS

3832 N. Lincoln Ave.
Chicago, IL 60613
773-525-5022
http://bigbrickschicago.com
Barbecue, pizza, and beer: When you put three of America's favorite culinary passions on the table, it better be good. We've heard so much good buzz about Big Bricks that we've gotta try it!

CIRCLE M

345 Martin Sausage Rd.
Liberty, SC 29657
864-375-9133
Barbecue buddy Ronny Lark told us about Circle M. He made it sound so good we wanted to hop on a flying hog jet to Sausage Road immediately. We haven't caught that hog yet, but Circle M is on our bucket list.

CRAIG'S

U.S. 70 West
DeVall's Bluff, AR 72041
870-998-2616
We're longtime fans of Craig's grainy vinegar-based sauce with a citrus accent, hot or mild. Craig's has a reputation for great barbecue that we're eager to try, along with pie from the Pie Shop across the road.

GRADY'S BARBECUE

3096 Arrington Bridge Rd.
Dudley, NC 28333
919-735-7243
Not to be confused with Grady's in the Texas Hill Country, another place we want to try, this joint is in North Carolina. Pronounced "Graddy's," Stephen and Geraldine Grady's very popular joint is one of the stops on the North Carolina Barbecue Society BBQ Trail. Our barbecue buddy Carl Rothrock told us Grady's is not to be missed. It's a whole hog place with "zing" in the sauce, and everything is made from scratch. The Gradys have been doing barbecue since 1986, so we know they're doing it right.

MOORE'S OLDE TYME BARBEQUE

36711 Dr. M. L. King Jr. Blvd.

New Bern, NC 28562

252-638-3937

http://www.mooresbarbeque.com

We know Moore's serves some of the finest chopped pork with slaw and hushpuppies this side of hog heaven. Tommy Moore's parents, John and Dot, would be proud that Tommy is continuing the Moore legacy that they started back in 1945.

OLE TYMER BAR B QUE

1000 N. Broad St. SE

Rome, GA 30161

706-234-8000

Vernee Green-Myers told us this is what locals will recommend for good barbecue in Rome. Julie Owens manages the downtown log cabin joint with her two daughters, Stephanie and Courtney. It is drive-thru or walk-up only, serving breakfast, lunch, and dinner. The other Ole Tymer in nearby Armuchee is drive-thru or dine-in, serving breakfast and lunch. We want to try the pulled pork sandwiches and Julie's special grilled chicken salad with blue cheese dressing and egg custard pie for dessert. Yum!

Q BARBEQUE

2077 Walmart Way

Midlothian, VA 23113

804-897-9007

http://www.qbarbeque.com

Tuffy Stone evolved from an apprentice in Richmond's La Maisonette restaurant to a championship barbecue competitor, nationally recognized barbecue judge, and barbecue businessman with a catering service and four Q Barbeque restaurants in greater Richmond. We haven't had the pleasure of dining in a Q Barbeque res-

taurant yet, but judging from what we've tasted from the Cool Smoke pit on the contest circuit, we know we won't be disappointed.

SMOKING PIG BBQ COMPANY

3340 Mowry Ave.

Fremont, CA 94538

510-713-1854

Our longtime friend Frank Boyer suggests that while in California this is a barbecue joint worthy of an excursion. The barbecue is good, and one item to try is the Parmesan Bacon Sausage Burger, a homemade sausage patty, smoked, then topped with bacon and smoked vegetables with a garlic aïoli sauce. Word is that you should also save room for their Peanut Butter Pie.

SPITFIRE BAR & GRILL

1660 13th Ave. East

West Fargo, ND 58078

701-478-8667

http://spitfirebarandgrillfargo.com

Paul met managing partner Tim Olson at the American Royal one year and sampled Tim's barbecue. It was, by far, some of the best barbecue that he tasted at the Royal. Fargo friends Tim and Paula Thompson, regulars at Spitfire, heartily agree, and we can't wait to try it.

WHOLE HOG CAFÉ

2516 Cantrell Rd.

Little Rock, AR 72202

501-664-5025

http://www.wholehogcafe.com

Becky Bryant, Ardie's friend in the Arkansas Department of Labor, highly recommended this place. We're long overdue for a Little Rock adventure!

ACKNOWLEDGMENTS

ur research for this book amounts to a collective total of more than a hundred years. It has been and continues to be a fun ride.

We owe a special thanks to Gretchen, Jessica, our children, and extended family for patience and understanding throughout the process of traveling, contacting pitmasters and restaurant proprietors, and writing and testing the recipes necessary to complete this second edition.

In all human endeavors we stand on the shoulders of those who have gone before us. This is especially true in the culinary realm. Therefore we offer a tip of the hat and sincere thanks to the millions of cooks, known and unknown, who have advanced today's culinary arts, especially barbecue, from humankind's primal beginnings.

Thanks to barbecue friends Steve Holbrook, Vince Staten, John Raven, Johnny White, Don McLemore, Chris Lilly, David Klose, Bill and Barbara Milroy, Guy Simpson, Carolyn Wells, Judith Fertig, Karen Adler, Rich Davis, Rick Browne, Bruce Bjorkman, Lolis Eric Elie, Roland Carrier, Paula Peck, Bob Lyon, Bill Herman, Daniel Vaughn, Renee and Frank Boyer, and many others. Gary Wells, Al Lawson, Cousin Homer, Jim Quessenberry, Charlie Vergos, Angelo Lucchesi, Tony Stone, John Willingham, Chef Louis Szathmary, and Giancarlo Gianelli and other late barbecue friends, we will always miss you. May you rest in peace.

Thanks also to our friends Ron Harwell, Ron Buchholz, and Vernee Green-Myers for help with text and pictures—Ron Harwell in Alabama, Ron Buchholz in Wisconsin, and Vernee in Georgia.

Special thanks to Dennis Hayes, our friend, our barbecue buddy, and our agent. Dennis had the original idea for this book more than a decade ago. It is due in large part to his vision and persistence and his passion for good eats, barbecue in particular.

Finally, it has been fun and a pleasure to work with the book division team at Andrews McMeel. Kirsty Melville, head of the book division; Lane Foster, our editor-at-large; Jean Lucas, senior editor; Tim Lynch, Diane Marsh, Maureen Sullivan, Carol Coe, and Andrea Shores, our hats are off to you!

PHOTO CREDITS

ABOUT THE AUTHORS

Paul Kirk, aka Barbecue Guru, Ambassador of Barbecue, Order of the Magic Mop, Certified Master Barbecue Judge, member of the Kansas City Barbeque Society Board of Directors, and inductee into the KCBS Hall of Flame, has won over 475 cooking and barbecue awards, among them seven world championships, including the prestigious American Royal Open, the world's largest barbecue contest.

For more than 12 years, Paul has operated the Baron's School of Pit Masters, teaching classes worldwide. He has also trained barbecue restaurant staffs across the United States and conducted seminars at national conventions for the International Association of Culinary Professionals (IACP). In 1998 and 2000, he was a member of The Julia Child BBQ Team of Ten at the IACP conventions, raising funds for the Julia Child Endowment Foundation.

Paul writes monthly columns for *Kansas City Bullsheet*, the *National Barbecue News*, and the *Goat Gap Gazette*. Paul has appeared on the *Today Show*, *Discovery Channel*, *CBS This Morning*, *Talk Soup*, and Anthony Bourdain's *In Search of the Perfect Meal*. He has been featured in the AARP's *Modern Maturity Magazine*, *Saveur*, and the *Calgary Herald*. For more on Paul, visit www.baron-of-bbq.com.

Ardie A. Davis, aka Remus Powers, PhB, founded the Diddy-Wa-Diddy national Barbecue Sauce Contest in his backyard patio in 1984. Three years later the contest became the American Royal International Barbecue Sauce, Rub & Baste Contest. He also founded the Great American Barbecue Sauce, Baste, and Rub Contest. A charter member of the KCBS and former three-term member of the KCBS Board of Directors, Ardie is now a board member emeritus, a certified master judge, and an inductee in the KCBS Hall of Flame (1992). He is also a certified Memphis in May barbecue judge, and in 2008, he was a featured judge at the 20th Annual Jack Daniel's World Championship Invitational Barbecue.

Ardie is a founder of Greasehouse University (1984) and serves as president, Diddy-Wa-Diddy Board of Barbecue at the university. He was interviewed and appeared in two History Channel shows: *Modern Marvels* and *America Eats*. He is a freelance writer for the *Kansas City Star* newspaper, the *Kansas City Bullsheet*, official newspaper of the KCBS, and the *National Barbecue News*, which awarded him a Spirit of Barbecue Award in 2003 at the Jack Daniel's World Championship Invitational Barbecue. In 2002, he was presented with a Judges Choice Award at the Jack Daniel's World Championship Invitational Barbecue.

INDEX

HOUSE PARK
BAR·B·QUE

WEED NO TEEF
O EAT·MY BEEF

MARKET
INCE 1900

OUR TRADITIONS
SINCE 1900.

NO BARBECUE SAUCE
(NOTHING TO HIDE)
NO FORKS
(THEY ARE AT THE END OF YOUR ARM)
NO SALADS
(REMEMBER NO FORKS)
NO CREDIT CARDS ALSO)
NK DOESN'T SELL BARBECUE
NO KIDDING
(SEE OWNERS FACE)
ST THE BEST BARBECUE

Van's
PIG STAND

COME BACK SOON

REAL BARBECUE

COMPLETELY UPDATED—
more recipes, even more photos!

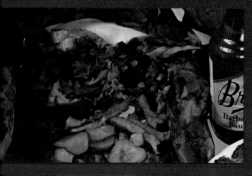

America's Best BBQ honors American restaurant barbecue and the people who make it. Food tastes better when you know the people and stories behind the recipes, and in this book you'll meet lots of famous and not-so-famous pitmasters and personalities as the Paul Bunyan and Johnny Appleseed of American barbecue take you on a tour of the best swine dining establishments from coast to coast.

Only Chef Paul Kirk, winner of seven world barbecue championships, and renowned barbecue historian and ambassador Ardie A. Davis (aka Remus Powers, PhB) could earn the trust—and the recipes—of some of the nation's top pitmasters. Here you'll find more than 100 recipes for out-of-this-world appetizers, tender and smoky meats cooked low and slow, sweet and spicy sauces and rubs, homemade sides, and even a few decadent down-home desserts—if you've saved room.

This all-new edition of the original bestseller offers more than just traditional ribs, beans, and slaw (although those are included too). You'll get recipes for the Badwich, the Q-Ban sandwich, Brunswick stew, barbecue brisket nachos, BBQ egg rolls, BBQ corn bread, Pig in a Puppy, crullers, and many more that will drive barbecue fans hog wild. If you love 'cue, then this is the only book for you.

Andrews McMeel
Publishing
www.andrewsmcmeel.com
Printed in China
Cover Design: Tim Lynch

$19.99 U.S.A. ($22.99 Canada)
ISBN: 978-1-4494-5834-8

51999

9 781449 458348